十二天突破系列丛书

十二天突破英语语法

（第三版）

武 峰 编著

内容简介

英语语法历来是英语教学中的难点。本书是作者在自己多年英语语法教学经验的基础上，针对学生希望尽快入门英语语法、顺利通过各种英语考试等需求编写而成。全书共分为十二天：第一天突破英语语法的基本知识和名词，第二天突破英语的代词和冠词，第三天突破英语的数词、形容词和副词，第四天突破英语的动词及其两种时态，第五天突破英语的时态（一），第六天突破英语的时态（二），第七天突破英语的被动语态、助动词和情态动词，第八天突破英语的非谓语动词，第九天突破英语的虚拟语气，第十天突破英语的介词、连词和基本句型，第十一天突破英语的复合句，第十二天突破英语的语序、主谓一致和 it 的用法。

本书重点突出语法难点，配有大量经典习题和参考答案与解析，适合英语自学者和准备参加英语四、六级考试及研究生考试等学生参考使用。

图书在版编目（CIP）数据

十二天突破英语语法/武峰编著. —3 版. —北京：北京大学出版社，2018.2
（十二天突破系列丛书）
ISBN 978-7-301-27638-9

Ⅰ.①十⋯ Ⅱ.①武⋯ Ⅲ.①英语—语法—高等学校—自学参考资料 Ⅳ.①H314

中国版本图书馆 CIP 数据核字（2018）第 013124 号

书　　名	十二天突破英语语法（第三版）
	SHI'ER TIAN TUPO YINGYU YUFA
著作责任者	武　峰　编著
责任编辑	吴坤娟
标准书号	ISBN 978-7-301-27638-9
出版发行	北京大学出版社
地　　址	北京市海淀区成府路 205 号　100871
网　　址	http://www.pup.cn　新浪微博：@北京大学出版社
电子邮箱	编辑部 zyjy@pup.cn　总编室 zpup@pup.cn
电　　话	邮购部 010-62752015　发行部 010-62750672　编辑部 010-62756923
印刷者	河北滦县鑫华书刊印刷厂
经销者	新华书店
	787 毫米×980 毫米　16 开本　18.75 印张　368 千字
	2008 年 9 月第 1 版　2014 年 2 月第 2 版
	2018 年 2 月第 3 版　2023 年 11 月第 8 次印刷(总第 19 次印刷)
定　　价	40.00 元

未经许可，不得以任何方式复制或抄袭本书之部分或全部内容。
版权所有，侵权必究
举报电话：010-62752024　电子邮箱：fd@pup.cn
图书如有印装质量问题，请与出版部联系，电话：010-62756370

序

  武峰是我的学生,但过去我并不了解他的个人经历与教学经验。一天他拿着这本《十二天突破英语语法》的书稿找我。听了他的介绍,看了部分书稿,我对他本人有了新的了解,对此书有了一定的评价。

  英语语法历来是英语教学中的难点。难,不是因为英语语法复杂,而是因为传统的教法使语法教学变得枯燥、机械,使学生失去兴趣,其结果就是语法关成为一道难关。

  当前英语教学面临两种教法、两个市场。其中一个就是培训渠道、应试市场。参加培训的学生目的明确:考试过关。面对这样的市场、这样的要求,教师就要研究如何用最简便的方法使学生抓住要点、顺利过关。武峰的这本书就是针对这种需求编写的。

  武峰长期在培训领域教语法,经验比较丰富,又善于积累、总结、研究,故形成了自己的"套路",经实践检验,比较有效。随着他自己英语水平和教学水平的提高,把做法、想法以书稿的形式表现出来,就成了今天这本书。这种努力应该肯定。虽然这不是学术著作,但只要有利于学习就是好事。相信此书会成为英语培训百花园中的一朵小花。只要努力,小花也会变成艳丽的花朵,吸引人们的目光。

北京外国语大学英语学院

梅仁毅

2008年7月11日

第三版前言
——这本书为什么要做第三版

这本书第一次出版是在2008年，时间过得真快，一转眼十年过去了。我还记得十年前我去找恩师梅仁毅先生"讨要"这本书序言时的样子，他当时说："你小子这种辅导书写得不错，要多写，要多写！"十年过去了，"十二天突破系列丛书"中的《十二天突破英汉翻译——笔译篇》《英汉翻译教程新说》和《考研英语翻译新说》等书相继出版，而且《十二天突破英汉翻译——笔译篇》还经常名列各大翻译类图书排行榜的前茅。但是也有遗憾，就是这本《十二天突破英语语法》之后的习题始终没有附上解析，第二版修订时，时间匆忙，没有做这个工作，甚是遗憾。

2017年是忙碌的一年，但是想到读者的一再要求，我们再忙也要抽出时间把这本书的习题解析做出来。在这个过程中，我们对书稿重新进行了完善，来来回回地审校，除了把习题答案解析附在书后，我们还发现了许许多多的小瑕疵，修改得很费心，不过我们都挺过来了，用我的话说，本书到第三版将不再改动了，以后也就是这个版本了，因为做语法书还是一个非常细致的工作，其中细节的烦琐有时候真的令人非常头疼。本书经过第三版的修订和完善，最终希望广大读者能够满意。

在本书第三版的修订过程中，有很多同人给予了专业的指导和帮助，在此要感谢吕婧雯女士和吴心月女士在百忙之中抽出时间提出了宝贵的意见和中肯的建议，还要感谢北京大学出版社的吴坤娟编辑、同事和领导给予的帮助，更要感谢各位读者提出的修改意见。

其实，一本书修订三版看上去已经很完美，但是小的问题一定还会存在，也请各位读者不吝赐教，让这本书成长得更快更好！

作者微博：Brotherfive

作者公微：Brotherfive教翻译

武 峰

2018年1月19日 于北京市海淀区

第二版前言
——我想把这本书做得更好

2008年的夏天是一个让人难忘的夏天,我在奥组委从事翻译工作,忙得焦头烂额的时候,"十二天突破系列丛书"的第一本——《十二天突破英语语法》经过增删修改几次后终于顺利上市。上市之后,销量很好,受到了很多读者的好评,也得到了大量的读者反馈。因为此书是这个系列丛书的第一本,所以我很重视读者的意见。从反馈中知道,由于编写时间匆忙而导致了部分笔误和印刷错误,我心中十分愧疚,但由于各种原因,没有时间勘误,在此要对所有读者说声抱歉。

后来几年我又陆续出版了《十二天突破英汉翻译——笔译篇》和《英汉翻译教程新说》等学习英语的书籍。根据这本书的经验,我没有匆忙交稿,而是慢工出细活,打造精品。确实,后来这几本书的错误很少,当然这得益于读者的监督。我也在修正错误中成长,编写时更加细心,尽量避免出现错误,即使是标点、大小写、字号大小等问题都不能出现。

不过,修订这本语法书却一直是我的一个心愿。2013年夏天,我在天津新东方授课时,遇到一位江西的高中老师,他说当年就是受到我这本语法书的启发,才把高中的语法知识讲得滚瓜烂熟。我听完之后感到无地自容,因为我知道书中有不少差错没及时修订。2013年秋天,我在美国波士顿做一个项目,终于有了一点时间,和北京大学出版社联系后得到再版此书的允许,十分开心。无论有多忙,修订此书便是我这一年最重要的事。夜以继日,加班加点,如今终于完成了。这次修订并没有增加很多新的知识点,因为我一直崇尚语法教学使用结构加知识点的方法,这一点在第一版的前言中做了很多的解释。这次修订主要是更正各种错误,甚至是标点错误,希望再版后能让更多的英语语法学习者从中获益。

在此,要感谢吴心月女士在此书修订过程中给予的巨大帮助,吕婧雯女士在各章练习解析中给予了认真修订,感谢她在百忙中抽出时间给我提出了许多宝贵的意见。同时,要感谢北京大学出版社吴坤娟编辑在修订此书过程中所给予的极大帮助。

最后，在使用此书过程中，如果您发现仍有错误或是别的任何问题，请您及时联系我，您的意见将让本书变得更完美。

武 峰

2013年10月15日

于美国马萨诸塞州阿灵顿市

第一版前言
——语法是十二天可以学成的

今天我能坐在这里写本书的前言，很感慨，也很激动。这本书的出版可谓是历经曲折，增删几次，最后才得以在北京大学出版社出版。这也应验了那句好事多磨的古语。我从事英语教学多年，最早接触的就是语法这个科目。由于这个科目是大家最难突破的，我一直在思考该怎样把这门课教好。最早萌发写这本书的时间是在2002年年底，我那时在安徽合肥建人学校教授成人高考和专升本的课程，在教学的过程中常常涉及语法项目，也在思考该怎么样把这门课教得更好，慢慢形成了一些心得体会并用文字的形式记录下来。2006年，我在西安新东方学校开始了实用英语语法课程的教学，并逐渐形成了《十二天突破英语语法》这本书的雏形。在几年的教学过程中，我的教学思路和教学方法得到大部分学生的认可和赞同，于是有了出版这本书的冲动。但是任何一家出版社都知道语法系列的书是很难销售的，所以我一直在不断地碰壁，不断地增删本书的内容，甚至一度放弃了出版本书的念头。在北京外国语大学几年的学习和在新东方学校教授语法的几年教学实践，让我对语法的教学又有了新的认识，在教学和学习上有了很大的进步。于是我对本书的内容作了较大的调整，最后形成了今天的《十二天突破英语语法》的蓝本，可谓十年磨一剑。语法书和其他书籍不一样，词汇书可以参照字典或别的工具书，但是语法书如果和大师们写的一样，那就是抄袭了，所以我一直秉承原创的态度。除了这些以外，本书还有以下两个特点。

（一）非学术化

我本身是一名英语学习者，在北外学习时从来不敢提自己是一名英语教师，因为在课堂上见过太多的英语大师用不同的方式来给我们诠释语言。这本书只是我在教学过程中的一些体会，根本谈不上是什么著作，我打着所谓"非学术化"的口号，就是想告诉所有英语学习者，在短期内突破英语语法是可以实现的。本书不敢和薄冰、张道真、章振邦等大师的著作相提并论，他们在几十年的教学过程中形成了自己对于语言的看法和诠释方法，其著作可谓是经典中的经典，对中国的语法教学起到了重要的作用。本书不是从研究的角度来讲解语法的，而是采用尽量简单的讲解，我相信，这能让学习语法的人一目了然。

（二）非例举化

现在大多数语法书的一个特点就是举例，在给出一条语法条目之后就是不停地举例，毫不考虑读者的习惯和思想，以为例子可以告诉所有人该怎么样学习语法。但是他们都忽略了英语语法学习的一个重要点——结构的重要性。我会在后面重点阐述这个问题。例子不在多，而在于精，本书并没有给出很多例子，所以显得和传统语法书有所不同。传统语法书有点类似于工具书，给出的例子很多，但是在本书中基本上是一个语法点只举一个例子，甚至一些不重要的语法点都没有举例。我在教学过程中发现，语法教学应该是让学生先理解，再举例说明，这样做会取得更好的效果。

近年来，在中国兴起了一股学习英语的热潮，但是在这股热潮中大家都把语法的教学忽视了，甚至很多大学都把语法课程取消了。我想这是很不科学的。如果语言的学习仅仅通过听和说就能解决的话，那也太简单了。当我们再把语法捡起来的时候也就不是那么回事了，操着中国式的英语，那么多雅思、托福、GRE的高分学员出了国还是不会使用语言，难道这就是我们所谓的学习语言吗？我要在这里呼吁：应重视语法教学。连时态都分不清的语言还敢拿出来说？说给外国人听，别人可以宽容咱们是非英语国家的人；说给中国人听，自己感觉还不错。但这不是学习英语之道。我把语法简化到如此简单的地步，就是为了让所有的人可以不把语法学习当作负担，可以通过简单的例子把英语当中所有的现象都清楚地认识和记住，以后就可以好好地使用了。

这两点就是本书的特点了。下面谈谈学习语法多年后我自己认为最重要的结构性含义。

从当老师开始我就一直在教语法，这么多年我一直强调语言的结构性特征。其实这不是我编造出来的，这些只是我在学习和教学的过程中根据前人告诉我们的知识，结合自己的一些心得，所形成的一套结构性的教学法。

在我看来，语言最重要的两个环节是结构和语义，这两者之间也是相互联系、不可分割的。语言学大师们把语法学从语言学或者说语义学当中分离出来，这是一件很了不起的事情，因为语法有了自己的生命，也可以说语言的结构真正地脱离了语义的范畴。不难发现，在教学的过程中，语言的结构和语义又是无法分开的。比如，在讲述从句中使用虚拟语气的时候，我会说其实语言的结构是固定的，因为任何动词和形容词的词根所导致的虚拟语气都是固定的，但是因为语义的不同而产生了虚拟语气，所以可以看出两者之间的相辅相成性。语言结构的丰富和美丽是一般人难以理解的。

最近在讲授高级英语语法时，一个学生忽然和我探讨起中学老师所讲述的语法和我所讲述的语法的区别。这个问题我在很多年前就开始思考了，其实也早已有了答案，因为中学老师所教的是语义意义上的语法，而我完全没有走这条路。在现代转换–生成语法中所强调的是结构的重要性，而不是语义的重要性。通俗地说就是中学老师可以讲授词的用法，甚至在精读的课文中讲述语法，但是我所讲的是纯粹（sheer）的结构。而在大多数人看来，这些结构是枯燥无味和乏力的，甚至觉得缺少一种实用感。因为人们往往比较容易界定和掌握具体的事物，而对于抽象事物的理解则比较困难。我以前喜欢用一些看上去比较"低俗"的例子去讲述这些知识，让大家比较容易理解，不知道从什么时候开始，我不再用这些例子，而把自己在大学里学习到的那套东西拿出来给学生讲了。

在这里要说的是，学习语法时真正要掌握的还是结构和层次。比如学习虚拟语气中if条件句的用法就要掌握一、二、二、四的结构框架，以后如果学到什么新的知识和内容，只要往里面填就可以了，没有必要把大师们的语法书都给背熟了。因为大师写书和我们学习是两回事，他们用的方法是"列举法"，语言中出现的任何现象都会出现在他的书中。而我们的教学内容不可能那么完善和齐备，只要把主要的框架拿出来讲和记忆就可以了，想成为那样的学者和大师是不太可能的。这也许就是宏观结构和微观知识的区别和联系吧。

在叙述完语言的结构性含义之后，我想大家应该已经知道我为什么要讲这个了。打开本书，从一开始看就要知道本书的结构框架，我建议大家能把书的目录好好地钻研一下，从中可以知道语法究竟应该学习什么。刚才花了这么多笔墨说我怎样教语法，现在要谈谈我们应该怎么样学习语法了。

说到英语的语法，我相信大家一定很头疼，而且谁也不会想到它和中文语法的联系。这正是学好英语语法的关键所在。我在这里没有比较两种语言的意思，我不是语言学的学者，更不是语法学的大师，我只是告诉大家中文的语法也很重要。就像我们看两个人一样，我们一般会看两个人之间的差异，而不会看相同点。所以，学习语法当然是要看两种语言的差异。正是因为两种语言在结构上有着本质的区别，我们才需要在学习过程中看到它们的不同点。例如，中文中把定语从句前置，而英语中却放在后面，这就是为什么我们要学习定语从句的原因，这一切都是源于结构。所以，我们要看的是中文和英文两者的语法。

我一直在推荐王力先生的《中国语法理论》。读完这本书之后，我的想法很多。我们日常生活中的有些语言结构是错误的，这就解释了为什么到英语中那样的结构也是错误的。我们研究中西方文化方面的人实在是太少了，因为学西方的说西方的一套，学中文的说中文的一套，最后谁都说不全。中国语言博大精深，想真正学好英语语法真不是一件很容易的事情，还需要在中文结构的学习上下功夫。讲了这些之后，希望所有学语法的同学都要意识到，脑袋里需要装着知识的体系和结构，不能只学几个单词的写法和用法，这些不是学好英语的根本途径。举个例子：在盖楼的时候，不能只看到砖块和金属材料等，最重要的是要看到图纸上的结构和奠基之后显示出来的结构。至于后期如何打磨自己的语言，那就是另一回事了。

那么英语和中文的区别又在什么地方呢？实际上我认为主要有两方面的差异。

（一）词汇上的差异

中文的词汇在词尾一般没有什么大的变化。在表达任何语法现象的时候都是通过语序的调整和换词来达到目的的。例如，中文在表达名词复数的时候一般是通过数量词来实现的，一本书是单数，两本书则是复数，但是在英语中却是通过词尾的变化来实现的，a book，two books，当我们看见名词的后面有s的时候，我们就知道它一定是名词的复数。这和中文有极大的差异，我们在学习语法的时候知道这样的差异就好学习了。在词法这一章中主要看的就是词尾的变化，名词有词尾复数的变化，动词有五种形式的变化，形容词有比较级和最高级的变化等。书中提到这些知识的时候大家一定要注意和认真学习。

（二）句型上的差异

中文多用短句，而英语多用长句。英语中，长难句产生的根本原因很多，涉及的语法现象主要有三点：代词的频繁使用、从句的频繁使用和插入语的频繁使用。中文中经常出现在句子中重复某类词语，特别是名词；但是英语中常常出现代词，这样就造成对于上下文的不理解，而在代词中又以it和that的用法为主，我在讲授这一部分时会重点讨论这两个词的用法。从句的使用也是产生英语长难句的一个重要原因。中文中出现从句的时候，大多用了标点符号，而英语中则用了连词，这样使句子显得很长。更重要的是，英语当中还有很多插入语，这和中文中前后语句用逗号隔开也是不一样的。

所以，当我们察觉到这些差异的时候，也就是我们学好英语语法的时候了。只要我们细细地"咀嚼"代词和从句的知识，利用少量的例句来辅助学习、理解这些知识点，就一定会取得成功。我经常挂在嘴边的五句话请大家能够记住：（1）一句话中不能同时出现两个动词，有两个动词时需要有连接，或者进行形式上的改变；（2）两个句子之间必须要有连词；（3）疑问词引导的不一定是疑问句；（4）以-ing结尾的词不一定表示进行；（5）以-ed结尾的词不一定表示过去。对于这五句话，在看完这本语法书之后请再好好地琢磨，如果都能理解的话，那么你的英语语法也就学习得差不多了！

我在这里还想谈谈学习语法的心态和方法问题。

1. 语法和任何一门课都不一样，它虽然可以在短期内突破，但是要达到熟练使用，却需要很长的时间，切勿放弃。本书的名字叫做《十二天突破英语语法》，很多人会怀疑地说："真的可以在短期内突破英语语法吗？"这是完全可能的，学习和使用是两回事情。学习完了之后，将这些知识应用于各种考试当中才是真正的目的，而不是靠天天把这些语法条目背得滚瓜烂熟，我想这样是没有什么效果的。任何一个理论，只有运用到实践当中，才可能有意义。我曾经把初中升高中的语法题和GMAT的语法题拿出来给我的学生做，最后的正确率是差不多的。所以，我想说，没有什么所谓神秘的东西，只有我们未发现的东西。语法的规则只有那么多，放在一个结构下，我们看不见什么很难掌握的内容，只要我们去实践，就一定能够掌握它。

2. 希望大家把书上的每个例句都背下来，这样无论对学习语法来说，还是对学习写作来说，都有很大好处。我不主张用什么很难的文学句子或很多例句来凑字数，而是要用最简单的句子来告诉大家这个语法点的现象是怎么出现的，以后在考试中将会以怎样的形式出现。

3. 希望大家把后面的习题认真地做完。一般来说，我挑选的习题都是历年的高考题以及大学英语四、六级的语法真题，这些题目都是我在平日的教学中积累下来的，很珍贵。在学习完语法知识之后，大家再把这些题目多加练习，就一定能达到事半功倍的效果。

我希望在前言中讲明本书的意图和学习方法。**任何想学习语法的英语学习者都可以使用本书，从零起点学习英语者到准备考托福、雅思和GMAT的学生**，我想这本书的包容性是不言而喻的，因为我在其中所强调的学习语法的理念和方法是永远不会变的。

说了太多关于这本书和学习英语语法的事情，在这里也该结束前言部分了。尽管在多年的语法教学过程中我也积累了一些经验，但还是有很多不足的地方。在我教学和生活、学习不顺利的时候总会有那么多人在默默地帮助我。为了这本书，我绞尽脑汁，喜怒哀乐已经不足以形容我这么多年编写此书的心路历程。当我得知这本书将在2008年的夏天由北京大学出版社出版时，我仿佛平静了许多，不再是一开始的单纯的欣喜，而是在心中积淀下那么久以来对于一种新生活的渴望。这本书对我来说是一个起点，我要继续努力，把语法这门课教授得更好。人生的幸福不在于结果，这样的过程恰恰是我们所需要的。

首先要感谢我的妈妈这么多年来对我无私的关怀，我无以为报，唯有认真生活、用心工作！更要感谢我的授业恩师北京外国语大学梅仁毅教授在百忙之中为我的拙作题写序言。还要感谢合肥师范学院、北京外国语大学和新东方科技教育集团的老师们以及北京大学出版社的编辑和领导们在出版本书过程中给我极大的帮助和支持。最后，我还要感谢这么多年以来关心过我、爱护过我、提携过我的所有人，谢谢大家！

书中难免有错误之处，恳请读者批评指正，我将感激不尽。

武 峰

2008年6月28日

于北京外国语大学东院

目 录

第一天 突破英语语法的基本知识和名词 1
  1.1 英语语言概述 1
  1.2 基本词法知识点 6

第二天 突破英语的代词和冠词 16
  2.1 代词 16
  2.2 冠词 25

第三天 突破英语的数词、形容词和副词 40
  3.1 数词 40
  3.2 形容词和副词 43

第四天 突破英语的动词及其两种时态 61
  4.1 动词 61
  4.2 动词的时态 68

第五天 突破英语的时态（一）...... 79
  5.1 一般将来时 79
  5.2 过去将来时 81
  5.3 现在进行时 83
  5.4 过去进行时 86
  5.5 将来进行时 88

第六天 突破英语的时态（二）...... 91
  6.1 现在完成时 91
  6.2 过去完成时 95
  6.3 将来完成时 97
  6.4 现在完成进行时 98

第七天　突破英语的被动语态、助动词和情态动词 ... 111
　　7.1　被动语态 ... 111
　　7.2　助动词和情态动词 ... 116

第八天　突破英语的非谓语动词 ... 134
　　8.1　不定式 ... 134
　　8.2　动名词 ... 138
　　8.3　分词 ... 140

第九天　突破英语的虚拟语气 ... 154
　　9.1　虚拟语气 ... 154
　　9.2　虚拟语气和条件句 ... 155
　　9.3　虚拟语气和从句 ... 156
　　9.4　虚拟语气的特殊用法 ... 158

第十天　突破英语的介词、连词和基本句型 ... 162
　　10.1　介词 ... 162
　　10.2　连词 ... 169
　　10.3　基本句型知识点 ... 170

第十一天　突破英语的复合句 ... 185
　　11.1　主语从句 ... 185
　　11.2　宾语从句 ... 186
　　11.3　表语从句 ... 188
　　11.4　同位语从句 ... 189
　　11.5　定语从句 ... 190
　　11.6　状语从句 ... 194

第十二天　突破英语的语序、主谓一致和it的用法 ... 210
　　12.1　语序 ... 210
　　12.2　主谓一致 ... 213
　　12.3　it的用法 ... 217

附录　参考答案与解析 ... 230

第一天

突破英语语法的基本知识和名词

语法是怎么回事？语法到底包括哪些内容？英语中最简单的名词需要掌握哪些知识？这是我们在第一天的学习中需要掌握的内容。

1.1 英语语言概述

英语是盎格鲁-撒克逊人的民族语。它属于印欧语系的日耳曼西部语支，大约形成于公元5世纪。

英语共有26个字母，48个音标。其重要特征是：① 屈折变化少，除名词、代词、形容词、副词、动词等有少数变化外，其他无变化；② 词汇具有开放性，引进外来语较多；③ 句法较灵活，共有三种句型（简单句、复合句、并列句）。

1. 英语词汇可分为实词和虚词两大类

实词	名词（noun）*n.*	e.g.: book	desk
	代词（pronoun）*pron.*	e.g.: I	yours
	形容词（adjective）*adj.*	e.g.: perfect	beautiful
	数词（numeral）*num.*	e.g.: one	third
	动词（verb）*v.*	e.g.: catch	hold
	副词（adverb）*adv.*	e.g.: happily	here
虚词	冠词（article）*art.*	e.g.: the	a
	介词（preposition）*prep.*	e.g.: on	under
	连词（conjunction）*conj.*	e.g.: but	and
	感叹词（interjection）*interj.*	e.g.: oh	hi

2. 英语的构词法主要来源于以下四种方法

（1）前缀法（prefixion）：词根前加前缀，词性不变，意义常改变。

（2）后缀法（suffixation）：词根后加后缀，意义不改变，词性常改变。

前缀法和后缀法如表1-1所示。

表1-1 英语的构词法

项 目	前 缀	例 词
意义	dis-（表否定） in-（有变体：il-, im-, ir- 表否定） un-（表否定） super-（超……） re-（再……）	disobey dislike incomplete irregular impossible unknown unexpected superman supermarket rewrite rebuild

项 目	后 缀	例 词
名词	-ism（表主义） -er（表人） -ess（表女性） -ese -(i)an（表某国人） -ness（与形容词连用形成名词）	socialism materialism booker worker actress waitress Chinese Russian meanness happiness
形容词	-ful（多由抽象名词构成） -less（表否定） -y（具有某特性）	useful helpful careless homeless sunny cloudy
副词	-ly	extremely personally
动词	-ise -ize -en	modernize nationalize harden loosen
数词	-th -ty -teen	fourth fifth thirty eighteen

（3）转类法（conversion）：一个单词由一种词性向另一种词性转变，而形式不变。

love（爱）n. — love（爱）v.　　　　bottle（瓶）n. — bottle（用瓶装水）v.

（4）合成法（compound）：一个单词是由两个或两个以上的词构成的新词。形式上可分为以下三种。

A	B	C
sunrise	bee-wax	washing machine
girlfriend	mail-delivery	post office
classroom	self-control	tax cut

3. 句子成分

一个句子一般由两个部分组成,即主语部分和谓语部分。

✏️ e.g.: He teaches us English.
　　　　主语　　谓语

句子成分即在句子中起一定作用的部分,一般可分为以下六种:

(1) 主语(subject):是一个句子的主体,是全句述说的对象。常用名词或相当于名词的词担当,一般置于句首。

✏️ e.g.: *The sun* is shinning in our faces.
　　　　主语

太阳正照着我们的脸。

(2) 谓语或谓语部分(predicate or predicate verb):是说明主语动作或状态的。常用动词担当,置于主语之后。

✏️ e.g.: I *go* to the park every day.
　　　　　　谓语

我每天去公园。

(3) 宾语(object):是表示及物动词的动作对象或介词所联系的对象的。常用名词或相当于名词的词担当,置于及物动词或介词后。

✏️ e.g.: He received *a letter* five days ago.
　　　　　　　　　　　宾语

他五天前收到一封信。

(4) 补语(complement)和表语(predicative):补语用于补充、说明主语和宾语的意义,一般说明其特征,常由名词或形容词担当。表语是位于主语后的主语补足语。

✏️ e.g.: I saw an old man *come across the street*.
　　　　　　　　　　　　　　　宾语补语

我看见一个老人过马路了。

I am *a good student*.
　　　主语补语(表语)

我是一个好学生。

（5）定语（attributive）：定语是用来限定或修饰名词或相当于名词的短语。常由形容词或相当于形容词的短语来担当。

✎ e.g.: She is a very *beautiful* girl.
　　　　　　　　　　定语

她是一个美丽的女孩。

（6）状语（adverbial）：是修饰动词、副词、形容词或全句的一类语法成分。常由副词或相当于副词的短语来担当。

✎ e.g.: *Unluckily*, she met a white elephant in the park.
　　　　状语

很不走运，她在公园里遇见了一头白象。

Tips 另外还有一种独立成分（independent element），它不做语法成分，如感叹词、插入语和称呼。

✎ e.g.: *Generally speaking*, he is a good man.
　　　　　插入语

大体上说，他是一个好人。

4. 短语（phrase）

短语是一类具有一定意义但不构成分句或句子的一组词，可单独做句子成分。它可分为名词短语、动词短语、形容词短语、副词短语、介词短语（**注意和短语介词的区别**）、不定式短语、动名词短语、分词短语等。

✎ e.g.: a university student（名词短语）　　walking home（分词短语）
　　　　get up（动词短语）　　　　　　　quite warm（形容词短语）
　　　　to see（不定式短语）　　　　　　work hard（副词短语）
　　　　watching TV（动名词短语）　　　at the gate（介词短语）

5. 从句（subordinate clause）

具体见第十一天的内容。

6. 句子（sentence）

（1）句子是包含主语部分和谓语部分并有完整意义的可以独立的一组词。英语中有五种基本句型。

① 主+谓 — (S+V)

✏️ e.g.: Day dawns.
　　　　天亮了。

② 主+谓+宾 — (S+V+O)

✏️ e.g.: He teaches English.
　　　　他教英语。

③ 主+谓+宾+宾补 — (S+V+O+C)

✏️ e.g.: John found her very clever.
　　　　约翰发现她很聪明。

④ 主+谓+宾+宾 — (S+V+O+O)

✏️ e.g.: He gives me a pen.
　　　　他给我一支钢笔。

⑤ 主+谓+主补 — 主+系+表 — (S+L+P)

✏️ e.g.: She is a good nurse.
　　　　她是一个好护士。

（2）根据结构可把句子分为以下三种。

① 简单句（simple sentence）：一个含有主语（并列主语）和谓语（并列谓语）的句子。

✏️ e.g.: Five and five is ten.
　　　　五加五等于十。

② 并列句（compound sentence）：由一个或一个以上的连词把两个或两个以上的句子合成的句子。

✏️ e.g.: I came early, but she wasn't happy.
　　　　尽管我回来很早，但她还是不高兴。

③ 复合句（complex sentence）：由关联词把主句和一个或一个以上的分句合成的句子。

✏️ e.g.: He is the man whom I want to talk with.
　　　　他是我想说话的那个人。

（3）根据句子的用途可分为：陈述句、疑问句、祈使句、感叹句。

小 结

在本章中，主要讲述了英语的基本知识，希望大家了解语法结构中的主要成分——主、谓、宾、定、状、补，而且句子的五种形式也是大家在日后经常遇到的。这些都是为以后的学习打下坚实基础的主要成分。在不配任何练习题的情况下，希望大家能将书中的每一个例句记牢，便于以后学习。努力吧！

1.2　基本词法知识点

1. 名词的定义、特征和种类

（1）名词是表示人、事物及抽象概念的词。

e.g.: book（书）　　railway（铁路）　　bear（熊）　　the Great Wall（长城）

（2）名词的特征。

① 有复数-s词尾的屈折变化。

e.g.: student—students

② 有冠词在前说明名词。

e.g.: in the sky　　　on the desk

Tips 在这里一定要注意"说明"和"修饰"两个词的不同，说明性的词是不可以省略的，而修饰性的词是可以省略的。

（3）名词的分类。

名词
- 普通名词
  - 个体名词：book　　bag ⎫
  - 集体名词：group　　family ⎭ 大多数可数
  - 抽象名词：work　　love ⎫
  - 物质名词：water　　milk ⎭ 大多数不可数
- 专有名词：用来说明某个具体事物的名称

Tips 实际上词汇的分类是一种人为行为，并没有特别的规定，也就是为了把可数和不可数名词进行大概的分类。

2. 名词的数

数是名词中最重要的语法现象之一。名词的数分为可数名词和不可数名词两种。

Tips 区分这两种名词切不可以数量的多少（特别是观念的影响）为依据，一定要以字典为依据。

e.g.: duty（责任）在中文中是不可数，但在英文中为可数——duties。

soap（肥皂）在中文中是可数，但在英文中为不可数——a cake of soap。

（1）可数名词的数（如表1-2所示）。

表1-2 可数名词的数的变化

情况	例词
一般情况：加-s清辅音后 读/s/ 浊辅音后 读/z/	book—books bag—bags
在/s/、/z/、/ʒ/、/ʃ/、/dʒ/、/tʃ/后加-es读/iz/ 注：在很多语法书的讲解中是以单词的词尾字母来加屈折变化的，但是如果用词尾发音来记忆会更加简单	brush—brushes orange—oranges watch—watches
在辅音字母+y结尾，去y变i加-es读/iz/ 在元音字母+y结尾，直接加-s读/z/	factory—factories boy—boys
在字母o后直接加-es 读/z/ （有生命的加-es，无生命的加-s） 注：实际上括号内的说法并不是专业的说法，在英语中应该是本族词汇要求加-es，外族词汇和新构成的词汇要求加-s，这点不要求非英语专业学生掌握	hero—heroes potato—potatoes tomato—tomatoes photo—photos radio—radios

续表

情 况	例 词
以f, fe结尾的变f为-ves,读/vz/ 　　注：但是cliff, chief, handkerchief 以及roof 后面一般加-s，大家可以记忆成"一个头领站在屋顶的悬崖边拿着手绢"	knife—knives leaf—leaves loaf—loaves
不规则变化： （1）元音内部变化	foot—feet man—men woman—women goose—geese mouse—mice
（2）辅音尾部变化	ox—oxen child—children
（3）通形名词 　　① 用修饰可数名词的词进行修饰 　　② 单数与复数形式相同 　　③ 它们也可以加-s，但表示种类	many sheep many fish a sheep—many sheep a sheep 一只羊 many sheeps 许多种羊
（4）民族词变化 　　注：中日不变，英法变，其余复数加后面	Chinese—Chinese Japanese—Japanese Englishman—Englishmen Frenchman—Frenchmen German—Germans
（5）少数需要记忆的特殊变化	house—houses belief—beliefs chief—chiefs piano—pianos safe—safes proof—proofs kilo—kilos photo—photos

（2）不可数名词的数。

不可数名词也要表达数量的多少，它们遵循以下规则。

① 单数：不定冠词 + 量词（单）+ of + 不可数名词

     a piece of paper

② 复数：数词 + 量词（复）+ of + 不可数名词

     two pieces of paper

当然，可数名词也有以下这种用法（注意词尾变化）：

a box of apples

two boxes of apples

（3）复合名词的数。

① 复数变化在最后 afternoon——afternoons

② 主要部分发生变化 looker-on——lookers-on

③ 由man，woman构成的词，两部分都发生变化 a man doctor——some men doctors

（4）集体名词的数。

① 集体名词的数要遵循"整体是单数（a），个体是复数（b）"的原则。

 e.g.:（a）The family is large.   （b）The family are large.

    这个家族很大。   这个家里成员很多。

② 有几个和冠词连用的词，谓语只用单数形式。

the majority   the minority   the public

③ 有几个词只有单数形式，而其谓语用复数形式。

people   police   cattle

3. 名词的所有格

Tips 所有格是和名词的数同样重要的语法现象之一。

（1）所有格的含义和种类。

① 所有格指的是两词之间所属关系的一种语法现象。

✏️ e.g.: Bruce's wife（布鲁斯的妻子）　　a cover of the book（书的封面）

② 种类（两种形式）：一是由名词后加's构成（有生命）　Xiaoming's desk

　　　　　　　　　二是由名词和 of 构成（无生命）　a leg of the desk

（2）'s格的用法。

① 表示共同拥有的关系时，'s加在最后一个词上；表示每个人各有的关系时，'s加在每个词之后。

✏️ e.g.: (a) Xiaoming and Wanghai's desk　(b) Xiaoming's and Wanghai's desks

---

Tips　　（a）句和（b）句的区别在于前者是两个人共有一张桌（单数），后者是两个人各有一张桌（复数）。

---

② 's格可表示有生命的东西，有时候也可表示无生命的东西。

A 表度量衡：today's newspaper

B 表自然现象：the tree's branch　（当然也可以用 a branch of the tree）

C 表国家、城市、星体：a city's park

③ 如出现家庭、商店、诊所这些词时，都可以省略。

✏️ e.g.: the doctor's clinic = the doctor's
　　　　Uncle Wang's house = Uncle Wang's

④ 当可数名词的复数形式做定语时，'s省略为'。

✏️ e.g.: the teachers's college = the teachers' college

（3）of 属格的用法（主要用于无生命的东西）。

✏️ e.g.: a subject of the sentence　句子的主语

（4）双重属格：of +'s 的属格形式称为双重属格。

✏️ e.g.: a picture of Xiao Li's（侧重于整体中的一个，不一定有小李）

请与这种形式做比较：a picture of Xiao Li（侧重于小李的画像，一定有小李）

Tips 实际上还有一种比较难的情况：

my father's big red nose 和 a big red nose of my father's

前者就是说我爸爸有个大红鼻子，但是后者更有一种感情色彩，请注意这样的短语: a lovely baby of my sister's。

---

4. 名词的性

名词的性可分为：阳、中、阴三种。如 boy（阳），teacher（中），girl（阴）。

Tips 在英语中已经基本不区分阴阳性，这点和其他印欧系的语言有所区别。

小 结

在这一节中主要学习了名词的概述、数、格、性。其中最重要、最常见的是数和格。
请大家回答下列问题：
（1）名词主要包括哪些？
（2）名词单复数是如何区分的？
（3）名词如何变成复数形式？（重点中的重点是九种变法）
（4）名词属格包括哪些？
（5）用's格代替of属格的情况是哪些？
（6）双重属格怎么用？
针对以上问题，如果大家能在很短的时间内回答出来，并且记住一些我给出的口诀，那么名词这章就没有问题了。

练 习

1. The student is so clever; he has _____.
   A. brain   B. a brain   C. brains   D. the brain
2. Could you give me _____ on how to learn math well?
   A. many advice   B. many advices
   C. a lot of advices   D. a piece of advice
3. — Let's go to the cinema.
   — I'm sorry. I have _____ tonight.
   A. many homeworks   B. much homeworks
   C. many homework   D. much homework
4. — Why are you so late?
   — I was delayed by _____.
   A. any heavy traffic   B. heavy traffic
   C. some heavy traffic   D. a heavy traffic
5. Mr. White is _____.
   A. a old friend of my father   B. an old friend of my father
   C. an old friend of my father's   D. my father old friend
6. Henry went into the _____ to buy a pair of shoes.
   A. shoes store   B. shoe store
   C. shoe's store   D. shoes' store
7. He is the only one among the _____ teachers who _____ from Beijing.
   A. man; comes   B. man's; come
   C. men; come   D. men; comes
8. — Please don't be late again next time.
   — I didn't intend to but it is _____ from my home to the station.
   A. two hours' walk   B. two hour walk
   C. two hours walk   D. two hour's walk
9. You have to climb up the _____ tree to fetch the kite.
   A. thirty foots high   B. thirty-feet-high
   C. thirty-foot-high   D. thirty feet high

10. Mr. Green entered a shop that only sells _____.
    A. men shoes　　　　　　　　　B. man's shoes
    C. men's shoes　　　　　　　　D. the shoes of men
11. _____ happy life people in the small village live today!
    A. What　　B. How　　C. How a　　D. What a
12. Farmers raise _____ on their farms.
    A. geese　　B. gooses　　C. geeses　　D. goose
13. This new car is _____.
    A. Ricky and Bruce　　　　　　B. Ricky's and Bruce
    C. Ricky and Bruce's　　　　　D. Ricky's and Bruce's
14. There are a large number of _____ in the street.
    A. passer-by　　　　　　　　　B. passer-bies
    C. passers-bys　　　　　　　　D. passers-by
15. My favorite food is some _____ and _____.
    A. potatos; bread　　　　　　　B. potatoes; bread
    C. potatos; breads　　　　　　　D. potatoes; breads
16. — You are _____, aren't you?
    — No, we are _____.
    A. Frenchman; Germen　　　　B. Frenchmen; Germans
    C. Frenchmen; Germen　　　　D. Frenchmans; German
17. There are lots of _____ eating _____ at the foot of the hill.
    A. sheep; grass　　　　　　　　B. sheeps; grass
    C. sheep; grasses　　　　　　　D. sheeps; grasses
18. That bookstore sells _____.
    A. children book　　　　　　　B. children books
    C. children's books　　　　　　D. childs books
19. It's bad _____ to speak with your mouth full of food.
    A. manners　　　　　　　　　　B. manner
    C. methods　　　　　　　　　　D. way
20. I give my _____ to her on her birthday.
    A. the congratulation　　　　　B. congratulations
    C. a congratulation　　　　　　D. congratulation

21. She is the one of _____ doctors who _____ from America.
    A. woman; comes   B. women; comes
    C. women; come   D. woman; come
22. I'm very surprised that a work ant has two _____.
    A. stomach   B. stomaches
    C. stomacs   D. stomachs
23. He is the best _____ teacher.
    A. chemistry   B. chemistry's
    C. chemical   D. chemical's
24. A thief is a harm to _____.
    A. the society   B. society
    C. societies   D a society
25. _____ is waiting for you, John.
    A. Mr. Smith   B. A Mr. Smith
    C. The Mr. Smith   D. Sir. Smith
26. What do you think about _____ advice?
    A. any one's else   B. anyone else's
    C. any's one else   D. anyone else
27. He went on doing his homework after _____.
    A. a moment rest   B. moments rest
    C. a moments' rest   D. a moment's rest
28. Cattle _____ eating in the field at that time.
    A. are   B. is   C. was   D. were
29. The village is about _____ ride from here.
    A. one and a half hour's   B. one-half-hour
    C. one and half hour   D. one and a half hours'
30. Tom's _____ as white as pearl.
    A. tooths are   B. teeth is   C. tooth is   D. teeth are
31. There is _____ on my back.
    A. pain   B. a pain   C. of pain   D. pains
32. Paper was first invented in _____.
    A. east   B. East   C. the East   D. the east

33. Lucy does _____ homework than any other _____ in the class.
    A. much; student			B. most; student
    C. more; student			D. more; students
34. _____ an important subject in university.
    A. Politics are			B. The politic are
    C. Political is			D. Politics is
35. He has two _____ bills in his pocket.
    A. ten-dollars			B. ten-dollar
    C. ten dollar			D. ten dollars
36. He spent _____ money on novels.
    A. a great deal of			B. a plenty of
    C. many				D. a number of
37. This piece of _____ is enough for him to make a suit.
    A. cloth		B. cloths		C. clothing		D. clothes
38. She seems to be _____, but as a matter of fact she is very clever.
    A. a girl of a fool			B. a fool of a girl
    C. a fool of the man		D. a man of my fool
39. How time flies! I find she has _____.
    A. a little gray hair			B. a few gray hairs
    C. some gray hair			D. much gray hair
40. Is _____ I visited last month?
    A. this school where		B. this school one
    C. this the school			D. this school

第二天

突破英语的代词和冠词

在第二天的学习中,我们将接触到代词和冠词这两部分,其中代词是比较容易的,主要应该注意不定代词的用法,而冠词是中文当中所没有的,所以三种冠词的用法在书中讲了多少,希望大家就要牢牢记住多少,不需要再多去学习。很多英语学者曾经用大量的笔墨讲解冠词的用法,但实际上一般学习者没有必要学习那么多用法。

2.1 代　词

1. 代词的定义及分类

（1）代词是代替名词以及起名词作用的短语、分句或句子的词。

（2）代词可分为人称代词、物主代词、指示代词、反身代词、相互代词、不定代词、疑问代词、连接代词和关系代词等。

2. 人称代词

人称代词是人称范畴,它们有屈折变化形式,有人称、数和性的变化（如表2-1所示）。

表2-1　人称代词

人称	单　数				复　数	
	主　格		宾　格		主　格	宾　格
一	I		me		we	us
二	you		you		you	you
三	阳性	he	阳性	him	they	them
	阴性	she	阴性	her		
	中性	it	中性	it		

注：主格用于主语,宾格用于宾语。

宾格常用于动词和介词之后。

✏️ e.g.: *He* stood in front of *her*.
　　　主格　　　　　　　　宾格
　　　他站在她的前面。

Tips 在这里要注意英文和中文的区别，中文第三人称单数（他、她和它）的读音都是一样的，只要不写出来，很难区分是男是女，甚至还是动物。

　　Could *you* go with *us*?
　　　　　主格　　　　宾格
　　你能和我们一起去吗？

3. 物主代词

物主代词是表示所属关系的代词，类似于名词的属格。它可分成形容词性物主代词和名词性物主代词（如表2-2所示）。

表2-2　物主代词

形容词性物主代词	my	your	his	her	its	our	your	their
名词性物主代词	mine	yours	his	hers	its	ours	yours	theirs
中文意思	我的	你的	他的	她的	它的	我们的	你们的	他（她）们的

（1）形容词性物主代词。

这一类代词相当于形容词，可以做定语。

✏️ e.g.: *My* shirt is blue.
　　　我的衬衫是蓝色的。

　　His bike is broken.
　　他的自行车坏了。

　　Your teacher has just come into the classroom.
　　你们老师刚刚进教室。

（2）名词性物主代词。

这一类代词相当于名词，可以做主语、表语和宾语。

> e.g.: There are three apples. I have two. *Mine* are red.
> 我有三个苹果中的两个。我的（苹果）是红的。
>
> Her blouse is green. We don't like *hers*.
> 她的毛衣是绿色的。我们不喜欢她的（毛衣）。
>
> There is a gray pencil and a black pencil on the desk. The gray one is *yours*.
> 桌上有一支灰色和一支黑色的铅笔。灰色的是你的（铅笔）。

4. 指示代词

指示代词一般包括this（这个，近指单数）、that（那个，远指单数）、these（这些，近指复数）、those（那些，远指复数），此类代词较简单。

> e.g.: *This* is a desk.　　　　　　*That* pen is black.
> 这是一张桌子。　　　　　　那支笔是黑色的。
>
> *These* are trees.　　　　　　　*Those* apples are red.
> 这是一些树。　　　　　　　　那些苹果是红色的。

5. 不定代词

Tips 英语中最重要的代词，这里采用比较的方法来讲解，请大家注意要比较清楚。

不定代词是用来代替不确定的一类事物的代词。此类词的用法较难，它一般包括some, any, no, none, many, much, few, little, each, both, all, either, neither, one, another, the other 等。

（1）some和any。

① some和any都表示"一些"时，some用于肯定句，any用于否定句和疑问句。

> e.g.: There are *some* people at the gate of the theater.
> 有一些人在剧院门口。
>
> I haven't *any* pencils.
> 我没有铅笔。

② some也可用于疑问句，表示一种客气的请求。

● e.g.: Would you like *some* cups of tea?

　　　　你要喝茶吗？

③ any也可用于肯定句，它表示"任何"的意思。

● e.g.: *Anyone* can do it.

　　　　任何人都能做。

（2）each和every。

each和every 都表示"每一个"。each的指向可少于三个，可以是两个，而且注意力在个体上；every的指向至少是三个或是三个以上，它主要集中在整体上。

● e.g.: *Each* teacher will give a speech in the meeting.

　　　　每个老师都将在会上做报告。

　　　　Every student can pass the exam.

　　　　每个学生都能通过考试。

（3）many和much。

many 和much 都表示"许多"的意思，只是 many 修饰或代替可数名词，much修饰或代替不可数名词。

● e.g.: *Many* students are playing on the playground.

　　　　许多学生都在操场上玩。

Tips　　many a man 这种用法也比较特殊，因为虽然表示"许多人"，但是后面的谓语动词用的是单数形式。一般只有可数名词有这种用法。

He has *much* money, so he can buy anything he likes.

他有很多钱，所以他可以买任何他喜欢的东西。

Tips　　一般很少提many和much这两个词的根本性区别，实际上many是一个具有形容词词性的单词，而much则是一个具有副词词性的单词。从词性上判断词的用法是最好不过的。

（4）a few和a little。

a few和a little都表示"一些"的意思，比some要少，它们可修饰或代替名词，但a few是和可数名词连用，而a little则和不可数名词连用。

Tips 它们的否定形式是将前面的a去掉。

e.g.: *A few* bananas are on the desk.
桌子上有一些香蕉。
Few bananas are on the desk.
没有多少香蕉在桌上。
A little water is in the glass.
杯子里有一点水。
Little water is in the glass.
杯子里没有多少水。

Tips 一般很少提a few和a little这两个词的根本性区别，实际上a few是一个具有形容词词性的单词，而a little则是一个具有副词词性的单词。从词性上判断词的用法是最好不过的。

（5）no, none, no one和nothing。

① no相当于形容词，它相当于not a (any)，可修饰不可数或可数名词。

e.g.: We have *no* lessons in the afternoon.
= We have *not any* lessons in the afternoon.
下午我们没有课。
I have *no* book. = I have *not a* book.
我没有书。

② none可指人或物（指三个或三个以上）。none后面的动词谓语可以用单数，也可以用复数。

✏️ e.g.: *None* of us know(s) French.
我们中没有人懂法语。

③ no one可以指人，不可指物。

✏️ e.g.: *No one* can do this job.
没有人能做这项工作。

④ nothing一般只能指物，不能指人。

✏️ e.g.: Nothing can be done easily.
没有事情可以轻易地做成。

Tips 一般来说，none, no one和nothing这三个词中，只有none后面可以加of，其余两个一般不用。

（6）both和all。

① 强调两个人或物时（不是一个），才用both。

✏️ e.g.: I have two brothers. *Both* are students.
我有两个兄弟，他们都是学生。

both…and…是常用词组。

✏️ e.g.: *Both* you *and* she are teachers.
你和她都是教师。

② all强调"所有""一切"的意思，强调三个或三个以上。

✏️ e.g.: *All* the people are men.
所有的人都是男的。

*Not all the people are men.
并非所有人都是男人。（部分否定）

*All the people are not men.
所有人都不是男人。（全部否定）

Tips not在不同的位置会产生不同的效应，在本书后面的一些章节也会提到。有部分否定和完全否定，还有否定的前置问题。

（7）other, another, the other 和 the others。

① other 是一个形容词，而不是副词。如： other people（另一些人）。

② another 指的是"另一个"，一般是指三者或三者以上的另一个。

e.g.: I have three magazines. *One* is white and black, *another* is red, *still another* is blue.

我有三本杂志，其中一本是黑白色的，另一本红色的，还有一本是蓝色的。

Tips 第三个用 still another 来表示。

③ the other 指的是"另一个"，一般是指两者之间的另一个。

e.g.: I have two books. *One* is on history, *the other* is on politics.

我有两本书，一本是关于历史的，一本是关于政治的。

④ the others 指的是"另一些"，一般是指两部分之间的另一些。

e.g.: There are many people in the park. *Some* are running, *the others* are playing football.

公园里有很多人，一些人在赛跑，另一些在踢足球。

（8） either 和 neither。

① either 指的是"两个中其中一个"。neither 指的是"两个都不"。

e.g.: *Either of* them can draw a picture.

他们中有一个会画画。

Neither of them can draw a picture.

他们中没有会画画的。

② 还有两个重要的词组：either ... or 和 neither ... nor。

e.g.: *Either* he *or* I am a student.

他和我有一个是学生。

Neither he *nor* I am a student.

他和我都不是学生。

（9）复合不定代词。

复合不定代词是由any，body，every，no，one，some，thing构成的。共有十二个（anybody，anyone，anything，everybody，everyone，everything，no one，nobody，nothing，somebody，someone，something），这些词做主语时其谓语动词用单数形式。

e.g.: *Someone* is in the classroom.
有人在教室里。

Tips 一般来说，anybody和anyone, everybody和everyone，somebody和someone在现代英语中一般没有区别，但是现在使用someone更多。如果有形容词修饰它们时，形容词一般放在它们后面。

I have *something* important to tell you.
我有重要的事告诉你。
You need to do *everything* necessary.
你需要做任何有必要做的事情。

6. 疑问代词

Tips 注意疑问代词和疑问副词的区别。

疑问代词有what, who, whom, which和whose。
（1）what的用法：用来问某问题的性质，可做主语、宾语和表语。

e.g.: *What*'s your father? = *What* does your father do?
你父亲是干什么的？

（2）who的用法："谁"的意思，可做主语和表语，问人称。

e.g.: *Who* are they?
他们是谁？

Who is that boy standing under the tree?

那个站在树下的小男孩是谁？

（3）whom的用法："谁"的意思，做宾语。

e.g.: *Whom* were you talking with?

刚才正在和你说话的是谁？

（4）which的用法："哪一个"的意思，做宾语和表语，一般和or连用。

e.g.: *Which* fruit do you like better, oranges or apples?

你更喜欢哪一种水果，橘子还是苹果？

（5）whose的用法："谁的"意思，做定语。

e.g.: *Whose* shirt is white?

谁的衬衫是白色的？

7. 关系代词

关系代词详见第十一天的内容。

小 结

在本章的学习中，应该注意代词的基本用法，人称代词和物主代词需要大家记忆，还要分清指示代词的近指和远指，疑问代词中which和what的根本性区别，最重要的就是不定代词。

请大家回答下列问题：

（1）a few 和 a little 的本质性区别是什么？

（2）many 和 many a 的区别是什么？

（3）some 是否全部用于肯定句？any是否完全用于疑问句和否定句？

（4）no 是什么词性？ none，nothing和no one的区别是什么？

（5）either和neither的区别？

（6）other的词性？ another，the other和others 的区别是什么？

（7）复合不定代词有哪两个特征？

代词的关键是不定代词，不定代词的关键是以上七个问题，回答出以上这些问题就可以了。

2.2 冠　　词

1. 冠词的含义

冠词应包括以下三层含义。

（1）冠词是一种虚词。

（2）冠词不能单独使用，而且不能构成句子成分。

（3）冠词是用来说明名词的，而不是修饰名词，这一点要注意。

> **Tips**　所谓虚词指的是不能在句子中单独构成成分的几类词，包括冠词、连词和介词等。在这里要强调的是：副词在英语中是实词，做状语，而在中文中却是虚词。

2. 冠词的分类

冠词可分为定冠词（the），不定冠词（an和a）和零冠词。

3. 不定冠词的用法

不定冠词可分为a和an两种。a一般用于辅音音素前，发作/ə/，而an用于元音音素前，发作/æn/。

 e.g.: an hour　　　an honest boy
　　　　a university　　a big apple

> **Tips**　元音音素和元音字母是两回事，所以不是以元音字母开头的单词前都要用an。

There is _____ "s" and _____ /s/ in this word "smile".

用a和an填空，前者填an，后者填a，因为前者是字母，读作/es/，是元音音素开头的；后者是音素，读作/s/，所以用a。

（1）不定冠词表示单数"一"或不确定时使用，源于数词one。

 e.g.: *A* boy is standing under the tree.

　　　一个小男孩正站在树下。

"a"在这里既指一个小男孩，又是表示不确定男孩是谁。

（2）不定冠词用于单数名词前表示一类东西。

> e.g.: *A* horse is smaller than *an* elephant.
>
> 马比象小。（并不是一匹马比一头大象小）

Tips

可数名词的类指实际上有三种方式。

A horse is smaller than *an* elephant.

The horse is smaller than *the* elephant.

Horses are smaller than elephants.

这三句都是"马比大象小"，在用法上可以在可数名词单数前加定冠词或不定冠词以及把它们变成复数形式。

（3）固定词组。

as a matter of fact 事实上	a few 一些（修饰可数名词复数）	
as a result 结果	a little 一些（修饰不可数名词）	
a bit 一点	a little bit more 一点点	
a lot of 许多	a great deal of 许多	a great number of 许多

4. 定冠词的用法

定冠词the用于辅音音素前，发作/ðə/，而the用于元音音素前，发作/ði:/。

> e.g.: the boy   the apple

（1）定冠词源于that，用于专指和特指。

> e.g.: *The* boy is my son.
>
> 这个男孩是我儿子。
>
> Take *the* apple.
>
> 拿这个苹果。

（2）定冠词用于单数名词前。

- e.g.: *The* horse is smaller than *the* elephant.

  马比大象小。（并不是这匹马比这头大象小）

（3）定冠词用于形容词最高级前和序数词前。

- e.g.: *The* most important is that we need deal with this problem first.

  最重要的是首先我们要处理这个问题。

  The boy is *the* same as his father.

  这个男孩和他爸爸长得一样。（same前须用the）

  It is *the* first time that I have heard of it.

  这是我第一次听说这件事。

Tips 不定冠词和定冠词用于形容词最高级前和序数词前的比较。

It is a most useful book.
这是一本非常有用的书。
It is the most useful book.
这是一本最有用的书。

I won a first prize in politics exam.
我在政治考试中得了一个第一名。
I won the first prize in politics exam.
我在政治考试中得了第一名。

（4）定冠词用于形容词和过去分词前，表示一类人，且谓语用复数形式。

- e.g.: *The* poor often hate *the* rich.

  穷人总是很讨厌富人。

  The injured were sent to hospital at once.

  受伤的人马上被送往医院。

（5）定冠词用于乐器之前。

- e.g.: play *the* piano   play *the* violin

> **Tips**: 现在如果是中国乐器，且用拼音表示的话，那么一般来说不用冠词，例如：play Yangqin 和 play Hulusi 等。

（6）定冠词用于世界上独一无二的东西，通常须记住以下几个。

e.g.: *the* star　　*the* sun　　*the* earth　　*the* moon

> **Tips**: 实际上世界上所有的东西都是独一无二的，只是在这里让大家记住这样几个最常用的词，不是绝对的用法。

（7）定冠词用于专有名词前。

① 用于复形/复数名词前，表示一类人。

e.g.: *the* Chinese people　中国人　　　　　*the* Germans　德国人
　　　the Browns　布朗一家人　　　　　　*the* Grays　格里一家人

② 用于某些江河湖海等地理名词前。

e.g.: *the* Great Wall　长城　　　　　　　*the* Changjiang River　长江
　　　the Pacific Ocean　太平洋（大洋前用the）　*the* Alps　阿尔卑斯山
　　　the United States　美国　　　　　　*the* Bible　《圣经》

（8）固定词组。

e.g.: in *the* morning/afternoon/evening　在早晨/下午/晚上
　　　to tell you *the* truth　老实说
　　　in *the* middle of　在中间
　　　in *the* east/west/north/south　在东边/西边/北边/南边（方向前用定冠词）
　　　go to *the* theater　去看电影（某些娱乐活动用定冠词）
　　　the Spring Festival　春节（中国传统节日前要定冠词）

5. 零冠词的用法

零冠词在英语中运用得相当广泛，零冠词不代表没有冠词，而是省略用法。

（1）泛指人类或男女时。

e.g.: Man is mortal.
　　　人总有一死。

（2）用于"kind (sort) of"后。

e.g.: What kind of deer it is?
　　　这是哪种鹿？

（3）用于职务、职位和头衔前。

e.g.: He was elected our president.
　　　他被选举为我们的主席。

（4）用于复形名词前，表一类。

e.g.: Horses are smaller than elephants.
　　　马比大象小。（并不是许多马比许多大象小）

（5）用于月份、星期、节假日（国际性节日）和四季。

e.g.: January　New Year　Christmas Day
　　　National Day　　in winter/summer/spring/autumn

（6）用于一日三餐、球类运动前。

e.g.: have supper　play football　play basketball

但有限定词修饰时要用冠词。

e.g.: have a delicious meal

（7）用于"by+交通工具"前。

e.g.: by car　by plane

Tips　注意by water和by air等词的用法，不是表示"通过水"和"通过空气"，而是表示"通过水路"和"坐飞机"。

（8）名词前有代词修饰时不用冠词。

e.g.: Some apples are red.　　　　They are doing their homework.
　　　一些苹果是红的。　　　　　　他们正在做家庭作业。

（9）固定词组。

catch fire 起火	lose heart 丧失信心	take place 发生
by chance 偶然	by day 整天	from time to time 有时
on foot 步行	one by one 一个接一个	heart and soul 全心全意
in time 及时	on time 按时	in front of 在前面
in spite of 尽管	take part in 参加	make use of 利用

6. 某些词前的冠词使用情况

（1）"radio"作"电台"时，不加冠词 radio station；
作"无线电广播"时，加冠词 listen to the radio。

（2）"society"作"社会"时，不加冠词 in our society；
作"社会主义国家"时，加冠词 the societies。

（3）"nature"作"自然"时，不加冠词 keep the balance of nature。

小 结

冠词是一个比较难理解的语法点，因为它在中文里是不存在的。在学习时切记不要和中文中的某些词比较使用，一定要记牢冠词的使用方法。不定冠词不是非常重要，记住固定用法即可；定冠词和所谓不使用冠词（零冠词）的用法则特别重要。

请大家回答：

（1）类指的三种方法是什么？
（2）过去分词和形容词最高级前面用什么冠词？
（3）江、河、湖、海前用什么冠词？
（4）乐器前用什么冠词？
（5）职称、称谓前用什么冠词？
（6）物质名词和抽象名词前是否用冠词？
（7）一日三餐、球类运动、假日前用什么冠词？

以上七种是我们最常见的冠词用法，定冠词和零冠词要好好地区分开来。

代词练习

1. If people pay attention to protecting environment, _____ money will be saved.
   A. a large number of   B. the number of
   C. many   D. a great deal of

2. Listening and speaking are both necessary to English; _____ practices our oral English and _____ makes us know what other people say.
   A. that; this   B. this; that
   C. one; the other   D. one; another

3. Though the African people are very poor, _____ has been done to help them.
   A. little   B. enough   C. few   D. many

4. _____ made a big mistake.
   A. You, Jim and I   B. You, I and Jim
   C. I, Jim and you   D. I, you and Jim

5. _____ is exciting. I enjoy it very much.
   A. Both lectures   B. Neither lecture
   C. Both of lectures   D. Either of lectures

6. Mr. White has three sons, _____ is doctor, _____ are teachers.
   A. one; another   B. one; the others two
   C. one; other two   D. one; the other two

7. — Could you lend me your ink?
   — Sure. But I'm afraid that there is _____ left.
   A. little   B. much   C. a little   D. many

8. — Do you want an apple or an orange?
   — _____. I don't mind.
   A. Both   B. Neither   C. Either   D. All

9. A few of _____ are planning to have a picnic during the summer holiday.
   A. us boys   B. we boys   C. boys we   D. boys us

10. I have two pens, one is red; _____ is black.
    A. other   B. the other   C. another   D. others
11. — What do you think about this book?
    — So difficult that I think not _____ of students understand it.
    A. all   B. some   C. few   D. any
12. In America, there is a great deal of food, in fact, sometimes _____.
    A. too many   B. much too
    C. too more   D. too much
13. _____ of the students in my class do their best to improve their spoken English.
    A. Which   B. All   C. Each   D. Every
14. _____ of the classroom is full.
    A. Either   B. All
    C. Everyone   D. Every one
15. — How many tickets for the film did you buy yesterday?
    — _____.
    A. None   B. No one   C. Nothing   D. Nobody
16. — Is _____ OK with you to go swimming Saturday?
    — Sure. Any time will be OK.
    A. there   B. this   C. that   D. it
17. This work is too much for us. We need _____ people.
    A. another   B. other two   C. two more   D. more two
18. — Who is in the house?
    — _____.
    A. None   B. Nothing   C. Nobody   D. Every
19. I want to know _____ the book is.
    A. of which   B. whose   C. who   D. whom
20. America is a country _____ is rich in natural resources.
    A. who   B. what   C. in which   D. that
21. Sherry got high marks in the examination, _____ had been expected.
    A. as   B. what   C. that   D. who

22. He is the only one of the best writers _____ praised four times by the government.
    A. who have   B. who has
    C. that has been   D. who have been
23. China is the one of the countries _____ nuclear weapons.
    A. who has   B. which has   C. that have   D. that has
24. She has _____ interesting novels than I have.
    A. much more   B. many   C. much   D. many more
25. — Do you speak English?
    — Yes, but only _____.
    A. little   B. few   C. a few   D. a little
26. If this dictionary is not yours, _____ can it be?
    A. what else   B. who else
    C. which else's   D. who else's
27. Shanghai is larger than _____ city in Africa.
    A. any   B. another   C. other   D. any other
28. Shanghai is larger than _____ city in China.
    A. any   B. another   C. other   D. any other
29. I have decided to do it and anything _____ you say will not change it.
    A. that   B. whose   C. which   D. about which
30. _____ is known to all, war is serious.
    A. That   B. It   C. As   D. Since
31. Could you tell me the reason _____ you were upset?
    A. which   B. for that   C. for why   D. why
32. Would you like _____ tea?
    A. any   B. much   C. little   D. some
33. Little John visits his grandparents every _____.
    A. a few days   B. another day
    C. other day   D. few days
34. China is famous for _____ history.
    A. his   B. him   C. its   D. it is

35. Everyone has gone, _____?
    A. hasn't he   B. don't they   C. haven't they   D. doesn't he
36. All the homework, _____ my teacher gave to me, should be finished tonight.
    A. that   B. which   C. what   D. they
37. The population of China is larger than _____ of America.
    A. that   B. those   C. the   D. it
38. There is a wide road in front of my house, but _____ of the side has trees.
    A. both   B. every   C. neither   D. none
39. These trousers are too small, please give me a bigger _____.
    A. set   B. one   C. piece   D. pair
40. I have two watches, _____ are made in Japan.
    A. both   B. both of them
    C. both of which   D. neither
41. — How shall I take this medicine?
    — Two pills _____.
    A. three times every day   B. three times day
    C. three time everyday   D. three times one day
42. I have many friends, but _____ could help me when I was in trouble.
    A. all of them   B. each of whom
    C. not all of whom   D. none of them
43. Leifeng was so kind that he always helped other people; but he never thought of _____.
    A. himself   B. his   C. him   D. his own
44. — What can I do for you?
    — I want to have a job, _____ sort of job.
    A. one   B. any   C. other   D. the same
45. — Who is knocking the door?
    — _____ must be Paul.
    A. He   B. She   C. That   D. It

46. — Could you want _____ to eat ?
    — Oh. Yes, I have not been having _____ all day.
    A. something; nothing   B. anything; something
    C. anything; nothing   D. something; anything
47. — Do you have _____ to state?
    — No.
    A. something important   B. important something
    C. anything important   D. important anything
48. Everyone took off _____ hats.
    A. her   B. his   C. their   D. its
49. — What about these two books ?
    — I think that _____ of them is interesting.
    A. both   B. none   C. neither   D. all
50. I have already eaten two cakes, but I still want _____ cake.
    A. other   B. the other
    C. another   D. the others
51. There are _____ apples in the basket.
    A. a plenty of B. plenty of   C. lot of   D. much
52. Her skirt is more beautiful than _____.
    A. my   B. mine   C. I   D. me
53. — Why don't we take a break?
    — Didn't we just have _____?
    A. it   B. that   C. one   D. this
54. I think _____ wrong to take _____ for granted that _____ is very difficult to learn a foreign language.
    A. that; something; it   B. it; it; it
    C. it; it; that   D. it; nothing; it
55. John said he'd been working in the office for an hour, _____ was true.
    A. he   B. this   C. which   D. who
56. _____ the houses were destroyed during World War Two.
    A. Both   B. Most of   C. Any   D. All

57. _____ are there _____ true.
   A. That they; is   B. They; is
   C. That they; are   D. They; are

冠词练习

1. It is known that _____ main material for building houses has been brick, but _____ metal and wood have also been used today.
   A. the; /   B. /; /   C. /; the   D. the; the
2. _____ is the only animal that can think.
   A. Man   B. A man   C. The man   D. Men
3. Madame Gurie was _____ first person who was given _____ second Nobel Prize.
   A. the; a   B. the; the   C. a; the   D. a; a
4. She is _____ girl we are waiting for.
   A. the right   B. a very   C. very   D. a right
5. _____ having a wonderful supper.
   A. The Smith is   B. The Smiths are
   C. A Smith is   D. The Smith are
6. It was reported that _____ satellite would be sent into _____ space.
   A. a; the   B. a; a   C. /; the   D. a;/
7. _____ wants to see you.
   A. The Green   B. The Greens
   C. A Mr. Green   D. Mr. Green
8. It would be _____ wonderful world if all nations lived in _____ peace with each other.
   A. a; /   B. the; /   C. the; the   D. the; a
9. — How _____ is the population of India?
   — India has _____ population of more than 1,100,000,000.
   A. large; the   B. large; a   C. many; a   D. many; the
10. Rice is usually sold by _____ weight, while eggs are sometimes sold by _____ dozen.
    A. the; the   B. /; the   C. the; a   D. /; a

11. _____, he knows much about electricity.
    A. A child is   B. As a child
    C. Child as he is   D. As a child he is
12. Some people still think advertisement is _____ waste of money instead of _____ industry.
    A. the; the   B. a; /   C. a; the   D. /; an
13. _____ it is to attend the party!
    A. What funny   B. What a fun
    C. How a fun   D. What fun
14. As the development of economy, _____ between China and America has increased since 1987.
    A. the trade   B. trade
    C. a trade   D. trades
15. John has a pen _____ mine.
    A. the same as   B. the same like
    C. same like   D. the same
16. One day _____ fire broke out in the forest near my house and the firefighters tried to put out _____ fire.
    A. the; a   B. a; a
    C. a; the   D. the; the
17. Professor Wang is still in _____ habit of smoking in _____ places.
    A. the; the   B. the;/   C. a; the   D. /; the
18. — What is _____ with you?
    — I've got _____ in my right arm.
    A. a matter; pains   B. the matter; the pain
    C. the wrong; a pain   D. the matter; a pain
19. Pay attention to _____ main idea when reading _____ English novel.
    A. a; the   B. the; an   C. the; the   D. a; an
20. _____ Middle Autumn is _____ traditional festival in China.
    A. The; a   B. A; a   C. A; the   D. /; a

21. I prefer _____ milk to _____ tea.
    A. a; a   B. /; a   C. a;/   D. /;/
22. Most girls like to play _____ piano while most boys like to play _____ football.
    A. the;/   B. the; the   C. a;/   D. /;/
23. — Have you seen _____ hat?
    — Is it _____ red one? I saw it in your bedroom.
    A. a; the   B. the; a   C. the; the   D. a; a
24. Do you know _____ man who is talking with _____ president?
    A. the; the   B. a; the   C. the;/   D. /;/
25. — Tom, are you in _____ washroom?
    — No, I'm in _____ bed.
    A. the;/   B. the; the   C. a; a   D. a;/
26. _____ bad information I have got yesterday!
    A. How   B. What a
    C. How a   D. What
27. He looked at me _____ as if I was wrong.
    A. in my eye   B. in an eye
    C. in eyes   D. in the eye
28. She told me that she would come _____.
    A. next day   B. the next day
    C. a next day   D. last day
29. She was working in _____ field when _____ sun was rising.
    A. the; the   B. /; the   C. /;/   D. the;/
30. He is _____ tallest boy in our class.
    A. a   B. the   C. /   D. one
31. _____ soon sent to _____ hospital.
    A. The injured is; /   B. The injured were; /
    C. An injured is; the   D. The injured were; the
32. Mary is _____ in our class.
    A. Leifeng   B. the Leifeng
    C. a Leifeng   D. one Leifeng

33. My grandparents always go to _____ church on _____ Sundays.
    A. the; a   B. /; the   C. /; /   D. /; a
34. _____ Pacific Ocean is _____ largest ocean in the world.
    A. The; the   B. /; the   C. /; a   D. /;/
35. It is _____ quick means to go to Beijing by _____ plane.
    A. a; a   B. the; a   C. the; a   D. a;/
36. After _____ lunch I have _____ wonderful supper.
    A. /; a   B. the; a   C. /;/   D. /; the
37. There are many trees _____ of our classroom.
    A. in front   B. in the front
    C. in a front   D. in fronts
38. I never read _____ because of my terrible eye-sight.
    A. at night   B. in night
    C. at the night   D. on night
39. I want to have _____ holiday, but I must go on _____ business.
    A. /; a   B. a; a   C. a;/   D. /;/
40. Becky got _____ second in _____ physics examinations.
    A. the;/   B. the; a   C. a;/   D. a; a

第三天

突破英语的数词、形容词和副词

3.1 数　　词

　　对于数词，学生要掌握其表达方法。其实考试时不会单纯考数词的表达法，最多是在中高级口译中可能会出现，但即使是这样，也不会考写法，而是考如何口头表达。所以，在这一章中，我们重点要掌握的是数词的几种特殊的用法。当然，如果大家有兴趣以后做翻译的话，那么数词这一章就是特别重要的了。

1. 数词的定义及特征

（1）数词是表示数目多少以及顺序的一类词。

（2）数词可以分为基数词（表示数目多少）和序数词（表示数目顺序）两类。

2. 基数词（如表3-1所示）

表3-1　基数词

类　别	举　例
1—12分别是	one two three four five six seven eight nine ten eleven twelve
13—19分别后加-teen	thirteen fourteen fifteen sixteen seventeen eighteen nineteen
20—90分别后加-ty	twenty thirty forty fifty sixty seventy eighty ninety
几十几中间有"-"	21　twenty-one　　　　　　94　ninety-four
一百以上的表达法	100 = a hundred 1 000 = a thousand 10 000 = ten thousand 100 000 = a hundred thousand 1 000 000 = a million 10 000 000 = ten million 100 000 000 = a hundred million 1 000 000 000 = a billion

续表

类 别	举 例
数字表达的方式，如：23, 684, 345, 369 注：在逗号之间不用and，逗号内部and连接	twenty-three billion six hundred and eighty-four million three hundred and forty-five thousand three hundred and sixty-nine

3. 序数词

（1）序数词第一、第二、第三分别为first，second，third，其他的后面都是加-th，如forth，fifth，sixth等。

（2）十位数序数词的构成方法是：将-ty变y为i加-eth。如twenty变成了twentieth，thirty变成了thirtieth等。这也是一种比较特殊的词尾变化。

（3）多位数的序数词是将前部保留为基数词，只有末尾变为序数词。如第2323个，即two thousand three hundred and twenty third。

4. 数词用法（几种特殊的表达）

（1）编号的表达遵循以下方式，需要记住以下两个公式。

① "the+编号（序）+号码名称（首字母大写）"　　the 203rd Room (203房间)

② "号码名称（首字母大写）+编号（基）"　　Room 203 (203房间)

（2）倍数、分数、小数、百分数的表达法。

① 倍数：This room is three times as large as that one.

　　　　这间房间的大小是那间的三倍。

　　　　This room is three times larger than that one.

　　　　这间房间比那间大三倍。

② 分数表达法：$\dfrac{1}{3}$ — one — 基数词　　$\dfrac{2}{3}$ — two — 基数词

　　　　　　　　　3 — third — 序数词　　　　3 — thirds — 序数词（复数）

③ 小数表达法：5.36　five point three six　　　　1.26　one point two six

④ 百分数表达法：5% five per(cent)　　　　　　　60% sixty per(cent)

（3）数式的表达法。

加法：One and one is two.　　　　　　减法：One minus one is zero.

乘法：Two times two is four.　　　　　除法：Two divided by two is one.

（4）年、月、日的表达法。

1986年8月7日用英语表达为August 7th 或7th August，nineteen eighty-six。

> **Tips**　2008年应该说成two thousand and eight而不是twenty eight。

> **Tips**　十二个月份的写法（缩写）：
> Jan. Feb. Mar. Apr. May. Jun. Jul. Aug. Sept. Oct. Nov. Dec.
> 一般不要求大家掌握其全部拼写，即使是在考试中，用缩写也就可以了。

（5）时间表达法。
① 直接表达法（美式）。　　9∶20　nine twenty
② 间接表达法（英式）。　　9∶45　a quarter to ten

> **Tips**　过半用to，不过半用past，一半用half，一刻用a quarter。

e.g.：9∶20 twenty past nine　　9∶30 half past nine　　9∶45 a quarter to ten

小　结

本章中数词的学习十分简单，大家不需掌握数字的具体表达法，但要清晰地掌握数字的各种特殊用法，特别是编号、倍数、分数等用法。

请大家回答下列问题：

（1）346294如何用英语表达？第34862077个用英语如何表达？

（2）编号表达法的公式是什么？

（3）数学上的加、减、乘、除、小数、分数、代分数、百分数和倍数用英语如何表达？

（4）时间、年、月、日用英语如何表达？

以上这些问题如果你能够毫不犹豫地回答出来，那么数词的学习目标也就达到了。

3.2　形容词和副词

形容词和副词是英语中做修饰成分最重要的两类词，经常有这样一副对联：
上联：形容词做定语翻译成"……的"修饰名词或代词
下联：副词做状语翻译成"……地"修饰动词、形容词或副词
横批：动词是谓语，谓语是动词

这样三行字指出了英语语法学习的根本方法，要想把语法学好，必须先把修饰成分分析清楚，这样才可能做到不受这些成分的影响而自由地把握句子的语法成分。形容词和副词的位置以及形容词、副词的比较级是本章最重要的部分。

1. 形容词

（1）形容词的定义及用法。
形容词是用来修饰名词或代词的一类词，一般是做定语、表语或宾语补足语。

> e.g.: She is a very *beautiful* girl.
> 　　　她是一个漂亮的姑娘。（定语）
> 　　　They are quite *friendly*.
> 　　　他们十分友好。（表语）
> 　　　I made the door *closed*.
> 　　　我把门关上了。（宾语补足语）

（2）形容词的位置。
① 一般形容词修饰名词时要放在它的前面。

> e.g.: He is a very *handsome* man.
> 　　　他是一个十分帅气的小伙子。
> 　　　a weak *small* old man
> 　　　一个虚弱的小老头

② 当形容词修饰复合不定代词时，要放在它的后面。

> e.g.: I have something *important* to tell you.
> 　　　我有重要的事情告诉你。

③ 当有多个形容词修饰名词时，遵循"美小圆旧黄，法国木书房"（重要口诀）的顺序。即：描绘性形容词、大小、形状、新旧、颜色、国别、材料和中心词。

e.g.: the first beautiful little white Chinese stone bridge
中国第一座美丽的小白石桥
some famous young Austrian reporters
一些著名的年轻奥地利记者

Tips 如果有冠词和数词修饰时，要将其放在首位。

2. 副词
（1）副词的定义。
副词是用来修饰动词、形容词、副词或全句的一类词。

e.g.: She is *quite* pretty.
她十分漂亮。（副词修饰形容词时放在其前面）
They ran *faster* than us.
他们比我们跑得快。（副词修饰动词时放在其后面）
Thank you *very* much.
非常感谢。（副词very修饰副词much时放在被修饰词前面）
Unfortunately, he lost his suitcase.
很不走运，他把箱子弄丢了。（一个副词修饰一句话时，放在句首或是句末）

（2）副词的种类。
① 副词按形式可分为三种。
● 简单副词：just（刚刚）　　only（仅仅）　　up（向上）
● 复合副词：therefore（因此）　　nonetheless（然而）
● 派生副词：happily（幸福地）　　interestingly（有趣地）

Tips 这一类副词是由形容词的词尾加-ly而变成的。如：slow → slowly，happy → happily

但有一类词既可以是形容词又可以是副词，且在加-ly后还有副词的形式，要注意它们的用法。

pretty	adj. 漂亮的 adv. 相当	prettily	adv. 漂亮地
hard	adj. 困难的 adv. 努力地	hardly	adv. 几乎不
high	adj. 高的 adv. 高地	highly	adv. 高地

e.g.: The bird can't fly that high.
鸟不能飞那么高。（high表示具体含义）
President Xi has highly praised the relationship between the U.S. and China.
习主席高度评价了中美之间的关系。（highly表示抽象含义）

Tips 所以，当副词和形容词同体时，由形容词在词尾加上-ly变成的副词表示抽象含义，而前者则是具体含义。

② 副词按意义可分为五种。
- 方式副词：interestingly（有趣地）　　happily（高兴地）
- 地点和方位副词：out（外面）　　up（向上）　　down（向下）
- 时间副词：today（今天）　　tomorrow（明天）
- 强调副词：very（非常）　　quite（十分）　　so（太）
- 频率副词：sometimes（有时）　　often（经常）　　usually（通常）

（3）副词的位置。
副词的位置不像形容词的位置较固定，它们的位置十分灵活，有以下几种规律。

① 频率副词一般用于be动词之后，实义动词之前。

✏️ e.g.: She *often* gets up at 6 every day.

　　　　她通常在六点钟起床。

　　　　She is *often* good at drawing.

　　　　她很擅长绘画。

② 表示地点和时间的副词一般都在句末或句首。

✏️ e.g.: He has already had supper *tonight*.

　　　　他今天晚上已经吃过饭了。

　　　　In the middle of the classroom there is a big tree.

　　　　教室中间有一棵大树。

③ 副词中时间副词和地点副词可修饰名词，放在被修饰词的后面。

✏️ e.g.: The people *there* are having lunch.

　　　　那儿的人正在吃饭。

　　　　The river *below* runs very fast.

　　　　下面那条河流得很快。

3. 形容词和副词的比较等级

Tips 比较级和比较等级是两个完全不同的概念，而且要注意两者之间的关系。

形容词和副词的比较等级一般分为三种：原级、比较级和最高级。
（1）三个比较等级的用法（基本用法）。
① 原级的使用。

✏️ e.g.: He is *as tall as* I (me).

　　　　他和我一样高。

形式：主语 + 动词 + as + 形容词原级 + as + 比较对象。
否定形式：主语 + 动词（not）+ so + 形容词原级 + as + 比较对象。
意义："……和……一样"。

② 比较级的使用。

e.g.: He is *taller than* I (me).

他比我高。

形式：主语 + 动词 + 形容词比较级形式 + than + 比较对象。

意义："……比……"。

Tips　在比较的过程中一定要注意是什么对象之间在比较，千万不要弄错比较对象。如下句：

The weather in Kunming is warmer than Beijing.

本句是将"昆明的天气"和"北京的天气"相比较，而不是将"昆明的天气"和"北京"比较。所以，本句正确的表达应是：

The weather in Kunming is warmer than that of Beijing.

昆明的天气比北京暖和。

③ 最高级的使用。

e.g.: He is *the tallest* of all.

他是所有人中最高的。

形式：主语 + 动词 + the + 形容词最高级 + 比较范围。

意义："……最……"（某一范围的最……）。

（2）形容词和副词的比较等级变化一般依据以下的规则。

① 形容词比较等级（如表3-2所示）。

表3-2　形容词比较等级

情　况	原　级	比较级	最高级
单音节词后加-er, -est	great	greater	greatest
重读闭音节双写词尾字母加-er, -est	big	bigger	biggest
辅音字母+y结尾，变y为i加-er, -est	happy	happier	happiest
不发音e结尾，直接加-r, -st	simple	simpler	simplest
双音节或多音节词，在词前加more和the most	beautiful	more beautiful	the most beautiful

此外，如表3-3所示的特殊变化是需要记忆的。

表3-3 形容词比较等级的特殊变化

原 级	比 较 级	最 高 级
good, well	better	best
bad, badly, ill	worse	worst
many, much	more	most
little	less	least
far	further, farther	furthest, farthest
old	older, elder	oldest, eldest

Tips 表3-3中further与furthest是far的比较级和最高级，但是further是"进一步"的意思，furthest现已很少使用。

e.g.: He jumps *farther than* I (do).
他比我跳得远。（在这里指具体的距离）
I want to get *further* information about it.
我想得到关于这件事情的进一步消息。（在这里指抽象的"远"）

e.g.: I have a *younger* sister and an *elder* sister.
我有个妹妹，也有个姐姐。（elder表示辈分上的，而不是年纪上的）
I am *older than* you.
我比你年纪大。（实际上指的是年龄上的）

Tips elder与eldest也是old的比较级和最高级，主要表示兄弟姐妹的长幼关系。

② 副词的比较等级要遵循以下原则：
- 它类似于形容词的比较级。
- 它的最高级前不加the。
- 由形容词派生出来的副词变化比较级时，要在词前加more和most。例如：slowly是由slow变化来的，它的比较级和最高级分别是more slowly和most slowly，而不是slowlier和slowliest。

Tips 在这里要考虑为什么不加the，因为副词和形容词的用法不一样，形容词是用来修饰名词的，而名词前必须有冠词来说明名词；但是副词则是用来修饰副词、形容词和动词的，所以不需要用冠词。

（3）形容词和副词的比较等级的用法（特殊用法）。

① 比较级前可用a bit，a few，a great (good) deal，a little，a lot，many，much等修饰。

e.g.: He is *a bit* better than before.
他比以前好一些了。
She is *a little* weaker than him.
她比他虚弱一点。

② 最高级可用序数词by far，much等修饰。

e.g.: Wangbing is *by far* the tallest of all.
王兵是所有人中最高的。
The Changjiang River is *the first* longest river in China.
长江是中国最长的河流。

③ "比较级+比较级"表示"越来越……"。

e.g.: more and more（越来越多）　　faster and faster（越来越快）

④ "the+比较级，the+比较级"表示"越……，就越……"。

e.g.: *The more*, *the better*.
越多越好。
The harder you work, *the more* progress you will make.
你越努力学习，你取得的进步就越大。

⑤ 用最高级表示比较级（the+形容词最高级+of是最高级的表达法，但是把形容词最高级变成比较级形式，这个结构仍然是最高级形式，但是表示"两者之间最高级"，也就是比较级）。

e.g.: Wangbing and Wanghai are brothers. Wanghai is *the taller* of the two.
王兵和王海是兄弟。王海是他们两个中最高的。

> **Tips** 此句型的结构是用of+比较范围表示最高级结构,但表示的是比较含义,因为两个人中最高的也就是一个比另一个高。特别要注意 the taller 的用法。

⑥ 用比较级表示最高级。

- e.g.: She is taller than *anyone else* in her class. = She is the tallest in her class.
  她在她们班比其他任何人都高。
  She is taller than *anyone* in Class Three. = She is the tallest in Class Three.
  她在三班比其他任何人都高。

> **Tips** 前一句是在范围内比较,而后一句却在范围外比较,注意区别不同情况。

⑦ 用原级表示比较级。

- e.g.: The rope is too long (than I needed/expected).
  这根绳子太长了。(实际上表示的含义是比需要的绳子长)

- e.g.: It is rather hot.
  天气太热了。(实际上可能表示比前几天要热)

⑧ 最高级前使用数词的情况。

- e.g.: The Changjiang River is *the first* longest river in China.
  长江是中国最长的河流。(使用序数词时后面的名词使用单数)

- e.g.: The Changjiang River is *one* of the longest rivers in China.
  长江是中国最长的河流之一。(使用基数词时后面的名词使用复数)

小 结

在本章中我们学习了形容词和副词的基本用法,最重要的是形容词和副词的位置及其比较等级。其中,形容词和副词比较等级的用法在考试中出现频率最高。

请大家回答下列问题:

（1）形容词修饰名词时的位置一般有几种？
（2）副词修饰副词、动词或形容词时的位置有几种？
（3）形容词和副词比较等级的基本形式如何？
（4）形容词和副词比较等级的特殊形式如何？

如果大家对这几个问题没有疑惑的话，那么第三天的学习就很成功了。下面几天的学习任务将会很重，因为明天要进入英语中最重要的动词的学习。不过，没有关系，只要大家坚持，就一定能够在短时间内突破这些看起来很难的语法现象了。

数词练习

1. — How soon can I take a bus downtown?
   — There is a bus passing here _____.
   A. every five minute   B. five minutes
   C. every fifth minute   D. every five minutes

2. David is ten years old and his cousin is just _____.
   A. twice as older as he   B. as twice old as he
   C. twice his age   D. twice elder than he

3. The _____ died three weeks ago.
   A. two-head-baby   B. two-heads-baby
   C. two-head baby   D. two-head babys

4. Uncle Wang bought _____ eggs yesterday.
   A. two dozens   B. two dozen
   C. two dozens of   D. dozens

5. _____ soldiers died during World War Two.
   A. Ten thousand of   B. Tens of thousands of
   C. Ten-thousands of   D. Tens of thousand of

6. There are _____ words we have learned this term.
   A. five thousand   B. five thousands
   C. five thousands of   D. the five thousand

7. He has been to Shanghai _____.
   A. at twenty old   B. at the age of his twenties
   C. in his twenties   D. in his twenty

8. The Nanjing Changjiang Bridge is about _____.
   A. 6, 700 metre long
   B. 6, 700 metres of long
   C. 6, 700 meters long
   D. long 6, 700 meters

9. Please turn to _____.
   A. page ten
   B. page of ten
   C. page tenth
   D. tenth page

10. She taught in this school in _____.
    A. 1980's
    B. 1980s'
    C. the 1980's
    D. the 1980s'

11. About _____ people disagreed with what president said.
    A. three seventh
    B. three of seven
    C. three sevenths
    D. three seven

12. _____ geese died of disease.
    A. Scores
    B. Scores of
    C. The scores of
    D. Score of

13. _____ dollars is a large sum.
    A. Eight thousands hundred
    B. Eight hundred
    C. Eight hundreds of thousand
    D. Eight hundred of thousand

14. _____, please allow me to introduce Professor Fan.
    A. Of all first
    B. First all of
    C. All of first
    D. First of all

15. Ten years _____ a long time.
    A. is
    B. are
    C. to be
    D. being

16. Your books _____ as many as mine.
    A. are five times
    B. is five time
    C. is fifth time
    D. are fifth time

17. The output of steel in May makes up _____ the total.
    A. 10%
    B. 10% of
    C. 10% in
    D. 10% for

18. It took me _____ to finish my homework.
    A. one and half hours
    B. a half and an hour
    C. an hour and half
    D. one and a half hours

19. — Do you have money?
    — I have a _____ note.
    A. hundred dollar B. hundred-dollars
    C. hundred-dollar D. hundreds-dollar

形容词和副词练习

1. Their beautiful smiles showed that they were having a _____ picnic.
   A. serious   B. friendly
   C. lively   D. wonderful
2. I find that records are often _____ an actual performance.
   A. as good   B. as good as
   C. good as   D. as well as
3. — What do you think of his speech?
   — Oh, it is _____.
   A. a great fun   B. quite a interesting
   C. very interesting   D. much interesting
4. If the doctor came earlier yesterday, _____ babies would not have been dead.
   A. the all poor little   B. all the little poor
   C. all the poor little   D. the all little poor
5. The old lady lived in a _____ house.
   A. two-storied big red   B. red two-story big
   C. two-story red big   D. red big two-storied
6. — I love your garden and it's so neat.
   — Well, the smaller the garden is, _____ to look after it.
   A. it is easier   B. the easy it is
   C. it is easily   D. the easier it is
7. I'm surprised that you should have been fooled by such a (an) _____ trick.
   A. ordinary   B. easy   C. smart   D. simple
8. In that case, there is nothing you can do _____ than wait.
   A. more   B. other   C. better   D. any

9. It was _____ five people seemed crowed.
   A. so small a car that   B. so a small car
   C. such small a car that   D. a such small car

10. — Let's go for a walk?
    — I'm sorry. I'm too busy now, please phone me _____ time.
    A. some other   B. some others
    C. any other   D. the other

11. Please tell me _____ about this trip.
    A. something interested   B. interested something
    C. interesting something   D. something interesting

12. The two boys look exactly _____.
    A. the same as   B. like   C. alike   D. likely

13. There are apples and oranges. Which do you like _____?
    A. better   B. well
    C. much   D. very much

14. We have six teachers. Who do you like _____?
    A. better   B. best   C. the best   D. the better

15. Please be quiet. The baby fell _____.
    A. asleeping   B. sleepy   C. asleep   D. slept

16. I have never seen _____.
    A. a three-hundreds-year-old tree
    B. a three-hundred-year-old tree
    C. a three hundred year old tree
    D. a three-hundred-years-old tree

17. Our school will hold a sports meeting _____ the next week.
    A. some time   B. sometime
    C. sometimes   D. some times

18. _____ place!
    A. What a lively   B. What lively a
    C. How lively   D. How a lively

19. Although he was not very clever, his teacher spoke _____ of him.
    A. high   B. highly   C. bad   D. badly

20. — Did you buy those trousers?
    — No, the price is _____ expensive for me.
    A. very much   B. too much   C. so much   D. much too
21. — How big are your shoes?
    — My shoes are _____ yours.
    A. as twice big as   B. as big twice as
    C. as big as twice   D. twice as big as
22. Keep your feet _____ while I fasten your shoes.
    A. quiet   B. silent   C. calm   D. still
23. — What can I do for you?
    — May I have _____ coffee?
    A. some   B. any   C. anyone   D. many
24. — Do you know _____?
    — They will be our classmates.
    A. the two beautiful young girls   B. the beautiful young two girls
    C. the two young beautiful girls   D. the young beautiful two girls
25. His suggestion is worthy _____.
    A. to consider   B. of considering
    C. of being considered   D. considering
26. My handwriting _____ yours.
    A. is not as good as   B. are not as good as
    C. is not good as   D. is not as well as
27. She is _____ of my two sisters.
    A. the cleverest   B. the cleverer
    C. cleverer   D. as clever as
28. He went to school much _____.
    A. late yesterday   B. yesterday late
    C. lately yesterday   D. yesterday lately
29. The family _____ is so noisy.
    A. which next door   B. it was next door
    C. next to the door   D. was next door

30. My friends are _____ teachers.

 A. mostly B. many C. most D. more

31. He is one of _____.

 A. the greatest alive poet

 B. the greatest alive poets

 C. the greatest poets who are still alive

 D. the greatest poet who are still alive

32. The Yellow River is _____ in China.

 A. the second longest river B. the second longest rivers

 C. a second longest river D. the second longer river

33. We were _____ when we won the football match.

 A. rather pleasing B. rather pleased

 C. rather pleasure D. rather please

34. Although Albert Einstein was a great scientist, you can't say he is _____.

 A. wonderful B. perfect

 C. complete D. splendid

35. Work hard and you'll be _____ in the future.

 A. succeed B. success

 C. successful D. successfully

36. All people in the world are trying their best to make the earth more _____.

 A. beauty B. beautify

 C. beautifully D. beautiful

37. Would you please give me some _____ information besides this?

 A. far B. farther C. farthest D. further

38. Mary is a _____ girl and John is a _____ boy.

 A. handsome; beautiful B. beautiful; handsome

 C. handsome; handsome D. beautiful; beautiful

39. A _____ lecture often makes students _____.

 A. boring; boring B. bored; boring

 C. bored; bored D. boring; bored

40. John is ill badly, please send for a doctor _____.
    A. as sooner as possible   B. as soon as possibly
    C. as soon as possible   D. soon as possible

41. — Would you like to have a dinner with me?
    — Are you _____?
    A. free   B. careful
    C. serious   D. true

42. Henry said that he was _____ able to water the flowers himself.
    A. too   B. much   C. very   D. quite

43. Peter is _____ fun that we all like him very much.
    A. such a great   B. such great
    C. so great   D. so a great

44. He is the only boy _____ for the monitor position.
    A. lively   B. probably
    C. possibly   D. possible

45. The village is only three hundred meters _____ from here.
    A. away   B. far away
    C. far   D. faraway

46. — Could you tell me where the nearest post office is?
    — Go _____ and turn _____ at the first turning.
    A. straightly; left   B. straight; left
    C. straight; the left   D. straightly; the left

47. All the _____ are interested in the _____.
    A. present students; present situation
    B. present students; situation present
    C. students present; present situation
    D. students present; situation present

48. Some students are playing basketball while the other students _____.
    A. are still doing their homework
    B. are already doing their homework
    C. are now doing their homework
    D. are doing their homework now

49. Light travels _____ than sound.
    A. too fast   B. much fast   C. very faster   D. much faster
50. The weather was _____ hot yesterday.
    A. very   B. pretty   C. rather   D. fairly
51. Jenny did _____ well in her exam, but you did _____ badly.
    A. rather; more   B. rather; fairly
    C. fairly; rather   D. pretty; too
52. He is _____ to go to school by himself.
    A. old enough   B. enough old
    C. young enough   D. enough young
53. I'm _____ at English while my sister does _____ in politics.
    A. good; good   B. well; well
    C. good; well   D. well; good
54. — Are you excited about your university life?
    — _____.
    A. Yes, very excited   B. Yes, very exciting
    C. No, very bored   D. No, nothing at all
55. — There are no mistakes in your paper.
    — Yes. I can not be too _____.
    A. nervous   B. careful   C. careless   D. happy
56. The town was so _____, and I didn't know where to go.
    A. strange   B. large
    C. interesting   D. beautiful
57. I can't put this big television _____.
    A. everywhere   B. somewhere
    C. anywhere   D. nowhere
58. You look _____ than you are.
    A. a more younger   B. more younger
    C. very younger   D. much younger
59. He is _____ fatter than me.
    A. very   B. much   C. so   D. too

60. The old lady lived _____, but she never felt _____.
    A. alone; lonely   B. lonely; alone
    C. lone; lonely   D. alone; lone
61. This is a _____ building in this city.
    A. much tall   B. pretty tall
    C. prettily tall   D. tall pretty
62. Was the dog _____ or dead?
    A. alive   B. lively
    C. live   D. living
63. He hurt _____ in a _____ night.
    A. bad; dark   B. badly; dark
    C. bad; darker   D. badly; darkly
64. Who can manage to do this job with _____ money and _____ people?
    A. little; less   B. little; fewer
    C. less; fewer   D. less; few
65. This picture was painted one thousand years ago. So it is _____.
    A. costless   B. worthless
    C. valuable   D. priceless
66. He is _____ of his _____ behavior.
    A. shameful; ashamed   B. shameful; shameless
    C. shameless; ashamed   D. ashamed; shameful
67. The apples are _____ pears.
    A. twice as many as   B. as many as twice
    C. twice as much as   D. as twice many as
68. Please keep _____ when you meet a sudden dangerous situation.
    A. quite   B. calm   C. still   D. silent
69. Although it was raining _____, yet _____ no one stopped working.
    A. heavy; nearly   B. heavily; nearly
    C. heavy; almost   D. heavily; almost

70. — Will the exam be difficult?

    — No, it's _____ that all of the students can pass it.

    A. surely　　　B. certainly　　　C. sure　　　D. certain

71. I have never spent a _____ day.

    A. more worrying　　　B. most worrying

    C. more worry　　　D. most worried

72. When we got to Mountain Tai, we saw the _____ sun rising.

    A. burnt　　　B. gold　　　C. golden　　　D. brightly

73. _____, I think you are wrong.

    A. Honest　　　B. Be honest

    C. To be honest　　　D. Honest to say

74. How delicious it is! I've never eaten a _____ dinner.

    A. good　　　B. excellent　　　C. worse　　　D. better

75. — When shall we meet?

    — Make it _____ you like. It's the same to me.

    A. sometime　　　B. any time　　　C. sometimes　　　D. every time

76. He didn't go to see a film. I didn't go, _____.

    A. too　　　B. also　　　C. to　　　D. either

77. South Africa is _____ country.

    A. an English-spoken　　　B. a speaking-English

    C. a spoken-English　　　D. an English-speaking

78. Those who are _____ with the progress they have made will not have greater success.

    A. proud　　　B. afraid　　　C. popular　　　D. content

79. — Who is _____ to win the game?

    — I think it is _____ for Peter to win.

    A. probably; likely

    B. possible; probably

    C. likely; probably

    D. likely; possible

80. I have four sisters, all _____ than me. _____ Jenny is a teacher.

    A. elder; The eldest　　　B. older; The older

    C. elder; The old one　　　D. older; The eldest

第四天

突破英语的动词及其两种时态

4.1 动　　词

　　动词是英语中最重要的语法现象，在英语所有的句型结构中，动词是必然出现的。在英语中，任何一个句子可以没有主语、宾语、定语等，但是谓语是必然要有的。这一点和中文的语法有所不同，例如用中文说：他今年十八岁了。这句话中主语是他，谓语可以理解为十八岁，也就是说数词是可以作为谓语的。如果这句翻译成英语，则是：He is eighteen years old this year. 而不是He eighteen years old this year. 可见英语中谓语动词的重要性。

　　在3.2中提到了一个对联，它的横批是"动词是谓语，谓语是动词"。希望大家能掌握的就是动词必然用来做谓语，谓语必然是动词的道理。一个句子如果没有了谓语，也就不成为句子。既然动词这么重要，那么我们学习的方法是什么呢？大家要在脑海里深深地刻下这样一条主线：动词的定义—分类—基本形式—动词词组—时态—语态—助动词和情态动词—非谓语动词—虚拟语气。把结构性的框架放在脑海里之后，只要我们把其他的内容往里面填就可以了。现在就让我们一起先进入动词的定义、分类、基本形式以及动词词组的学习吧。

一、动词的定义和分类

1. 动词是用来表示动作和状态的词

   🖊 e.g.: He *gets up* at 6 every day.
   　　他每天在6点钟起床。（在这里"起床"实际上是一个动作）
   　　The earth *moves* around the sun.
   　　地球绕着太阳转。（在这里"绕着"实际上就是一种状态）

2. 动词的分类

动词按照其在句子当中的用途可以分为以下四类。

（1）实义动词（notional verb，又称行为动词），是用来表动作或状态的，能单独做谓语。

> e.g.: I *wash* my hair every day.
> 我每天洗头。
> He often *goes* to school at 7 o'clock.
> 他经常7点钟去上学。

① 实义动词按照其后可否带宾语又可分为及物动词和不及物动词两种。

> e.g.: I *got up* early so that I could *catch* the bus.
>   不及物动词（vi.）   及物动词（vt.）
> 我起得早是为了能赶上汽车。

但有时这种情况也会出现，即：一个动词既是及物动词又是不及物动词（以 fly 为例）。

> e.g.: The boy *flies* a kite.
> 男孩放风筝。（及物动词）
> Birds can *fly*.
> 鸟儿会飞。（不及物动词）

A. 及物动词：在动词后直接出现人或物的动词。

> e.g.: I am *reading* a book.
> 我正在读书。
> They are *cleaning* the blackboard.
> 他们正在擦黑板。

B. 不及物动词：有两种理解方式。

● 在动词后不出现宾语，直接构成主谓结构。

> e.g.: I can *fly*.
> 我会飞。（后面没有宾语，can fly就是谓语部分）

● 在动词后加上介宾短语做状语的动词。

> e.g.: He is *standing* on the top of the mountain.
> 他正站在山顶上。（动词后面跟了一个介词短语直接构成状语）

Tips 在这里要强调的是，及物动词和不及物动词可以单独做谓语，而且不及物动词一般不能用于被动语态当中。

② 实义动词按照动词的持续性来分类，又可以分为持续性动词和短暂性动词。比方说 eat，go，play，watch等都是持续性动词；buy，die等就是短暂性动词。

Tips 一般来说，短暂性动词后不能接表示持续性时间的词。

e.g.: I *have* already *finished* my homework.
我已经完成家庭作业了。（finish是持续性动词，所以可以用于现在完成时态）
I *have bought* this car for three years.（错误）
我已经买这辆车三年了。（buy不是持续性动词，所以这句话是错的，应该写成I *have kept* this car for three years.）

③ 实义动词按照动作位置的改变程度来分类，又可以分为位移动词和非位移动词。比方说come，go，leave等就是位移动词；buy，finish，listen，see等就是非位移动词。

Tips 一般来说，位移动词要用一般现在时态和现在进行时态代替一般将来时态。

e.g.: The train *will leave* at 3 o'clock.
火车三点钟就要走了。
因为leave是位移动词，在这里应该用一般现在时态和现在进行时态来代替一般将来时态，所以这句话可以写成：
The train *leaves* at 3 o'clock. / The train *is leaving* at 3 o'clock.

Tips 以上三种分类都是人为分类，是为了说明某种语言用法而分的，不是固定的。

（2）联系动词：是用来表示不定主谓语关系的动词，它说明真正的谓语（即表语），而且不可以单独做谓语。

> e.g.: He *is* a good student.
> 他是一个好学生。
> The trees *turned* green.
> 树变绿了。

联系动词可分为三类。

① be动词：am，is，are等。

Tips 在这里需要强调的是，be动词不一定是联系动词，因为be动词还可以做助动词；联系动词也不一定就是be动词，因为联系动词还包括感官动词和性质变化动词，这两者之间在一定程度上有交叉，在后面助动词的用法中我们还会重点讲解这个问题。

> e.g.: We *are* boys.
> 我们是男孩。
> I *am* thirsty.
> 我口渴了。

Tips 我们经常说的主语补足语实际上就是表语，因为表语在某些程度上就是说明主语的特征和性质的。

② 感官动词：由身体某器官可感知的动词，如：hear（听到，听说），look（看），smell（闻到），taste（品尝）等。

> e.g.: The piece of music *sounds* beautiful.
> 这首歌听起来很悦耳。
> The food *tastes* delicious.
> 这食物尝起来很好吃。

③ 性质变化动词：由某种状态变化到另一种状态时所用的一类动词，如become（变成，成为），grow（变得），get（变得），turn（变得）等。

> e.g.: The girl *became* a doctor.
> 这个女孩成了医生。
>
> The population *grows* larger and larger.
> 人口变得越来越多。

（3）助动词：用来帮助动词形成时态、语态、语气的一种动词，它本身无意义或意义不完全，不能单独做谓语。常见的助动词有be动词，do，have，shall，will，should，would等。

> e.g.: He *is* having lunch now.
> 他现在正在吃午饭。
>
> The woman *was* killed in the accident.
> 那个女人在事故中丧生了。

（4）情态动词：是用来表示陈述者态度的一种动词。

情态动词的意义不完整，必须和后面的实义动词连用，且必须和不带to 的动词不定式连用（have，ought 除外），它不能单独做谓语动词，且一般没有人称和数的变化。常见的情态动词有have to，must，need，ought to，should等。

> e.g.: You *mustn't* play with knife, because it is so sharp.
> 你不能玩小刀，因为它很锋利。
>
> The girl *need* finish her homework in five days.
> 这个女孩须在五天之内完成家庭作业。
>
> We *should* try our best to make contributions to our country.
> 我们要努力为国家做出贡献。

二、动词的基本形式

英语中动词的形式有五种，分别是动词原形、第三人称单数、现在分词、过去分词和过去式，这五种形式和助动词连用构成了不同的时态、语态和语气（如表4-1所示）。

表4-1　动词的基本形式

原　形	第三人称单数	现在分词	过去分词	过去式
be	is	being	been	was/were
have	has	having	had	had
go	goes	going	gone	went
look	looks	looking	looked	looked

动词的屈折变化比较多，特别是第三人称单数形式（在一般现在时中附注）、过去式（在一般过去时附注）、过去分词（在现在完成时中附注）、现在分词（在现在进行时中附注）比较复杂，我们将在以后的学习中进一步讨论。但是如果我们仔细想想，就会发现：实际上动词的第三人称单数只能在一般现在时态的第三人称单数中使用，动词的过去式只能在一般过去时态当中使用，所以也就剩下三个动词形式。这点在印欧语系中最简单。在其他语言中，以西班牙语为例，一个动词的基本变化达到了上百种之多。这样一想，实际上英语也就简单多了。

三、动词词组

动词词组的形式多种多样，有动词和副词构成的，有动词和介词构成的，也有动词和副词及介词构成的，等等。

look up　　动词+副词构成

look at　　动词+介词构成

look forward to　　动词+副词+介词构成

> **Tips**　很多英语大师曾经说过，能把英语中简单的动词词组牢记在心，也就不要背什么生词了。拿look这个单词来说，字典上列出了不下五十种的动词搭配，如果大家可以活学活用，英语的学习将不再是一件难事。当然，在这里不是讨论如何背诵这些词组的问题，而是要在这其中发现一些用法和规律。

请看以下八个短语并判断对错：

（1）look at the word　　　　　　（2）look the word at

（3）look up the word　　　　　　（4）look the word up

（5）look at it　　　　　　　　　　（6）look it at

（7）look up it　　　　　　　　　　（8）look it up

（1）是正确的，因为look at后面要带宾语。

（2）是错误的，因为look在这里是不及物动词，不能直接加宾语。

（3）是正确的，因为look up后面是可以带宾语的。

（4）是正确的，因为在这里look似乎可以认为是及物动词。

（5）是正确的，因为look at后面要带宾语。

（6）是错误的，因为look在这里是不及物动词，不能直接加宾语。

（7）是错误的，因为有代词的时候，在动词+副词的短语中，代词只能放在动词后，不能放在副词后。

（8）是正确的，因为有代词的时候，在动词+副词的短语中，代词只能放在动词后，不能放在副词后。

小 结

很多同学看完这段解释后还是不明白，那就再说得更明白些：实际上，look at是个动词+介词的词组，在这种词组中一般认为look是不及物动词，所以后面不能直接加宾语，不论是代词还是名词，当然look at是不能拆开来用的；然而look up是个动词+副词的词组，在这种词组中一般认为look是及物动词，所以后面可以直接加宾语，但是又出现代词的时候，在动词+副词的词组中，代词只能放在动词后，不能放在副词后。这时大家再看看我的解释，是不是更加明白了呢？

请大家回答下列问题：

（1）动词主要可以分为几大类？

（2）实义动词可以怎样进行分类？

（3）动词的基本形式有哪些？

（4）动词的词组，特别是动词+副词和动词+介词的词组各有什么样的特点？

如果大家可以把这些问题弄明白的话，那么动词的入门学习就已经达到目标了。在接下来的学习中还有很多动词的知识点需要加以琢磨和体会啊！

4.2 动词的时态

动词的时态、语态和语气一般被称为动词的三要素，在三个要素中又以动词的时态最为繁杂。大家在学习时态的时候，一定要遵循这样一条主线：定义—图示—结构—用法（基本用法和特殊用法）—比较。还是那句话，语法的结构性意义十分重要。

时态是动词的一个语法范畴，是以动词的不同的形式表达在不同时间和不同行为方式中所发生的不同动作。

按时间方面可分为：现在、过去、将来和过去将来四个部分。

按动作方面可分为：进行、完成、一般现在和完成进行四个部分。

这样一来，时态就可分为十六种，这里我们要讨论的是以下十一种。

1. 一般现在时

（1）定义：一般现在时是表示说话人经常发生或近一段时间内发生的动作或存在的状态。

e.g.: I *go to* school every day.

我每天去上学。

He *runs* faster than you.

他比你跑得快。

这样的句子都是在陈述一般性的事实和主语的某种状态。

（2）图示（下面以数学中的数轴来表示）：

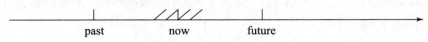

Tips　这种数轴表达时态的方法是我从牛津大学某本著名的语法书上借鉴来的，因为这样的方法可以让大家一目了然地了解到时态是怎样发生的。根据定义，可以把一般现在时在数轴上表示，一定要注意看数轴上的斜体部分，它既可表示在过去、现在，也可表示可能在将来发生的动作或存在的状态。所以，一般现在时在英语中可以说是时间跨度最大的时态之一。

（3）结构：在结构中，主要将动词分为实义动词（以work为例）和be动词两种情况（如表4-2和表4-3所示）。

表4-2 "单三"的动词变化

动词	肯定式	否定式
be	I am ... . He/She/It is ... . We/You/They are	I am not ... . He/She/It is not ... . We/You/They are not ... .
work	I work. He/She/It works. We/You/They work.	I do not work. He/She/It does not work. We/You/They do not work.

表4-3 疑问式和简答式

动词	第一人称	第二人称	第三人称
be	Am I ... ? Yes, you are. No, you are not. Are we ... ? Yes, we/you are. No, we/you are not.	Are you ... ? Yes, I am. No, I am not. Are you ... ? Yes, we are. No, we are not.	Is he/she/it ... ? Yes, he/she/it is. No, he/she/it is not. Are they ... ? Yes, they are. No, they are not.
work	Do I work? Yes, you do. No, you do not.	Do you work? Yes, I do. No, I do not.	Does he/she/it work? Yes, he/she/it does. No, he/she/it does not. Do they work? Yes, they do. No, they do not.

值得一提的是，在一般现在时中，我们要注意当遇到第三人称单数时，动词不能用原形，要用我们在学习动词基本形式时所提到的第三人称单数形式（又称"单三"或是"三单"）。"单三"形式的变化主要是在动词后加-s（类似于名词变复数），如表4-4所示。

表4-4 "单三"动词变化总结

情 况	例 词
一般在词尾加-s,清辅音后,读/s/。 浊辅音后,读/z/。	look—looks read—reads
在/s/, /z/, /ʃ/, /ʒ/, /dʒ/, /tʃ/后加-es,读/iz/。	teach—teaches watch—watches
以辅音字母加y结尾,变y为i加-es,读/z/。	fly—flies apply—applies

（4）用法（我们在介绍每种时态时,都会把用法分为基本用法和特殊用法）。

① 基本用法：

● 根据定义,一般现在时主要用于表示说话人这一段时间内所发生的动作和存在的状态。

e.g.: He *likes* China very much.
　　　他很喜欢中国。
　　　I *put* some apples on the desk.
　　　我把一些苹果放在桌子上。
　　　They *walk* to the park every day.
　　　他们每天走路去公园。

● 表示说话人的习惯和能力。

e.g.: My father *is* a worker.
　　　我的父亲是一个工人。
　　　I *swim* very well.
　　　我游泳很好。
　　　She *goes* to work by car.
　　　她开车去上班。

● 表示一般的客观事实。

e.g.: The earth *goes* around the sun.
　　　地球围着太阳转。
　　　Knowledge *is* power.
　　　知识就是力量。

Light *travels* faster than sound.

光比声音跑得快。

② 特殊用法：

● 一般现在时谓语中出现arrive, come, go, sail, start等动词（位移动词）时，要用一般现在时表示将要发生的事，且主要表示这类事是事先安排好的，即将要发生的。

✏ e.g.: The plane *arrives* at 9 a.m.

这架飞机早上九点钟到。

Where does she *go*?

她将要去哪儿？

The film *starts* at 7 p.m.

这场电影将在下午七点钟开演。

● 在时间或条件状语从句中，用一般时代替将来时。

Tips 这点实际上就是我们所说的"主将从现"的语法现象。

✏ e.g.: If it *rains* tomorrow, the sports meeting will be put off.

如果明天下雨，运动会就将推迟。

When I *become* an adult, I will be a doctor.

我长大了要成为一名医生。

2. 一般过去时

（1）定义：表示说话人在过去某一时间所发生的动作或存在的状态。

✏ e.g.: I *went* to the park yesterday night.

我昨天晚上去了公园。

She *saw* a man climb the hill last week.

她上周看见一个男的爬山了。

这些都是在过去的某个时间发生的事情，有具体的时间状语，句子的谓语用的是动词的过去式。

（2）图示：

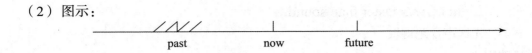

Tips 根据定义可将一般过去时反映在此数轴上的斜线部分。这样大家就会明白：原来动作是发生在过去的时间内，而且是和现在没有任何关系的，这和后面讲到的现在完成时态是有本质性区别的。

（3）结构。

简而言之，一般过去时就是谓语动词用过去式表示。

还是以be动词和实义动词work为例（如表4-5所示）。

表4-5　一般过去时中动词的变化

动　词	肯定式	否定式
be	I was… . You were… . He/She/It was… . We/You/They were… .	I was not… . You were not… . He/She/It was not… . We/You/They were not… .
work	I/You/He/She/It/We/You/They worked	I/You/He/She/It/We/You/They did not work.

动　词	疑问式	回　答
be	Was I… ? Were you… ? Was he/she/it…? Were we/you/they…?	Yes, you were./ No, you were not. Yes, I was./ No, I wasn't. Yes, he/she/it was./ No, he/she/it wasn't. Yes, you/we/they were./No, you/we/they weren't.
work	Did I work? Did you work? Did he/she/it/work? Did they work?	Yes, you did./No, you did not. Yes, I did./No, I did not. Yes, he/she/it did./No, he/she/it did not. Yes, they did./No, they did not.

动词的过去式一般常在动词结尾加-ed，但也有特殊用法（如表4-6所示）。

表4-6 动词过去式

情况	例词
一般在词尾加-ed	walk—walked look—looked start—started
以不发音的e结尾，直接加-d	care—cared live—lived like—liked
辅音字母+y结尾，变y为i加-ed	carry—carried satisfy—satisfied supply—supplied
重读闭音节的词后，双写词尾字母加-ed	stop—stopped plan—planned
不规则动词	break—broke catch—caught see—saw

（4）用法。

① 基本用法：

● 表示过去某个时刻发生的动作或存在的状态，且和过去具体时间连用（yesterday, last year /month/ week，in+年份、月份、on+过去某一天，... ago等）。

e.g.: I *lived* in Beijing three years ago.

三年前我住在北京。

They *repaired* the car last night.

他们昨天晚上修理了汽车。

Finally Mr. Smith *caught* the thief yesterday.

昨天史密斯先生最终抓住了小偷。

● 表示过去经常发生的动作，常和always，often等词连用。

Tips 实际上，英语中的不规则动词才是重点中的重点。一般来说，常用的动词都是不规则动词。

> e.g.: When I *was* at college, I always *went* to the library.
> 当我还在上大学的时候,我经常去图书馆。
> When she *was* a girl, she often *swam* in this river.
> 当她还是个小女孩时,她经常来这河里游泳。

Tips 我们经常讨论关于频率副词的问题,实际上频率副词always,never,often,sometimes等可以用于各种时态,不一定就要用于一般现在时态当中。

② 特殊用法:
表示过去常常发生某事时,常用used to do和would do两个词组,但这两个词组有区别。

> e.g.: I *used to* smoke, but I have stopped.
> 我过去常吸烟,但现在已经戒了。(表示过去常常发生,现在不发生了)
> I *would* smoke, and I smoke sometimes.
> 我过去常吸烟,现在有时还吸。(表示过去常常发生,现在不一定不发生)

 练 习

1. If you don't know the word, why don't you _____ in the dictionary?
   A. look at it B. look after it
   C. look up it D. look it up
2. The horrible noise from the man's room simply _____ me mad.
   A. put B. caused
   C. drove D. turned
3. I can hardly hear the radio. Would you please _____?
   A. turn it on B. turn it down
   C. turn it up D. turn it off
4. — Do you think this hall can _____ 1000 people?
   — I don't think so.
   A. sit B. manage C. take D. hold

5. I went to the forest to _____ the tiger there.
   A. recognize   B. search   C. study   D. learn
6. The wooden house was _____ by the flood.
   A. washed out   B. washed off
   C. washed up   D. washed away
7. The clothes _____ me one thousand Yuan.
   A. taken   B. took   C. used   D. spent
8. You must _____ the importance of studying foreign language.
   A. learn by heart   B. know by heart
   C. keep in mind   D. think of
9. When I invited him to have a dinner, he told me he was very busy and had not a minute to _____.
   A. spend   B. save   C. share   D. spare
10. Please help me _____ my book that is on the ground.
    A. keep up   B. lay up   C. look up   D. pick up
11. My father _____ me to become a teacher.
    A. thinks   B. says   C. hopes   D. wishes
12. All life on the earth _____ on the sun.
    A. depends   B. carries   C. keeps   D. goes
13. The guests are coming. I must _____ the dinner.
    A. get down to do prepare   B. get down to preparing
    C. get used to prepare   D. look forward to preparing
14. She _____ my pen, then she _____ it to Jack.
    A. borrowed; lent   B. borrowed; had lent
    C. lent; had borrowed   D. lend; borrow
15. You'd better _____ what is right before making a decision.
    A. look for   B. search for
    C. find out   D. find
16. The farmers _____ rice in the field.
    A. get along with   B. cut down
    C. cut up   D. get in

17. Father won't _____ us to use his recorder.
    A. have   B. let   C. agree   D. allow
18. I hope your speech can _____ some new points.
    A. bring in   B. make up   C. take in   D. give in
19. He _____ to make it, but he failed again.
    A. was trying   B. tried
    C. was managing   D. managed
20. Whenever I saw the pretty girl, my heart would _____ fast.
    A. run   B. beat   C. strike   D. hit
21. Many things are _____ iron.
    A. made up   B. made from
    C. made of   D. made into
22. David said he couldn't _____ one day away from studying.
    A. waste   B. spend   C. cost   D. afford
23. Fire-fighters spent two hours _____ the fire.
    A. putting on   B. putting up
    C. putting off   D. putting out
24. Who can _____ the differences between these two leaves?
    A. talk   B. tell   C. speak   D. say
25. Since you have made up your mind, you should _____ to carry out your plan.
    A. set about   B. set off   C. set up   D. set out
26. My mother is _____ the big meal.
    A. preparing for   B. preparing with
    C. preparing   D. preparing about
27. How many pages have you _____ so far?
    A. looked   B. seen   C. covered   D. turned
28. When you meet new words, you should _____ in the dictionary.
    A. look through them   B. look them up
    C. look up them   D. look down them
29. Reading books will _____ my taste for literature.
    A. add   B. add up   C. add to   D. add up to

30. World War One _____ in 1914.
    A. broke out   B. broke up   C. broke in   D. broke
31. The book _____ me.
    A. is belong to   B. is belonged to
    C. belongs to   D. belong to
32. That red suit _____ me.
    A. doesn't fit   B. isn't fit   C. fits for   D. doesn't fit for
33. Jack is _____ a black jacket today.
    A. having   B. put on   C. wearing   D. dressed
34. My mother always tells me to _____ my own things.
    A. put away   B. put aside   C. put on   D. put up
35. Cheap coal _____ a lot of smoke.
    A. gives up   B. gives in   C. gives away   D. gives off
36. All children should be _____ to having manners.
    A. brought out   B. brought through
    C. brought up   D. brought about
37. I _____ president to pay attention to pollution.
    A. suggest   B. hope   C. make   D. beg
38. — You should have stopped smoking.
    — Yes, but it is very difficult to _____.
    A. get off   B. do away   C. get on   D. get rid of
39. Mr. White's daughter _____ Henry for two years.
    A. married   B. was married
    C. has been married with   D. has been married to
40. I _____ a invitation, but I didn't _____.
    A. have received; accept   B. had received; accept
    C. have accepted; receive   D. had accepted; receive
41. I found my son _____ on the table when I returned home.
    A. laying   B. lying   C. lain   D. lied
42. Jenny _____ in the crowded street in order to find her friend.
    A. looked for   B. looked through
    C. looked around   D. looked forward to

43. The accident occurred when the plane was just _____.
    A. taking away   B. taking out
    C. taking off   D. taking up
44. The suit _____ me 100 dollars.
    A. spent   B. cost   C. paid   D. tooks
45. The other day I _____ a bird but missed it.
    A. shoot at   B. shot at   C. shoot   D. shot
46. I am _____ Beijing tomorrow morning.
    A. arriving at   B. arriving in
    C. getting   D. reaching at
47. How much did you _____ the radio?
    A. pay for   B. pay off   C. pay back   D. pay out
48. Our water supply has been _____ for two days.
    A. cut out   B. cut off   C. cut down   D. cut away
49. The bag is so heavy. Let me help you _____ it.
    A. bring   B. carry   C. take   D. fetch
50. — Will somebody go and get Dr. White?
    — He's always been _____.
    A. asked for   B. sent for   C. called for D. looked for
51. The old man can't hope to _____ his cancer in a few days.
    A. get away   B. get off   C. get out   D. get over

第五天

突破英语的时态（一）

本章主要突破英语中的一般将来时、过去将来时、现在进行时、将来进行时和过去进行时。这五个时态很简单，希望大家把所有的例句背下来。

5.1 一般将来时

1. 定义

一般将来时表示说话的人在将来某一时刻将要发生的动作或存在的状态。

将来时态（一般将来时、将来进行时、将来完成时和过去将来时）和其他时态不一样的地方在于：其他时态中的动作已经发生、正在发生或是经常发生，只有将来时态的动作并没有发生。所以，我们在后面会讨论哪种将来时态表示发生的可能性较大。

> e.g.: I *will enter* Peking University this summer.
> 我今年夏天将要去北京大学上学。
> They *are going* to the park tomorrow.
> 他们明天要去公园。

Tips be going to 也是一种表示将来时态的方法。

2. 图示

一般将来时图示如下：

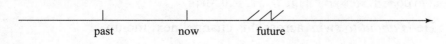

根据定义，可见一般将来时发生在数轴上的斜线部分。因为将来还没有发生，所以也就具有一定的预见性。

3. 结构

在这个时态中，我们不采用图表的方式来学习，其主要结构是：

主语 + shall（用于第一人称）/will（用于第二、三人称）+动词原形

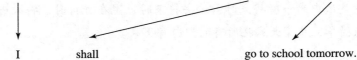

I   shall   go to school tomorrow.

疑问句是将will或shall提前即可，否定形式是在其后加not。

📝 e.g.: { *Shall* I go to school tomorrow?   { *Will* you go to America in 2019?
         Yes, *you shall*./ No, you *shall not*.   Yes, *I will*./ No, *I won't*.

4. 用法

（1）基本用法：表示主语在将来某个时刻发生的动作或存在的状态。

📝 e.g.: The sports meeting *will be held* in 2019.
运动会将于2019年举行。
We *will have* a picnic this weekend.
我们这周末有个野餐会。

（2）特殊用法：表示一般将来时，除了可以用will和shall的结构，还可以用以下几个结构，但要注意区别。

① be going to do表示即将发生的事或打算、计划、决定或很有可能发生的事。

📝 e.g.: I *am going to have* a holiday next week.
我下个星期准备去度假。
We *are going to spend* two months reading this book.
我们准备花两个月时间读这本书。

② be about to do表示安排好了的或筹备已久的事情。

📝 e.g.: He *is about to swim* across this channel next month.
他打算下个月横渡这个海峡。

Tips be about to这个结构一般还会和when连用，形成固定搭配。要特别注意：一般在when的结构中使用过去将来时态时，都用be about to do的结构。

🖋 e.g.: When it rained yesterday, I *was about to go* to the shopping mall.
昨天下雨的时候，我刚好要去购物中心。

③ be to do表示已安排好且是将来可能成为现实的事情。

🖋 e.g.: I *am to be* a doctor in a few years.
过几年我就会成为医生。
He *is to visit* Russia in 2019.
他将于2019年访问俄罗斯。

5.2 过去将来时

1. 定义

过去将来时表示说话的人在过去将来的某一时刻所发生的动作或存在的状态。

过去将来时也是一种用来预测将来发生事情的时态，它比一般将来时所表达的可能性要大一些，因为这是在过去的某个时刻说出的话，预示着将来要发生的事情。

🖋 e.g.: They said they *would have* a very important meeting next week.
他们说下周他们有个重要的会议。

Tips 在从句中所用的时态就是过去将来时，因为是在过去预测将来要发生的事情。

2. 图示

过去将来时可以图示如下:

从图中可看出,在过去某时之后的时间所发生的动作和状态都可叫做过去将来时。这个时态与现在和将来相连接,句子当中的时态既可以是现在发生,也可能是将来发生。所以也就导致过去将来时经常用于宾语从句当中。

3. 结构

疑问句是将would或should提前即可,否定句是在其后加not。

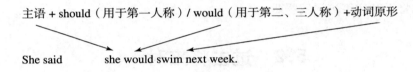

主语 + should（用于第一人称）/ would（用于第二、三人称）+动词原形

She said she would swim next week.

> 📝 e.g.: *Should* I *go* to school tomorrow?   *Would* you *go* to America in 2019?
> Yes, you *should*./ No, you *should not*.   Yes, I *would*./ No, I *would not*.

4. 用法

基本用法：主要用于间接引语（宾语从句）中,详见第十一天,主句谓语多用一般过去时。

> 📝 e.g.: She said that she *could go* to college next year.
> 她说她明年要上大学了。
>
> They hoped that they *could defeat* the enemies.
> 他们希望他们能打败敌人。

5.3 现在进行时

1. 定义

现在进行时表示主语即刻所发生的动作或存在的状态。

e.g.: Sherry *is playing* basketball.
　　　谢丽正在打篮球。
　　　Henry and Bruce *are writing* something.
　　　亨利和布鲁斯正在写东西。
　　　They *are cooking* dinner.
　　　他们正在做饭。

2. 图示

现在进行时图示如下：

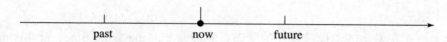

从图中可看出"即刻"是怎样表示出来的，表示在中心点和其边缘所发生的动作和状态。所以，现在进行时态不仅仅可以表示正在发生的动作，也可以表示动作的某种持续性，即动作可以在一段时间内发生。我们在比较时态的过程中会讨论这个问题。

3. 结构

现在进行时的结构如下：

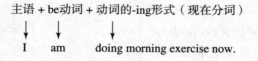

be动词形式要根据人称和数的变化而变化。在这里我们要讨论一下现在分词的构成（如表5-1所示）。

表5-1 分词构成

情 况	例 词
一般动词直接在词尾加-ing，读/iŋ/。	look—looking work—working see—seeing
重读闭音节词的词尾，双写词尾字母加-ing，读/iŋ/。	stop—stopping plan—planning
有辅音字母接不发音e的词尾，去e加-ing，读/iŋ/。	use—using live—living leave—leaving

现在进行时的疑问句是将be提到句首，回答时用yes或no。

e.g.: He *is playing* basketball at this moment.
Is he *playing* basketball at this moment?
Yes, he *is*. / No, he *is not*.

4. 用法

（1）基本用法。

① 表示主语正在发生的动作或存在的状态。它经常和at the same time，at this moment，now等词连用。

e.g.: What *is* she *doing*?
她正在干什么？
She *is having* a bath.
她正在洗澡。

Is she *having* a bath?
她正在洗澡吗？
Yes, she *is*./No, she *isn't*.
是的，她是。/不，她不是。

② 表示主语在最近一段时间内正在发生的动作或存在的状态，经常和these days, these weeks等词连用。

e.g.: He *is reading* this book these days.
这几天他一直在读这本书。
They *are trying* to look for this person these weeks.
几周来他们一直试图找到这个人。

（2）特殊用法。

① 用于表示将来发生的事，常表示"意图""安排"或"打算"的含义，特别表示最近

或较近事情的发生，常用于位移动词中。

> e.g.: The train *is leaving* at 7:45a.m.
> 火车早上7:45出站。
>
> He *is going* for a holiday.
> 他打算去度假。

② always可以用于现在进行时，用来表示说话人的某种感情色彩。

Tips 这种用法在英语的各大考试中出现的频率甚高，请注意。

> e.g.: She *is always criticizing* other people.
> 她总是喜欢批评别人。

always在这里表示的含义就是对她的这种做法不是十分满意，含有抱怨的情绪在其中，所以表达了一种感情色彩。

> e.g.: The teacher *is always laughing* at his students.
> 这位老师总是嘲笑他的学生。

5. 比较

（1）一般现在时可表示最近发生的事情。现在进行时也可表示最近发生的事情。

> e.g.: He *reads* a book these days.
> He *is reading* a book these days.

Tips 现在进行时更强调动作的持续性，表示主语最近几天都在进行此动作，而且连续不断；一般现在时表示主语可能在最近一段时间做此动作，并无持续性，可能是断断续续的。

（2）位移动词的代替用法。

在位移动词的使用过程中，既可以用一般现在时态代替一般将来时态，也可以用现在进行时态代替一般将来时态。请看例句：

e.g.: The train *is leaving* at 3 o'clock p.m.
　　　The train *leaves* at 3 o'clock p.m.

Tips leave是位移动词，所以我们要用以上两种时态代替一般将来时。前者更加强调动作发生的时间接近下午3点钟，现在可能是下午2:58；后者则更加强调现在可能是下午1点钟或是中午12点钟。在没有任何语言环境的情况下，我们无法判断用什么时态，这时两者都可以用。

5.4　过去进行时

1. 定义

过去进行时表示主语过去某个具体时间所发生的动作或存在的状态。

e.g.: He *was having* breakfast at 7 o'clock yesterday morning.
　　　他昨天早上七点正在吃饭。
　　　What *were* you *doing* when I came back?
　　　我回来的时候你正在做什么？
　　　While I *was having* lunch, the doorbell rang.
　　　当我正在吃饭的时候，门铃响了。

Tips 从这几个例句不难看出，过去进行时都要和一定的时间状语连用。一般来说，过去进行时不单独使用。在后面总结时态的时候，我们还会讲到必须和时间状语连用的几个时态。

2. 图示

过去进行时图示如下：

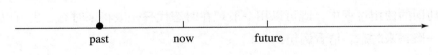

从图示中不难看出，过去进行时表示的是过去某一具体时刻发生的事情，和一般过去时不同的是：前者强调时间点发生的事，而后者强调时间段发生的事。这点实际上也是一般时态和进行时态的区别所在，一般时态（一般过去时、一般现在时、一般将来时和过去将来时）都是在时间段内发生的动作或存在的状态，而进行时态（现在进行时、过去进行时、将来进行时和过去将来进行时）都是在时间点上发生的动作或存在的状态。进行时态还可以用于表示时间段，请注意这种用法。

3. 结构

过去进行时的结构如下：

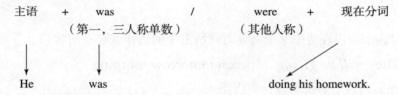

过去进行时的疑问句一般是把be动词提到句首，用yes或no来回答。

✏️ e.g.: He *was doing* his homework.

Was he *doing* his homework?

Yes, he was. / No, he was not.

4. 用法

（1）常和过去某一具体时间连用，表示正在发生的动作和存在的状态。

✏️ e.g.: He *was playing* football at 7 last night.

他昨晚七点正在踢球。

What *was* the boy *doing* when the thieves stole his clothes?

小偷偷他衣服时那个男孩在干什么？

（2）常有文中出现"when + 一般过去时，过去进行时"的结构。

✏️ e.g.: What *were* they *doing* when the accident happened?

当事故发生时，他们正在干什么？

She *was living* in Beijing when she was 8 years old.

她8岁时，正住在北京。

（3）主要用于间接引语（宾语从句）中，详见第十一天。

e.g.: I told you that she *was leaving* soon.
　　　我告诉你她不久就要走了。
　　　He told me that he *was having* lunch at that time.
　　　他告诉我他那时正在吃饭。

5.5　将来进行时

1. 定义

将来进行时表示主语在将来某个具体时间所发生的动作或存在的状态。

e.g.: They *will be giving* a speech tomorrow morning.
　　　他们明天早上将举行一个讲座。

> Tips: 将来进行时在表示将来所发生的动作和存在的状态时，相比较一般将来时来说，发生的可能性更大。

2. 图示

将来进行时图示如下：

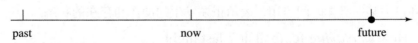

从图示中不难看出，图上的黑点部分就是将来进行时态所发生的时间点，在将来某个确定的时间，所以发生的可能性是较大的。

3. 结构

将来进行时的结构如下：

　　　　主语　　+　　shall / will　　+　　be　　+　　doing　　+　　宾语
　　　　　　　　　　（第一人称）（第二、三人称）

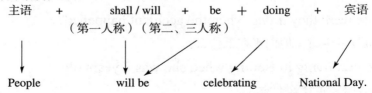

People　　　will be　　　celebrating　　　National Day.

将来进行时的疑问句是将助动词will提到句首,回答用yes或no。

🖊 e.g.: She *will be singing* at this time of next week.

Will she *be singing* at this time of next week?

Yes, she will. / No, she will not./ No. she won't.

4. 用法

(1) 基本用法:表示主语在将来的某一具体时刻所发生的动作或存在的状态。

🖊 e.g.: Henry *will be going* to the United States tomorrow to visit his girl friend.
亨利明天去美国看他的女朋友。

People *will be waiting* for the music band to give a performance in three days.
人们在等待三天后乐队的演出。

(2) 特殊用法:表示说话人的某种委婉说法。

🖊 e.g.: *Will* you *be waiting* for me?

Tips 这个句子所表达的含义要比Will you wait for me？更委婉一些。委婉的原因很简单。例如Could you help me？比Can you help me？委婉的原因我们可以理解为:could是can的过去式,表示已经发生过的事情,既然是已经发生过的事情,对于说者和听者来说不会觉得生硬,显得很有礼貌,这样就产生了委婉语气。当大家看到将来进行时比一般将来时要委婉时,其原因也就不言而喻:将来进行时是将来正在发生的事情,而一般将来时则是在将来有可能发生的事情。

📚 小 结

以上五种时态,包括昨天所讲的两种时态,是英语中最基本的时态,也是最简单和最常用的时态。在不配任何习题的情况下,希望大家能回答下列问题:

(1) 一般现在时的基本用法是什么？"主将从现"指的是什么？位移动词的替代情况是什么？

(2) 一般过去时中used to do和would do有什么区别？

(3) 一般将来时的几个特殊表达法有什么不同？

（4）过去将来时一般用在什么从句当中？它所表达的将来的可能性比一般将来时大还是小？

（5）现在进行时是否可以表示一段时间内所发生的事情？它又和一般现在时表示一段时间内发生的事情有什么不同？

（6）使用过去进行时时一般有什么要求？

（7）将来进行时是如何表达委婉语气的？为什么可以这样表达？

在不配任何练习的情况下，希望大家能对以上问题对答如流，然后在明天学习完时态之后，再去把后面的习题做完，就能把英语中所有的时态都弄懂了。加油！

第六天

突破英语的时态（二）

本章讲解英语中最难的四个时态，要特别注意最后的时态总结。这些总结是时态部分学习的精髓，而且还要对后面练习中经典的题目加以深入地分析，因为这些题目大都是高考和英语四、六级中的典型考题。

6.1　现在完成时

完成时是英语中最重要的时态之一，请务必认真学习。在中文里我们表达完成时态时一般使用"已经"一词，但是在英语中却不是只靠already就可以表示的，谓语部分必须有相应的变化，才可以形成正式的完成时态。此外，完成时也是表示过去发生的事情，但是和一般过去时态是完全不同的。

1. 定义

现在完成时跨越两个时间段，一个在过去，另一个在现在，具有三层含义：
① 主语的动作发生在过去（和一般过去时不一样）。
② 而影响或持续到现在（重点在这里）。
③ 句子所表达的目的在于强调动作的影响和持续（注意句子的意图是什么）。

> e.g.: I *have had* supper for three hours.
> 我已经吃过晚饭三个小时了。

Tips　这句话并不是想强调我什么时候吃饭，或是吃的什么饭，甚至吃了几个小时，只是想强调吃完饭了这件事情对于现在的影响。

> e.g.: She *has been* away since 1976.
> 她1976年就已经离开这里了。

> **Tips** 这句话表示她已经很多年不在这里了，和她什么时候走的并没有什么关系。

e.g.: The cat *has been* dead for two days.
这只猫已经死了两天了。

2. 图示

现在完成时图示如下：

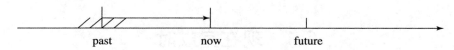

这张图示和我们以前所看到的图示都是不一样的，因为涉及两个时间，从图示可以看出，主语的动作发生在过去某个时刻，而它的影响却持续至今，我们并不想了解动作发生在哪个时间，而是想更多地了解动作如何影响或持续至今。

3. 结构

现在完成时的结构如下：

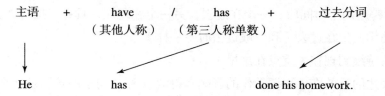

在这里我们必须讨论过去分词的构成（如表6-1所示）。

表6-1 过去分词的构成

情况	例词
在词尾直接加-ed	look—looked work—worked walk—walked
以不发音的e结尾，直接加-d	love—loved live—lived hope—hoped

续表

情　况	例　词
辅音字母+y结尾，变y为i加-ed	supply—supplied try—tried carry—carried
重读闭音节的词尾，双写词尾字母加-ed	stop—stopped plan—planned
不规则动词	see—seen fly—flown forget—forgotten

4.用法

（1）表示主语过去的动作对于现在的影响。

e.g.: I *have* already *typed* this letter.

我已经把这封信打好了。（表示动作"打印信件"发生在过去，而我们要知道的是"信件打印完了"，强调影响）

He *has* already *gone* there.

他已经去那儿了。（表示动作"走了"发生在过去，而我们要知道的是他不在这儿，不关心他什么时间走或到哪儿去了）

（2）在英语中只有持续性动词（动作可以持续的动词，如live，read，study等）才可用于现在完成时，而非持续性动词（动作不可以持续的动词，如 buy，die，get up，sell等）不可用于现在完成时。

e.g.: He *has been* dead for three years.

他已经死了三年了。

切不可说：He *has died* for three years.

Tips

die是非持续性动词，"死"不可能"死"三年，所以这里要用它的形容词形式来代替。这样的情况还适用于以下动词：

buy—keep　　go—be away　　come—be here　　join in—be a member of

像以上这样的结构还有许多，需要大家平时多收集并认真记忆。

✏ e.g.: He *has joined* the army for three years.（错误）

由于join不是持续性动词，所以我们应该写成以下的句子：

He *has been* a member of the army for three years.

他参军已经三年了。

（3）现在完成时常和时间段连用，常见的有以since和for两个词引导的时间状语。

✏ e.g.: He *has been* here since 1999.

他从1999年起就在这儿了。（since表示"从……开始"，它是表示时间点的词）

He *has been* here for 4 years.

他已在这儿住四年了。（"for+时间段"表示一段时间）

（4）现在完成时中常用的副词有already（"已经"，用于肯定句），yet（"还"，用于否定和疑问句），just（"刚刚"）。

✏ e.g.: She *has* already *finished* this subject.

她已经完成了这个课题。

The girl *hasn't had* a meal yet today.

小女孩今天还没有吃饭。

Lucy *has* just *gone* away.

露西刚刚才走。

（5）现在完成时用于表示主语过去的动作持续至今。

✏ e.g.: The Chinese people *have used* bamboos to make paper for several thousand years.

中国人已经用竹子造纸几千年了。（表示中国人几千年来一直用竹子造纸，而且很可能现在和将来还要用竹子造纸）

5. 比较

（1）一般过去时和现在完成时的比较。

✏ e.g.: ① My father *had* supper at 6 p.m. 我爸晚上六点吃饭。
② My father *has had* supper for three hours. 我爸已经吃过饭三个小时了。

①句表示"我爸在晚上六点吃饭"这个动作的发生,它和现在没有关系,只是指一个人发生一个动作。②句表示"我爸已经吃过饭三个小时了",它不强调动作的发生,而是强调动作对于现在的影响,可能我爸现在不想吃东西或不饿等。

(2) has been to 和 has gone to 的区别。

e.g.: ① I *have been to* Shanghai. 我去过上海。
② I *have gone to* Shanghai. 我去了上海。

①句和②句的区别在于:前者表示曾经去过,而现在说话人在现场,后者则表示已经去了某地,现在不在此地。

Tips 现在完成时是英语中最重要的时态,在本章中并没有分成基本用法和特殊用法,因为这些用法一定要完全记住,用法的比较也十分重要。后面要讲解的过去完成时和将来完成时都是在现在完成时的基础上延伸出来的。

6.2 过去完成时

1. 定义

简而言之,过去完成时,就是"过去的过去"。表示主语在"过去的过去"所发生的动作对于过去的影响。一般用于具体的时间状语中,不单独使用。

e.g.: He said he *had been* away for several days.
他说他已经走了几天了。

By the time of last summer the edifice *had been built* for five years.
到去年夏天这栋摩天大楼已经建成五年了。

Before 7 o'clock they *hadn't reached* the railway station.
七点之前他们还没有到火车站。

2. 图示

过去完成时的图示如下:

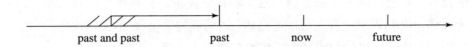

在图示中,过去的过去所发生的动作对于过去产生了影响,实际上相当于现在完成时向后倒退了一个时间段,所以它被形象地称为"过去的过去"。

3. 结构

过去完成时的结构如下:

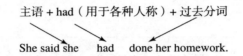

4. 用法(基本用法)

(1)用于表示"过去的过去"。

> e.g.: Before she went to bed Lily *had dealt* with everything that she needed to do.
> 在丽莉睡觉之前她处理好了一切她需要做的事。
> At the age of five, he *had played* the piano very well.
> 在他五岁时他钢琴弹得已经很好了。

(2)用于when引导的时间状语后和用于含有by引导的时间状语从句之后。

> e.g.: When I was a child, I *had had* to live alone.
> 当我还是个孩子时我就不得不一个人住。
> By the time of 1996, Bruce *had collected* more than six thousand stamps in all.
> 到1996年时,布鲁斯已经总共收集到了超过六千张的邮票。

(3)用于间接引语(宾语从句)中,详见第十一天的内容。

> e.g.: I said I *had* already *repaired* the broken desk.
> 我说我已经修好了坏的桌子。
> Ann told me that she *had told* her father something important about you.
> 安告诉我她已经把一些重要的关于你的事情告诉了她的父亲。

6.3 将来完成时

1. 定义

将来完成时表示主语在现在乃至将来发生的动作对将来产生的影响。

✏️ e.g.: By 2019, they *will have learned* about six thousand words.
到2019年,他们将会学习6000个单词了。

Tips 这句话的含义在于强调到2019年时的影响,而不是强调在将来能学习多少单词或是别的动作或状态。

2. 图示

将来完成时的图示如下:

从图示中不难看出,现在甚至将来发生的事情对将来产生了某种影响,这样的时态称为将来完成时。

3. 结构

将来完成时的结构如下:

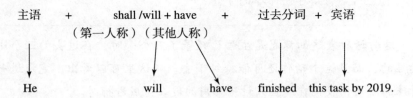

将来完成时的疑问句是将will提到句首,回答时用yes或no。

✏️ e.g.: He *will have finished* this task by 2019.
Will he *have finished* this task by 2019?
Yes, he *will*. / No, he *will not*.

4. 用法

基本用法：表示将来一定会发生的某件事情。

> **Tips** 在前面讲解一般将来时曾经讨论过将来时发生的可能性，在所有表示将来时的语法现象中，将来完成时所表达的动作是最有可能发生的。

e.g.: When he becomes an adult, he *will have been* a doctor.
他长大以后肯定会成为一个医生。

> **Tips** 这句话表达的事情发生的可能性实际上比 When he becomes an adult, he will be a doctor. 所表达的可能性要大得多。

6.4 现在完成进行时

1. 定义

现在完成进行时表示主语从过去发生一个动作持续到现在，并有可能持续下去。强调动作的持续性和影响性。

e.g.: He *has been waiting* for you for three hours.
他已经等你等了三个小时了。

> **Tips** 这句话所表达的意思是主语已经等了三个小时，在过去的三个小时里动作是持续性的，而且这个动作还可能持续下去。从这里可以看出，完成进行时是一组比较特殊的时态，我们在这里只讨论常用的现在完成进行时。

2. 图示

现在完成进行时图示如下：

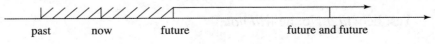

从图示可以看出，现在完成进行时表示在过去持续发生的事情，和完成时的不同之处在于：完成时是一定对现在或将来有影响，但是完成进行时不只会有影响，更多的是考虑到会不会持续的问题。在这里不讨论到底能不能持续的问题，因为这是一个深层的英语语法问题，我们假设都可以持续。

3. 结构

现在完成进行时的结构如下：

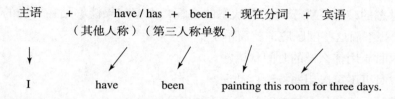

现在完成进行时的疑问句是将have提到句首，回答时用yes或no。

e.g.: He *has been painting* this picture for several days.

Has he *been painting* this picture for several days?

Yes, he *has*. / No, he *has not*.

4. 用法

（1）基本用法：表示过去发生的动作对现在产生的影响，并且这个动作将持续下去。

e.g.: This girl *has been living* abroad for many years.

这个女孩已经在国外生活了很多年。

（2）特殊用法：表示一种委婉语气。

e.g.: Too many things *have been happening* this fall.

真是个多事之秋啊！

小 结

时态实际上要表述时间和状态，不论什么时态，在句子中的体现都是先时间，后状态，比方说：

现在进行时　　am/is/are doing

过去进行时　　was/were doing

将来进行时　will be doing

大家会发现前面的助动词、时间在变化，后面的状态始终都是doing，没有任何变化。再看下面一组：

现在完成时　have/has done

过去完成时　had done

将来完成时　will have done

同时，大家也会发现前面的助动词、时间在变化，后面的状态始终都是done，没有任何变化。所以，时态的核心就在于时间和状态的搭配，大家如果能够站在这样的高度看待时态的话，那么回答下面这些问题应该就简单了：

（1）现在完成时要用什么样的时间状语？

（2）现在完成时可不可以用非持续性动词？

（3）过去完成时一般和什么样的时间状语连用？

（4）将来完成时表示将来的可能性比一般将来时大还是小？

（5）现在完成进行时表示持续的影响吗？

在完成了以上的问题和以下的习题之后，相信大家一定能够突破英语的时态了。努力！

练 习

1. By the end of this year, I _____ English in that middle school for three years.

    A. have taught　　　　　　　　B. will be teaching

    C. will have taught　　　　　　D. are teaching

2. — What happened to Tony?

    — He stepped on a nail while he _____ in the yard.

    A. was running　　　　　　　　B. is running

    C. runs　　　　　　　　　　　　D. had run

3. We promise that we'll meet again after we _____ our college education in three years.

    A. finish　　　B. will finish　　　C. have gone　　　D. goes

4. She often _____ to see her grandparents.
   A. is going   B. went   C. has gone   D. goes
5. It is the first time I _____ the Great Wall.
   A. will visit   B. had visited
   C. have visited   D. visit
6. It was the first time I _____ the Great Wall.
   A. will visit   B. had visited
   C. have visited   D. visit
7. She _____ in two hours.
   A. arrives   B. will arrive
   C. is arriving   D. is to arrive
8. I'll give him this message the moment I _____ him.
   A. will see   B. see   C. is seeing   D. is to see
9. As soon as I _____ New York, I'll write to you.
   A. am getting to   B. get to
   C. will get to   D. get
10. If it _____ rain tomorrow, we will have a picnic.
    A. won't   B. doesn't   C. will   D. wouldn't
11. John's brother _____ in bed all day because he had a headache.
    A. lay   B. lie   C. laid   D. lain
12. — What were you doing this time last night?
    — I _____ newspaper.
    A. am reading   B. was reading
    C. read   D. would read
13. I _____ my homework when the telephone _____.
    A. did; rang   B. was doing; was ringing
    C. was doing; rang   D. did; was ringing
14. Do you see the sign that _____ "keep off the grass"?
    A. is read   B. reads   C. is written   D. writes
15. Can you tell me when you _____?
    A. come back   B. will come back
    C. is coming back   D. would come back

16. When spring _____, the weather will be warmer and warmer.
    A. is coming   B. comes
    C. come   D. will come

17. — Do you know him?
    — Yes, I _____ him once before.
    A. met   B. meet
    C. have met   D. had met

18. Look out! The car _____.
    A. comes   B. is coming
    C. will come   D. is to come

19. You must water these flowers. Look, they _____ soon.
    A. will die   B. would die
    C. are dying   D. are being died

20. Hello! I _____ you _____ in London. How long have you been here?
    A. don't know; were   B. hadn't known; are
    C. haven't known; are   D. didn't know; were

21. Don't get off the bus until it _____.
    A. has stopped   B. stopped
    C. will stop   D. shall stop

22. That supper was the most delicious dinner I _____.
    A. would have   B. have ever had
    C. had never had   D. had ever had

23. Let's set off before the sun _____.
    A. will set   B. is setting   C. sets   D. set

24. — What will you do this weekend?
    — I don't know, but it's about time _____ it.
    A. I'm considering   B. I'll consider
    C. I had considered   D. I considered

25. — Dick sat in the back of the classroom.
    — Really? I thought he _____ in the front.
    A. sat   B. is sitting
    C. has been sitting   D. had sat

26. The last time I _____ her, she _____ at a medical college.
    A. was visiting; studied   B. visited; studies
    C. visited; was studying   D. was visiting; was studying
27. — _____ my pen?
    — Yes, I saw it on the desk a moment ago.
    A. Do you see   B. Had you seen
    C. Would you see   D. Have you seen
28. You can't watch TV until you _____ your homework.
    A. did   B. are doing
    C. have done   D. had done
29. My wish is _____ a teacher.
    A. becoming   B. become
    C. to become   D. being come
30. — Hi, Tracy, you look tired.
    — I'm tired, because I _____ the living room all day.
    A. painted   B. had painted
    C. have been painting   D. have painted
31. He insists that he _____ it by himself.
    A. manages   B. will manage
    C. manage   D. managed
32. You _____ upset, what's wrong with you?
    A. are looking   B. have looked
    C. look   D. looked
33. — He _____ here five days ago.
    — What _____ these days?
    A. came; did he do   B. came; was he doing
    C. came; has he been doing   D. has come; has he been doing
34. I phoned him that I _____ there next week.
    A. was going to   B. was going to be
    C. will get   D. would get to
35. You can't catch up with your classmates unless you _____ hard.
    A. work   B. are to work
    C. will work   D. is going to work

36. He suddenly remembered that he _____ his key at home.
    A. had forgotten   B. has left
    C. had left   D. has forgotten
37. The temple _____ for years.
    A. isn't repaired   B. hasn't repaired
    C. hasn't been repaired D. hadn't repaired
38. He _____ while he _____ his motorbike and hurt his leg.
    A. had fallen; rode   B. fall; was riding
    C. fell; was riding   D. had fallen; was riding
39. You should prepare the dinner before guests _____.
    A. will be arrived   B. are arrived
    C. arrive   D. will arrive
40. It _____ two years _____ I had been here.
    A. is; that   B. was; that   C. is; since   D. was; since
41. It _____ two years since I _____ here.
    A. is; have been away   B. is; had left
    C. was; have left   D. was; would leave
42. I don't know if she _____. If she _____, I'll let you know.
    A. will come; comes   B. comes; will comes
    C. comes; comes   D. will come; will come
43. My birthday _____ next week I _____ twenty-three years old.
    A. comes; is to be   B. is coming; will be
    C. comes; shall be   D. is coming; is going to be
44. Who do you think _____ him advice?
    A. give   B. gives   C. giving   D. to give
45. — Which big city have you visited?
    — I _____ New York.
    A. have gone to   B. have been to
    C. went to   D. go to
46. He _____ to New York three times last year.
    A. has been   B. has gone
    C. went   D. was going

47. He _____ for his ID Card, which he _____ for several days.
   A. has looked; has lost   B. has been looking; has lost
   C. has looked; has missed   D. has been looking; has missed

48. Some experts think these plays _____ written by Shakespeare.
   A. were not   B. has not been
   C. is not to be   D. had not been

49. Nancy _____ "Hello" to people who she meets.
   A. is always saying   B. was always saying
   C. always gave   D. would give

50. As she _____ the newspaper, Granny _____ asleep.
   A. read; was falling   B. was reading; fell
   C. was reading; was falling D. read; fell

51. Tom _____ into the house when no one _____.
   A. slipped; was looking after him
   B. had slipped; looked after him
   C. slipped; had looked after him
   D. was slipping; looked after him

52. You are still here, and I _____ you _____ America.
   A. think; are leaving
   B. think; have already left for
   C. thought; had already left for
   D. thought; would leave for

53. A new cinema _____ here. They hope to finish it next week.
   A. will be built   B. is built
   C. has been built   D. is being built

54. Look at the bad weather. It _____ heavily for two days.
   A. is raining   B. had rained
   C. has been raining   D. has been rained

55. _____ there likely _____ anyone to meet us at the airport?
   A. Does; to be   B. Is; being
   C. Has; that   D. Is; to be

56. — It's said that "Titanic" is a moving film.
    — I _____ it yet. I hope to see it soon.
    A. didn't see   B. hadn't seen
    C. don't see   D. haven't seen
57. I had a discussion with Mr. Blake and hoped he _____ us an early reply.
    A. would give   B. give
    C. gave   D. had given
58. He told me how to do after I _____ him twice.
    A. ask   B. have asked
    C. asked   D. had asked
59. John said that he would write to me but I _____ him so far.
    A. didn't hear from   B. hadn't heard from
    C. haven't heard from D. hadn't received
60. By the time I arrive at the station, the train _____.
    A. will start   B. starts
    C. will have started   D. is starting
61. — There are many people in the square.
    — What do you suppose _____?
    A. is happened   B. did happen
    C. would happen   D. has happened
62. — Hey, Henry! Where are you going?
    — Oh, I'm terrible sorry, _____.
    A. I'm not noticing   B. I wasn't noticing
    C. I haven't noticed   D. I don't noticing
63. Look! What _____ they _____ over there?
    A. did; do   B. do; do
    C. are; doing   D. will; do
64. — Professor Zhang has just arrived.
    — Really? I don't think he _____ until next month.
    A. is coming   B. has come
    C. will come   D. had come

65. Doctor Joan _____ in the hospital since she _____ from a university.
   A. has worked; graduated B. had worked; graduated
   C. was working; graduated D. worked; graduated
66. — Do you know anyone in Paris?
   — No, but I'll make friends once _____.
   A. I've been settled B. I'll be settled
   C. I had settled D. I'm settled
67. — Have you brought me a dictionary?
   — Oh, sorry. I _____ all about it.
   A. forget B. had forgotten
   C. forgot D. will forget
68. — Is Mary in?
   — She is out, and _____ back until eight o'clock.
   A. she comes B. she'll come
   C. she won't come D. she'll be
69. Health experts in many countries still _____ their ideas about the relationship between food and health.
   A. have tested B. tested
   C. are testing D. test
70. The old said the earth _____ round the sun.
   A. moves B. will move
   C. is moving D. is to move
71. It is 8 o'clock now. The plane _____ in half an hour.
   A. will leave B. were leaving
   C. leaves D. is to leave
72. Unless you _____ smoking, you'll not be healthy.
   A. give up B. will give up
   C. gave up D. will give in
73. — Where is John?
   — Oh, he _____ just now.
   A. goes out B. has gone to
   C. went out D. had gone to

74. It has been five years since he _____ smoking.
    A. gives up   B. gave up
    C. has given up   D. would give up

75. I _____ swim in the river when I was a child.
    A. went   B. used to
    C. am used to   D. was used to

76. He was recovered sooner than I _____.
    A. am expected   B. am expecting
    C. expected   D. have expected

77. We were all surprised when he made it clear that he _____ office soon.
    A. leaves   B. would leave
    C. left   D. had left

78. — We could have walked to the station; it was not very far.
    — Yes. A taxi _____ at all necessary.
    A. wasn't   B. hadn't been
    C. wouldn't be   D. won't be

79. He _____ the guitar when I went to see him last night.
    A. has been playing   B. had played
    C. was playing   D. played

80. My father said that he _____ the car for ten years.
    A. has bought   B. had bought
    C. has had   D. had had

81. Can you tell me what _____ next?
    A. will we do   B. we will do
    C. we would do   D. would we do

82. — Did you see Mary in the reading room?
    — No, _____ by the time I came in.
    A. she'd left   B. she's left
    C. she left   D. she would leave

83. To our surprise, we found that she _____ her English so rapidly.
    A. improves   B. improved
    C. has improved   D. had improved

84. Did you ask Nancy if she _____ tomorrow?
    A. left   B. had left
    C. is going to leave   D. was going to leave
85. David _____ to pass the examination but he failed.
    A. has hoped   B. hopes
    C. would hope   D. had hoped
86. She told me that she _____ there in two hours.
    A. will be   B. would be   C. was   D. has been
87. There _____ great changes in our hometown in the past twenty years.
    A. had been   B. will be   C. have been   D. were
88. I'll begin the dictation when you _____ ready.
    A. shall be   B. will be   C. are   D. have been
89. It _____ when we arrived at the station.
    A. has snowed   B. is snowing
    C. snowed   D. was snowing
90. — When will you finish your work?
    — I'll finish it before you _____ back.
    A. come   B. will come
    C. shall come   D. have come
91. — Why do you hurt her?
    — But I _____.
    A. mean to   B. didn't mean to
    C. meant to   D. would mean to
92. — Please help me post this letter.
    — OK, _____.
    A. I do   B. I would   C. I will   D. I did
93. I never imagined that Peter _____ such a good student.
    A. be   B. would be   C. is   D. will have been
94. Human beings _____ the moon and _____ to the earth again.
    A. have gone; came back   B. have gone to; came back
    C. have been; came back   D. have been to; came back

95. By the end of last year I _____ ten thousand English words.
    A. have learnt   B. had learnt
    C. would have learn   D. will learn
96. Hardly _____ the house when it began to rain.
    A. I had left   B. had I left
    C. I have left   D. have I left
97. I _____ to say my opinion, but the meeting was over.
    A. have hoped   B. was hoping
    C. had hoped   D. would hope
98. We _____ a walk when it started to rain.
    A. take   B. took   C. are taking   D. were taking
99. By the time I get to the airport, the plane _____ for Shanghai.
    A. will leave   B. leaves
    C. will have left   D. left
100. Not until I returned home _____ that my wallet _____.
    A. I found; was stolen
    B. had found; had stolen
    C. did I found; had been stolen
    D. had I found; has been stolen
101. There _____ a storm in this area next week.
    A. is   B. will be   C. is to be   D. is going to be
102. I _____ him for a relative. Why didn't you tell me earlier?
    A. have taken   B. took
    C. take   D. had taken
103. In the past ten years I _____ all the mountains in China.
    A. have traveled   B. traveled
    C. had traveled   D. was traveling

第七天

突破英语的被动语态、助动词和情态动词

被动语态是一个结构性语法的教学典范，只需要掌握本章中所讲的几大结构，然后把所学的知识放在其中就可以了。助动词和情态动词一直是难点，本章中罗列了主要助动词的用法，在学习情态动词的过程中可采取对比的办法。

7.1 被动语态

一、语态

语态是英语中的一个语法范畴。它主要表示主语和谓语之间的关系。英语中的语态可以分为两类，即主动语态和被动语态。

e.g.: I *cleaned* the classroom last week.
　　　施动者　　　　受动者
　　上周我打扫了教室。（主动语态）
　　The classroom *was cleaned* last week by I (me).
　　　受动者　　　　　　　　　　　施动者
　　上周教室被我打扫了。（被动语态）

二、被动语态

1. 定义

被动语态是受动者处于主语位置上，而谓语位置上由be+过去分词构成的一种语态。

e.g.: I *was invited* to your birthday party.
　　我被邀请参加你的生日晚会。

Henry *has been wanted* on the telephone several times.

已经有几个电话找亨利了。

2. 构成

被动语态的谓语部分是由"be+过去分词"构成的。

e.g.: The classroom *is being cleaned* by us.

教室正在被我们打扫。

The project *has* already *been finished*.

这项工程已经完成了。

They *were killed* in the accident.

他们在这场事故中丧生。

3. 主动语态变被动语态的方法

主动语态变被动语态要遵循以下规律："主（语）变宾（语），宾（语）变主（语），动词变'be + done'，其余部分带下来。"（注：done代表各种动词的过去分词）

e.g.: <u>The student</u>　　<u>broke</u>　　<u>the window</u>　　<u>yesterday</u>.

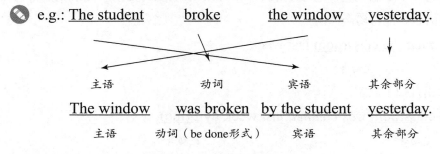

主语　　　　动词　　　　宾语　　　其余部分

　<u>The window</u>　<u>was broken</u>　<u>by the student</u>　<u>yesterday</u>.

主语　　动词（be done形式）　宾语　　其余部分

运用这种方法，我们可以把主动语态变为被动语态：

I *am carrying* a box into the room.

我正在把一个箱子搬进房间。

The box *is being carried* by me into the room.

一个箱子正在被我搬进房间。

> **Tips** 主语I变成by I (me)形式，宾语a box变成主语放在句首，动词am carrying变成is being carried形式，而其余部分into the room带到下句，一般可将by结构省略。

在这里，我们还可以用一种数学的表示方法让大家感受主动语态变被动语态。

✎ e.g.: I *am washing* my coat now.

其实谓语动词的变化最重要，示例如下：

```
抽象    be  doing              具体    am  washing
    +   be    done                 +   be   done
    ───────────────                 ────────────────
        be being done                    am being washed
```

即得：My coat *is being washed* by me. 这就一目了然了，句子中同时出现时态和语态时，必然先是时态，再是语态，两者相加，即得出一个完整的谓语部分。再如下一句：

✎ e.g.: He *has finished* this task for three days.

谓语动词的变化如下：

```
抽象    have  done              具体    has  finished
    +   be    done                  +   be   done
    ────────────────                 ──────────────────
        have been done                    has been finished
```

所以这句话变出的结果是：This task *has been finished* by him for three days.

4. 几种特殊句型的被动语态

（1）含有双宾语的被动语态。

✎ e.g.: I   gave   him   a pen.
         主语 动词   间接宾语 直接宾语

本句有两种变法，既可以将间接宾语变成主语，又可以把直接宾语变成主语。

　　　　He *was given* a pen.

　　　　A pen *was given* to him.

> **Tips** 将直接宾语变成主语，要用to来连接动词和间接宾语（宾格形式），切不可省略。

（2）含有复合宾语的被动语态。

e.g.: <u>We</u>　　<u>*elected*</u>　　<u>him</u>　　<u>our president</u>.
　　　主语　　　动词　　　宾语　　　宾语补足语

按照变化规律，本句应变化为：

He *was elected* our president by us (we).

但是有些情况（如下），要用to来连接宾语补足语和动词。

e.g.: ⎧ I *made* the door open.
　　　⎩ The door *was made* to open by me (I).

Tips 在上句中make是使役动词（包括感官动词），它的后面接不加to的不定式做宾语补足语，变成被动语态时要将to还原，不可省略。

e.g.: ⎧ She *saw* me walk along the street.
　　　⎩ I *was seen to walk* along the street by her (she).

（3）含有情态动词的被动语态。

e.g.: He *need look after* his mother in the hospital.

按照变化规律本句应变化为：

His mother *need be looked after* in the hospital by him (he).

含有情态动词的句子变被动语态的规律是：情态动词+be+动词过去分词。

e.g.: ⎧ You must finish this job tonight.
　　　⎩ This job *must be finished* tonight by you (you).

（4）含有动词词组的被动语态。

e.g.: He *looked at* the picture.

按照变化规律本句应变化为：

The picture *was looked at* by him (he).

Tips 在过去式looked后，切记不要忘记at这个介词，因为look at是完整的动词词组。

（5）含有宾语从句的被动语态。

e.g.: I *think* that she is a nurse.

按照变化规律变化上句时，宾语是一个句子，而不是词。这时可以有以下两种变化方法：

① 将宾语从句中的主语看作宾语而进行变化，即：

She *is thought* to be a nurse by me (I).

Tips 其实这也就是英语当中be done to do的结构。

② 将宾语从句用it这个形式主语来代替而进行变化，即：

It *is thought* that she is a nurse by me (I).

Tips 实际上这也就是英语中主语从句的形成方式，比如：

It is reported/thought/said/guessed/believed that ...

所以，对于句子：We *said* that he had been rich. 我们可以用以下两种变化方法：

{ He *was said to* have been rich.
{ It *was said* that he had been rich.

5. 几种含有被动意义而用主动语态来表达的句型

（1）含有某些连系动词的句子。

e.g.: The cloth *feels* soft.

这块布摸起来很柔软。（实际上"布"是被"摸"的）

> The songs *hear* very beautiful.
>
> 这些歌曲听起来很优美。（实际上"歌曲"是被"听"的）

（2）某些可和well, easily等副词连用的不及物动词，如：cook, draw, read, sell, wash, wear等。

> e.g.: The book *sold* well.
>
> 这本书很畅销。（实际上"书"是被"卖"的）
>
> The shoes *wore* out several days.
>
> 这双鞋穿坏几天了。（实际上"鞋"是被"穿坏"的）

6. 系表结构和被动语态的区别

系表结构是be动词+表语（可以是过去分词构成的形容词）；被动语态是be动词+动词过去分词。

> e.g.: The door *is closed*.

如果说这句话是系表结构，它的意思是"门关着"；而如果说这句话是被动语态，它的意思是"门被关上"。区别它们的最好的方法是根据具体情况和上下文的语境。

7.2 助动词和情态动词

一、助动词

助动词是帮助实义动词形成时态、语态和语气的一类动词。它本身无意义，要与动词的各种形式结合，才有完整意义。

常见的助动词有：be动词，do动词，have动词，shall（should）和will（would）等。

1. be 动词

（1）be动词的一般式和现在分词构成现在进行时态。

> e.g.: We *are* climbing the mountain.
>
> 我们正在爬山。
>
> They *are* doing their homework.
>
> 他们正在做家庭作业。

（2）be动词的过去式和现在分词构成过去进行时态。

e.g.: The river *was* being polluted by the factories.

这条河正在被工厂污染。

They *were* sleeping when it began to rain.

当开始下雨时，他们正在睡觉。

（3）be动词和过去分词构成被动语态。

e.g.: The room has never *been* entered by anyone.

这间房从未有人进去过。

We *were* always bothered by these people.

我们总是被这些人打扰。

2. have动词

Tips have动词的用法极其广泛，在这里把所有的用法都罗列出来，供大家记忆。

（1）have可以是实义动词，表示"拥有、举行"等含义。

e.g.: I *have* a beautiful box.

我有个很漂亮的盒子。

We will *have* our sports meeting this afternoon.

我们今天下午举行体育运动会。

（2）have动词和动词过去分词构成现在完成时、过去完成时以及将来完成时。

e.g.: We *have* already passed this exam.

我们已经通过这次考试。

He said he *had* had to go to work.

他说他不得不去工作。

By 2019, our factory will *have* produced more cars.

到2019年，我们厂将生产更多的汽车。

（3）have动词还可以形成三个经典短语。

① have something done（使某事情被做）

e.g.: I *had* my hair *cut* three days ago.
我三天前把头发剪了。

在这里，had表示被动语态，头发不能自己剪而是要被剪。

② have somebody do（让某人做某事）

e.g.: I *have* him *wait* for me now.
我让他现在等我。

在这里，have是使役动词的用法。

③ have somebody doing（使某人保持某种状态）

e.g.: I *had* her *waiting* for me for a long time.
我让她一直等了很久。

3. shall（should）和will（would）

shall（should），will（would）和动词原形构成一般将来时和过去将来时。

e.g.: Bruce *will* attend a meeting in Shanghai next year.
布鲁斯明年将要参加在上海的一个重要会议。

We *shall* deal with this affair.
我们将会处理好这件事。

I said I *should* go to school first.
我说我要先去上学。

Tom said he *would* listen to the music.
汤姆说他要听音乐。

4. do动词

（1）do动词的各种形式构成各种疑问句。

e.g.: *Do* you want to go home?
你想回家吗？

What *did* she do?
她是干什么的？

Did they really spend this money?

他们真花了这些钱吗？

（2）do动词构成各种否定句。

✏️ e.g.: He *doesn't* work hard.   She *didn't* like shopping.

    他工作不努力。   她不喜欢购物。

（3）do动词构成强调句型。

✏️ e.g.: I *do* love you forever.   *Do* sit down!

    我会爱你到永远。   请坐下！

二、情态动词

情态动词是用来表达主语的意愿、能力、愿望、请求、义务等语气的一类动词。它本身无完整的意义，只有加上动词原形（除ought 和have加不定式外）后，才构成完整的谓语部分。在这一节中我们用比较的方法来讲述。

1. can，could和be able to的用法

（1）can的用法。

① 表示某种能力。

✏️ e.g.: A bird *can* fly.

    鸟会飞。

② 表示允许。

✏️ e.g.: You *can* go now.

    你现在可以走了。

    Can I borrow your pen?

    我能借你的钢笔吗？

③ 表示请求、命令等。

✏️ e.g.: *Can* I help you?

    我能帮你什么？

    Can you help me?

    你能帮我吗？

（2）could的用法。

could实际上是can的过去式，也可以说是can的委婉说法。

① 用于过去时态中，特别是间接引语中可以表示can的过去式。

e.g.: She said she *could* finish this job in a short time.
　　　她说她一会儿就能把这工作做完。

My sister told me that she *could* eat five apples at one time.
我的姐姐告诉我她能一次吃五个苹果。

② 表示can的委婉说法。

e.g.: *Could* you help me?
　　　你是否能帮我一下？

Could you lend me a pen?
你能借我一支钢笔吗？

（3）be able to的用法：用于表示"能够"。

e.g.: He *is able to* pass CET-6.
　　　他会通过英语六级考试的。

Tips be able to和can的区别在于，前者有更多的时态变化，而后者没有。

e.g.: When he was 6 years old, he was able to swim very well.
　　　他六岁的时候就能游泳游得很好了。

2. may和might的用法

（1）may的用法。

① 用于表示可能。

e.g.: It *may* be cloudy tomorrow.　　　　What he said *may* be true.
　　　明天可能多云。　　　　　　　　　　他说的可能是真的。

② 用于表示允许。

e.g.: You *may* go now.　　　　　　　　　*May* I use your rubber?
　　　你现在可以走了。　　　　　　　　　我可以用你的橡皮吗？

（2）might的用法。

might是may的过去式，也可以说是may的委婉说法。

① 用于表示may的过去式，用于过去将来时。

> e.g.: She said he *might* telephone her at once.
>
> 她说他可以马上给她打电话。
>
> His mother said she *might* go to the school to see the teacher.
>
> 她妈妈说她要去学校见老师。

② 用于疑问句中表示委婉说法。

> e.g.: *Might* I use your rubber?
>
> 我可以用你的橡皮吗？
>
> *Might* she go with us?
>
> 她可以和我们一起吗？

3. must和have to的用法

must 和have to都表示"必须"，前者多表示主观，且动词形式较少；而后者表示客观，动词形式较多。

（1）must 的用法。

① 表示必然性。

> e.g.: He *must* be a worker.
>
> 他肯定是个工人。
>
> We *must* make contributions to our society.
>
> 我们必须为我们的社会做出贡献。

② 表示义务或强制。

> e.g.: You *must* catch the robbers.
>
> 你们必须抓住抢劫犯。
>
> He *must* remember to write home.
>
> 他要记住写信回家。

③ must用于疑问句时，问答如下。

> e.g.: *Must* I go now?
> 我必须走吗？
> Yes, you *must*.
> 是的，你必须走。
> No, you *don't have to*. (No, you *needn't*.)
> 不，你不必要走。

Tips 在这里一定要注意否定形式的回答。

（2）have to 的用法。

① have to 可用于各种时态和语态中，形式较多。

> e.g.: You can not imagine that they will *have to* do so much work.
> 你难以想象他们将不得不做这么多工作。
>
> Due to SARS people here seldom *had to* go out.
> 由于"非典"这儿的人不得不少外出。

② 表示客观需要，而非主观愿望。

> e.g.: It is too late, and we *have to* go home now.
> 太晚了，我们必须要回家了。

4. should 和 ought to 的用法

should 和 ought to 都表示有义务做某事，前者加动词原形，后者加不定式，它们都不及 must 那样具有信心。

> e.g.: We *should* work hard for our country.
> 我们必须为祖国努力工作。
>
> You *ought to* tell the truth to your mother.
> 你要把真相告诉你妈妈。
>
> They *ought to* run so quickly.
> 他们不得不快跑。

5. shall和should的用法

（1）shall的用法：用于第一人称，表示意愿。

✏ e.g.: I *shall* leave Shanghai for Tokyo.
我要从上海到东京。

We *shall* do this job for 5 years.
我们做这项工作要五年时间。

（2）should的用法。

① 用于表示shall的过去式，用于过去将来时。

✏ e.g.: We said we *should* go to Beijing to have a visit.
我们说准备去北京旅游。

② 也可表示"有义务做某事"。（见上一条）

6. will和would的用法

（1）will的用法。

① 用于各种人称，表示意愿或意图。

✏ e.g.: He *will* attend a very important meeting in Hangzhou.
他将要在杭州参加一个很重要的会议。

Xiaoli *will* take photo of you.
小李要给你照相。

② 用于Will you please ...?表示请求。

✏ e. g.: *Will you please* pass me the paper?
请你把纸递给我好吗？

Will you please open the window?
请你打开窗好吗？

（2）would的用法。

① 是will 的过去式，常用于过去将来时。

✏ e.g.: They exclaimed that they *would* give a lesson to U.S.
他们宣称将要教训一下美国。

She often said she *would* go abroad when she studied at college.

上大学时候她经常说她要去国外。

② 用于表示过去常常做某事,见"一般过去时"中的说明部分。

7. dare和need的用法

(1) dare表示"敢",作为情态动词时后面接动词原形,作为实义动词时后面也可接不定式。

e.g.: She *dare* go alone in the evening.

她敢晚上单独行走。

She *dares* to go alone in the evening.

她敢晚上单独行走。

Tips 它们的肯定句无区别,但是其否定句和疑问句则有区别。

否定句
- She *dare not* go alone in the evening.　　　　(dare为情态动词)
- She *doesn't dare* to go alone in the evening.　　(dare为实义动词)

疑问句
- *Dare* she go alone in the evening? Yes, she dare./ No, she dare not.
  (dare为情态动词)
- *Does* she *dare* to go alone in the evening? Yes, she does./ No, she does not.
  (dare为实义动词)

(2) need和dare的用法完全一致,(作为情态动词时)后面接动词原形,(作为实义动词时)后面也可接不定式,只是need表示"需要"。

Tips 因为在任何一个考试中,都很少考这两个单词的肯定句,所以否定句和疑问句只要记住"有to有do,无to无do"的用法就可以了。

8. "情态动词+现在完成体"的用法

在英语中,我们可以用"情态动词+现在完成体"表示对过去情况的推测。这包括以下几种情况：

（1）must have+过去分词，表示对过去情况的肯定推测。

（2）should have+过去分词，表示过去有义务做某事而未做。

（3）ought to have+过去分词，表示过去有义务做某事而未做。

（4）need have+过去分词，表示过去有必要做某事而未做。

（5）may (might) have+过去分词，表示过去有可能做某事而未做。

（6）could have+过去分词，表示过去有能力做某事而未做。

e.g.: He *must have passed* the exam.

他肯定通过了考试。（表示对过去情况的肯定）

She *should have finished* the housework.

她应该做完了家务。（表示她有义务做家务事，而她未做，表示一种委婉的批评）

You *need not have carried* so heavy boxes.

你没必要搬这些重的箱子。（表示本不必要搬这些重的箱子而搬了）

He *might have done* it very well.

他本来可以做得很好的。（表示他本可以做得好，而未做好，表示一种委婉的批评）

The sports meeting *could have been held* yesterday.

运动会可能昨天举行过了。（表示过去有可能举行的运动会）

小 结

本章共学习了三部分内容，其中被动语态部分，需要掌握一个口诀和五种特殊的变化方法；助动词部分需要掌握be，have和do动词的主要用法；情态动词部分需要掌握两点，一是各个情态动词的比较，另一个是情态动词+现在完成体的用法。学习完之后，请大家来回答以下几个问题：

（1）主动语态变被动语态的口诀是什么？

（2）被动语态中五种特殊的变化方法是什么？

（3）助动词中be，have和do分别怎么用？

（4）七组情态动词如何比较？

（5）"情态动词+现在完成体"表示什么？

如果大家对以上问题都可以做到心中有数，那么今天的任务就算完成了。

被动语态练习

1. The young man has _____ fit for this job.
   A. been proved
   B. proved to be
   C. been proved to be
   D. proved being

2. Satellites are made _____ by scientists.
   A. go into space
   B. to go into space
   C. go into the space
   D. to go into the space

3. I was told _____ my study.
   A. to continue
   B. continuing
   C. that continues
   D. go on with

4. The dish _____ delicious.
   A. is tasted
   B. tastes
   C. taste
   D. are tasted

5. The workers _____ their rights.
   A. deprived
   B. deprived of
   C. were deprived
   D. were deprived of

6. This is one of the best books _____ by O. Henry.
   A. that have ever been written
   B. that have written
   C. that had been written
   D. that was written

7. — What about your new house?
   — It is _____ now.
   A. painted
   B. being painted
   C. to be painted
   D. to have painted

8. — Come here. Where is your baby?
   — My baby _____ by his aunt.
   A. is taken care
   B. is being taken care
   C. is taken care of
   D. is being taken care of

9. In my opinion, the Great Wall is worth _____ again.
   A. visiting
   B. to be visited
   C. being visited
   D. to visit

10. I find French hard _____.
    A. learned
    B. learning
    C. to learn
    D. to be learned

11. The polluted water isn't fit _____.
    A. to be drunk   B. to drink   C. drunk   D. drinking
12. The manager entered the office and was happy to learn that four-fifths of the tickets _____.
    A. was booked   B. had been booked
    C. were booked   D. have been booked
13. In that village there are many sick people, so Doctor Green is always _____.
    A. asked for   B. waited for
    C. looked for   D. sent for
14. — Do you have anything more _____, Sir?
    — No, you can have a rest or do something else.
    A. typing   B. to be typed
    C. typed   D. to typing
15. All the books _____ before I got to the bookshop.
    A. had been sold out   B. have been sold out
    C. have sold out   D. had sold out
16. Peter is often seen _____ in the park.
    A. to read Chinese   B. read Chinese
    C. to read China   D. reading China
17. The fish _____ perfect.
    A. is smelled   B. are smelt
    C. smells   D. smell
18. "Titanic" was the largest ship that _____ at that time.
    A. was ever built   B. has ever built
    C. had ever been built   D. has ever been built
19. My radio _____ now.
    A. got repaired   B. is getting repaired
    C. is getting being repaired   D. is repaired
20. Jenny _____ a man who was her classmate.
    A. was married by   B. marries
    C. married   D. got married by

21. None of them _____ for the accident.
    A. should be blamed   B. should blame
    C. can be blamed   D. can blamed
22. The dictionary _____ me.
    A. is belonged to   B. belong
    C. belongs to   D. is belonged
23. "Do you have any clothes _____ today, Sir?" asked the servant politely.
    A. to wash   B being washed
    C. to be washed   D. be washing
24. Lots of _____ experiments _____ in our lab.
    A. interesting; carry out   B. interested; carry out
    C. interesting; are carried out   D. interested; are carried out
25. There will be speech on history _____ next week.
    A. given   B. to giving
    C. to be given   D. being given
26. The teacher _____ to the party last week came from England.
    A. invited   B. being invited
    C. to be invited   D. was invited
27. I have got enough room _____ all of us.
    A. to be seated   B. to seat
    C. seating   D. seated
28. Mr. Smith is the only doctor for you _____.
    A. sent for   B. sending for
    C. to send for   D. to be sent for
29. Hundreds of jobs _____ if the factory closes.
    A. lose   B. will be lost
    C. are lost   D. will lose
30. The United Nations, which _____ in 1945, is playing a more and more important part in international affairs.
    A. was set up   B. set up
    C. had set up   D. had been set up

31. Everything _____ if Albert hadn't called the fire department immediately after the fire broke out.
    A. would destroy   B. would have destroyed
    C. would be destroyed   D. would have been destroyed
32. — I don't know how to get there.
    — I'll show you the right road _____.
    A. to take   B. to be taken
    C. taking   D. taken
33. My daughter _____ a doctor three years ago.
    A. was married   B. married with
    C. married to   D. got married to
34. These dishes _____ easily.
    A. don't clean   B. are not cleaned
    C. have not been   D. are not to be cleaned
35. — My hair is so long.
    — You should _____.
    A. have you hair being cut   B. have your hair cut
    C. have you hair to be cut   D. cut your hairs
36. The homework I got down to do _____ yesterday evening at last.
    A. be finished   B. do was finished
    C. was finished   D. being finished
37. The old man phoned police that he _____ his money.
    A. robbed   B. robbed of
    C. was robbed   D. was robbed of
38. I have just called Peter and he _____ to return soon.
    A. expects   B. expected
    C. is expected   D. will expect
39. — When should I pay money?
    — The money _____ at once.
    A. should pay   B. should be paid
    C. be paying   D. should be paid for

40. — I'd like to go into the lab.
    — I'm sorry, John. Only scientists are _____ into it.
    A. required   B. admitted
    C. supposed   D. intended

助动词和情态动词练习

1. — The phone is ringing.
   — It _____ be David. He told me he would call me tonight.
   A. will   B. may   C. must   D. can

2. It is raining heavily now, so I _____ stay at home.
   A. must   B. have to   C. can   D. should

3. — Must I clean the window?
   — No, you _____.
   A. must not   B. needn't   C. can't   D. may not

4. Laws ought _____ by everyone including president.
   A. to obey   B. obey   C. be obey   D. to be obeyed

5. Look at your eyes. You must have cried, _____?
   A. mustn't   B. have not you
   C. wasn't you   D. didn't you

6. She _____ yesterday's examination, but she didn't.
   A. should have passed   B. would pass
   C. must have passed   D. should pass

7. I _____ go abroad next week.
   A. am to   B. could   C. can   D. may

8. — You hurt him deeply.
   — I _____.
   A. didn't mean   B. didn't mean to
   C. can't mean   D. mustn't mean

9. He was to _____ work next month, but he changed his mind.
   A. start   B. be starting
   C. got started   D. have started

10. Bruce spent as much as he _____ fishing.
    A. could   B. went
    C. could to go   D. could going
11. Although I've never seen your daughter, I guess this little girl_____ be your daughter.
    A. would   B. should   C. can   D. must
12. If you do as I tell you, you _____ be successful.
    A. shall   B. may   C. can   D. will
13. — May I use your pen?
    — No, _____.
    A. you can't   B. you mustn't
    C. you may not   D. you needn't
14. I _____ read books when I was four years old.
    A. can   B. could   C. may   D. might
15. Let's go for a walk, _____?
    A. shall we   B. will you   C. don't you   D. do we
16. Let us go for a walk, _____?
    A. shall we   B. will you   C. don't you   D. do we
17. — Could I borrow your bike?
    — Yes, of course you _____.
    A. will   B. could   C. might   D. can
18. I _____ eat apples than oranges.
    A. would rather   B. had better
    C. like better   D. prefer
19. You must be a football player, _____?
    A. must you   B. are you
    C. aren't you   D. mustn't you
20. — Will you go with David?
    — No, I _____.
    A. wouldn't   B. won't   C. shouldn't   D. shall not
21. I missed the first bus, so I _____ wait for the next bus.
    A. must   B. have to   C. may   D. had to

22. The room is dark; Ricky _____ to bed.
    A. should go   B. must go
    C. should have gone   D. must have gone
23. The football match was wonderful! You _____ it.
    A. must go to see   B. may see
    C. must have gone to see D. should have gone to see
24. You _____ start early.
    A. would better   B. had better
    C. had better to   D. have better
25. _____ a good time in America?
    A. Had you   B. Have you had
    C. Have you   D. Have you got
26. He had me _____ shy.
    A. feel   B. felt   C. to be   D. to feel
27. _____ so stupid as to repeat your mistakes.
    A. Do   B. Don't   C. Don't be   D. Do be
28. To be honest, I _____ like math.
    A. did never   B. don't never
    C. never would   D. do never
29. He likes music, and I _____ as well.
    A. do   B. do it   C. do so   D. do that
30. If you keep going on with your study, you _____ be successful.
    A. would   B. will   C. should   D. may
31. — Would you like to have a cup of tea?
    — Yes, _____.
    A. would like   B. like
    C. must have liked   D. please
32. He _____ to visit Beijing.
    A. used   B. use not   C. is not used   D. was not used
33. — Could you lend me your pen?
    — Yes, _____.
    A. I could   B. you could C. I can   D. you may

34. This question is rather difficult, so you _____ too careful.
    A. can't be   B. must be   C. should   D. can be
35. I can't help _____ that she was my classmate.
    A. remember   B. to remember
    C. but remember   D. remembering
36. John _____ be wrong, but I don't think he is.
    A. can   B. must   C. should   D. would
37. — May I break the rule?
    — No, you _____.
    A. wouldn't   B. may not   C. mustn't   D. needn't
38. _____ to say that you are against him?
    A. Do you dare   B. Need you dare
    C. Did you dare   D. Had you dared
39. I don't think you _____ about your son.
    A. need to worry   B. need to worrying
    C. need to being worried D. need worried
40. I _____ late, but the traffic was heavy.
    A. shouldn't have been   B. wouldn't have been
    C. should not be   D. would not be
41. It is five o'clock. We _____ so early.
    A. need not get up   B. need not have got up
    C. need not to get up   D. need not getting up

第八天

突破英语的非谓语动词

今天进入英语中最难的语法现象的学习,再难的语法点都是有办法掌握的。先来解释一下非谓语动词,实际上,如果把谓语的形式放在一边来说,单纯一个动词从语法功能上来说一定是谓语,但是当动词的形式发生变化,不再做谓语时,也就是非谓语动词了。

在英语中,动词是用于做谓语的,而谓语一般也是由动词来做的。但是却有一类动词形式,它们不做句中的谓语,而做句子的其他成分,我们把这种动词形式称为非谓语动词。非谓语动词包括:不定式、动名词和分词(过去分词和现在分词)。

Tips 有些语法书中把动名词和现在分词放在一起讲解,但在本书还是把它们分开讲解。

8.1 不 定 式

不定式是由"to(有时省略)+动词原形"所构成的(切记to be也是不定式),它虽然仍具有动词形式,但是已经失去了动词的功能。它在句中可做主语、表语、宾语、宾语补足语、定语和状语等。

> e.g.: *To see* is *to believe*.
> 眼见为实。(不定式做主语、表语)
> She likes *to go* to the park.
> 她想要去公园。(不定式做宾语)
> I want you *to have* a dinner with me.
> 我想和你一起吃饭。(不定式做宾语补足语)

There is something *to drink* in the fridge.

冰箱里有些喝的东西。（不定式做定语）

He got up so early *to catch* the first train.

他起得这么早是为了赶上头班火车。（不定式做状语）

Tips 在这里抛弃传统的语法学习方法，因为在讲非谓语动词时一般都是列举它们做句子成分的用法，而本章则是总结出在不定式的学习中需要注意的几个问题。

1. 及物动词后加不定式

（1）有些及物动词后必须加不定式做宾语。它们是：agree（同意），begin（开始），care（关心），choose（选择），continue（继续），decide（决定），desire（羡慕），expect（期望），fail（失败），hate（讨厌），hope（希望），intend（打算），learn（学习），like（喜欢），manage（设法），offer（提供），plan（计划），pretend（假装），promise（承诺），refuse（拒绝），start（开始），want（想要），wish（祝愿）等。

- e.g.: The policeman managed *to let* the thieves speak out the truth.

  警察设法让小偷们说出真相。

  They planned *to have* a picnic near the lake.

  他们计划在湖边搞一个聚餐。

（2）有些及物动词后必须加不定式做宾语补足语。它们是：advise（劝告），allow（允许），ask（问），cause（引起），encourage（鼓励），expect（期望），force（迫使），get（使），hate（讨厌），help（帮助），invite（邀请），leave（使），like（喜欢），mean（打算），order（命令），permit（允许），persuade（说服），prefer（宁愿），remind（提醒），request（要求），tell（告诉），want（想要），warn（警告），wish（祝愿）等。

- e.g.: He always encourages us *to try* best to do our jobs.

  他总是鼓励我们做好工作。

  The woman warned her son not *to drive* home after drinking.

  那女人告诫她儿子不要酒后驾车回家。

2. 用it代替不定式做形式主语，不定式做真正主语的情况

结构：It + be + adj. + 不定式

e.g.: It is impossible *to go* abroad.
　　　出国是不可能的。

Tips 不定式在句子中是真正的主语，它位于句末，而it为形式主语，位于句首，这样的替代关系是为了平衡句子。

It is necessary *to learn* English well.
学好英语是有必要的。

3. 使役动词和感官动词之后宾语补足语的情况

（1）使役动词是表示"使……"的一类动词，主要包括：get, have, let, make等。当不定式做它们的宾语补足语时，要将to省略（除了get）。

e.g.: I made the door (*to*) *open*.
　　　我把门打开了。

Tips 原句为"I made the door *to open*."因为make是使役动词，所以将to省略。

（2）感官动词是表示人体器官所能感知到的一类动词，主要包括：hear, see, smell, taste等。当不定式做它们的宾语补足语时，要将to省略。

e.g.: I saw an old man (*to*) *walk* past the road.
　　　我看见一个老头过马路。

Tips 原句为"I saw an old man *to walk* past the road."因为see是感官动词，所以将to省略。

4. 不定式做定语时的不同情况

e.g.: ① The last question *to be discussed* is very easy.
　　　　最后一个讨论的问题很简单。
　　　② The last question is very easy *to discuss*.
　　　　最后一个问题很容易讨论。

Tips　①句表示"被讨论的问题很简单",所以用被动的不定式;而在②句中,问题仍然是被讨论,但我们却用主动语态,原因在于②句中的不定式在句中修饰表语且句子结构为系表结构,所以不定式用主动语态代替被动语态。

e.g.: There is something *to eat* on the desk.
　　　桌子上有些吃的东西。
　　　The problem is hard *to solve*.
　　　这个问题很难以解决。

5. 不定式的否定式、被动式、完成体和复合结构

(1) 不定式的否定式为not to+动词原形。

e.g.: I asked him *not to touch* that wall.
　　　我让他不要碰那面墙。

Tips　非谓语动词的否定形式是一定要在完整结构前进行否定,不可以把to do拆开再去否定。

(2) 不定式的被动式为to be+过去分词。

e.g.: This job is *to be done* next week.
　　　这项工作下周做完。

(3) 不定式的完成体为to have+过去分词。

e.g.: He is very sorry *to have missed* the meeting last week.
　　　他对于上周没有参会表示非常抱歉。

（4）不定式的复合结构为for somebody to do something。

e.g.: It is impossible *for her to go abroad*.
　　　她出国是没有可能的。
　　　It is very kind *of you to do* it.
　　　你这样做太好了。

Tips 这里用的是"of somebody to do something"，当形容词是用来表示某人的品质、性格时，用此结构。

e.g.: It is rather foolish *of her to want* to go to university.
　　　她想去上大学实在是太傻了。

8.2 动 名 词

动名词是由动词原形在词尾加-ing构成的。它的作用相当于名词，在句中可做主语、宾语、表语、宾语补足语和定语等。

e.g.: *Seeing* is *believing*.
　　　眼见为实。（动名词做主语、表语）
　　　He likes *playing* basketball.
　　　他喜欢打篮球。（动名词做宾语）
　　　I saw a cat *coming* across the road.
　　　我看见一只猫正在过马路。（动名词做宾语补足语）
　　　His *walking* stick is long.
　　　他的手杖很长。（动名词做定语）

在动名词的学习中需要明白以下几个问题。

1. 有些及物动词后必须加动名词做宾语

这样的及物动词包括：avoid（避免），can't help（忍不住），consider（考虑），delay

（延迟），enjoy（喜欢），finish（完成），give up（放弃），imagine（想象），mind（介意），miss（想念），require（要求），practice（练习），suggest（建议）等。

- e.g.: Everyone can't avoid *making* mistakes in our society.
  社会中的每个人不能避免犯错误。
  She couldn't *help laughing* when she heard the news.
  当她听见这个消息时，她忍不住笑了。

2. 用it代替动名词做形式主语，动名词做真正主语时的情况

- e.g.: It's no use *doing* like this.
  这样做没有用处。
  It's no good *helping* them cope with this affair.
  帮助他们处理这件事没有好处。

Tips 只有在use和good后用it代替动名词做形式主语。

3. 动名词做宾语补足语和不定式做宾语补足语的区别

- e.g.: ① I saw him *going* upstairs.
  我看见他正在上楼。
  ② I saw him *go* upstairs.
  我看见他上楼了。

Tips 在①句中，动名词做宾语补足语表示"正在发生的动作或看见动作发生的全过程"，而在②句中，不定式做宾语补足语则表示"已经发生的动作或只注意动作的结果"。

I heard her *sing*.　　我听见她唱歌了。
I heard her *singing*.　　我听见她正在唱歌。

4. 有些及物动词后既可接不定式做宾语又可接动名词做宾语，注意它们的区别

stop	to do	停下来去做另一件事	mean	to do	打算做某事
	doing	停下正在做的事		doing	意味着
like	to do	想要做某事	try	to do	努力做某事
	doing	喜欢做某事		doing	试图做某事
need	to do	需要做某事	go on	to do	继续做另一件事
	doing	需要某事被做		doing	继续做同一件事
want	to do	想要做某事	forget	to do	忘记做某事
	doing	想要某事被做		doing	忘记做过某事
remember	to do	记住做某事			
	doing	记住做过某事			

5. 动名词的否定式、被动式和完成体

（1）动名词的否定式为not+动名词。

🔖 e.g.: *Not going* to the park is very reasonable.
不去公园是十分有道理的。

（2）动名词的被动式为being+过去分词。

🔖 e.g.: She prided herself *on being* called "beauty".
她因为被叫作"美人"而感到自豪。

（3）动名词的完成体为having+过去分词。

🔖 e.g.: He denied *having seen* this film.
他否认看过这部电影。

8.3 分　　词

分词包括现在分词（由动词原形在词尾加-ing构成）和过去分词（由动词原形在词尾加-ed构成）两种。分词具有形容词和副词的一些性质，它们在句中可做定语、表语、宾语补足语和补语等。

e.g.: *Boiling* water is hot.

　　　开水很烫。（现在分词做定语）

　　　The door is *broken*.

　　　门坏了。（过去分词做表语）

　　　I saw an old lady *climbing* the hill.

　　　我看见一个老太太正在爬山。（现在分词做宾语补足语）

　　　Arriving at the railway station, we missed the train.

　　　当我们到达火车站时，我们错过了火车。（现在分词做状语）

在分词的学习中我们需要明白以下几个问题。

1. 现在分词和过去分词做定语的区别

　　　developing countries　　发展中国家　　　　*boiling* water　　开水
　　　developed countries　　发达国家　　　　　*boiled* water　　开过的水

现在分词做定语时表示"正在、主动"的意义，而过去分词做定语时则表示"被动、完成"的意义。这两种不是都要同时出现的，也就是说，现在分词既可以表示"正在"，又可以表示"主动"，不一定要在一个分词中把两个含义都表达出来。

2. 分词做定语修饰中心词时，它们位置的情况

e.g.: the *missing* boy

　　　丢失的孩子（分词是一个词时，放在被修饰词的前面）

　　　the boy *standing* by the table

　　　站在桌边的男孩（分词是一个词组时，放在被修饰词的后面）

3. 分词短语做状语时的情况

这一点是英语中最难的语法现象，英语中的三大难点：分词、虚拟语气和定语从句。实际上分词做状语的现象是最难学的。在这里需要注意以下三个问题。

（1）分词短语做状语，其逻辑主语的情况。

e.g.: *Arriving* at the railway station, they missed the train.

　　　当他们到达火车站时，他们错过了火车。

Tips   arriving at the railway station是现在分词做时间状语，它必然会有动作的发出者。有人说这不是非谓语动词吗，怎么会有主语呢？实际上，难点就在这里，因为在非谓语动词中，不定式和动名词已经基本失去了动词的性质，被称为"完全非谓语动词"，但是分词没有完全失去动词的性质，它有一半副词的含义，一半动词的含义，被称为"非完全非谓语动词"。所以，在分词做状语的时候，当然要寻找所谓的"主语"，也即"逻辑主语"。分词做状语时，逻辑主语要和主句的主语保持一致，所以arriving at the railway station的逻辑主语就是they，而不能按照中文中的翻译方式："Arriving at the railway station, the train left. 到了火车站，火车走了。"

e.g.: *Seeing* from the top of the hill, I saw the beautiful view.
从山顶上我看到美丽的风景。（seeing的逻辑主语是I，所以用现在分词）
Seen from the top of the hill, the city is beautiful.
从山顶看，城市很美丽。（seen的逻辑主语句the city，所以用过去分词）

（2）分词的一般体和完成体做状语时的区别。

e.g.: *Having had* breakfast, we started to have a meeting.
吃完饭后我们开始开会。

Tips   having had breakfast发生在we started to have a meeting之前，而不是同时进行。前面的分词短语相当于时间状语从句after we had breakfast。

e.g.: *Having seen* the film, Tom and I needed to have a shower.
在看完电影后，汤姆和我需要洗澡。（having seen the film发生在needed to have a shower之前）

e.g.: ① *Washing* my hands, I had lunch.
我边洗手边吃午饭。
② *Having washed* my hands, I had lunch.
我先洗手后吃午饭。

Tips ①句是分词的一般式，它所表示的动作和主句表示的动作是一起发生的，但是②句用的则是分词的完成体，它所表示的动作和主句表示的动作是先后发生的。

（3）分词的独立主格结构。

在具体的句子中也会遇到这样的句型：

Arriving at the railway station, the train has been away for several minutes.

实际上这句话是错误的，需要把它改正过来，主要的方法是在状语的前面加上一个逻辑主语，这样就变成了：

We *arriving* at the railway station, the train has been away for several minutes.

奇怪的结构出现了："名词/代词+分词"的结构。这样的结构被称为"分词的独立主格结构"。

e.g.: This *done*, he left the room.

这事做完后，他离开了房间。

Tips 前后主语不一致，但是正确。前面一个是词组，而不是句子，是分词的独立主格结构。

e.g.: That *being* the case, we had better make another plan.

因为事情总是这样，我们最好还是有另外一个计划。

Tips 前后主语不一致，但是正确。前面一个是词组，而不是句子，是分词的独立主格结构。

小 结

在这章中主要讲解非谓语动词的知识，而且也没有用传统的教学法来给大家讲述，希望大家能记住讲述的几个问题，这些知识点需要记忆。请大家回答以下问题：

（1）非谓语动词分为几类？分别是什么？
（2）学习不定式时应注意的几个问题是什么？分别怎么学习？
（3）学习动名词时应注意的几个问题是什么？分别怎么学习？
（4）学习分词时应注意的几个问题是什么？分别怎么学习？
（5）分词做状语时要注意几个问题？
（6）分词的独立主格是什么含义？怎么使用？

希望大家能够认真地回答以上问题，牢牢地记住以上问题的答案是今天学习最大的收获，也是突破非谓语动词的法宝。

练 习

1. Don't you remember _____?
   A. seeing the man before   B. to see the man before
   C. saw the man before   D. to have seen the man before

2. Paul from normal university practiced _____ in the middle school.
   A. to teach   B. to be teaching
   C. teaching   D. having taught

3. I decided _____ a teacher.
   A. not to become   B. not to have become
   C. to have become   D. to have not become

4. I'm glad to _____ an opportunity to interview you.
   A. give   B. be giving
   C. be given   D. have not been given

5. _____ a windy day, we gave up our plan to sail.
   A. With it   B. It being
   C. Being   D. Because it being

6. I'm going to have my radio _____.
   A. fixed   B. to fix   C. fix   D. fixing

7. I preferred to _____ at home rather than _____.
   A. stay; camp   B. staying; camping
   C. stay; to camp   D. staying; to camping

8. I preferred _____ at home to _____ such a party.
   A. stay; join
   B. staying; joining
   C. to stay; joining
   D. staying; join
9. _____ in front of it, this old house needs _____.
   A. To see; repairing
   B. Seen; repairing
   C. Having seen; making repairs
   D. Seeing; to be repaired
10. The moon was shining brightly _____ everything there _____ more romantic.
    A. having; look
    B. to have; looked
    C. and had; looks
    D. having; be looked
11. The girl kept on _____ when her mother came in.
    A. to write
    B. lying in bed
    C. dancing to the music
    D. to dance to the music
12. He ran away quickly, _____ his friend _____ in the middle of the playground.
    A. to leave; standing
    B. to leave; to stand
    C. leaving; to stand
    D. leaving; standing
13. The boy wanted to ride his bicycle in the street, but his mother told him _____.
    A. not to
    B. not to do
    C. not do it
    D. do not to
14. I'm enjoying _____ the vacation in Qingdao with my parents last year.
    A. being spent
    B. to have spent
    C. having spent
    D. having been spent
15. Having a walk along the seaside, I felt like _____ in the sea.
    A. to go swimming
    B. go swimming
    C. going swimming
    D. to go to swim
16. He did nothing but _____.
    A. to read
    B. reading
    C. read
    D. to have read

17. I was heard _____ that I fell in love with her.
    A. say   B. to saying   C. to say   D. said
18. _____ what you say, he is an honest man.
    A. Judging from   B. Judged from
    C. Having judged   D. To judge
19. _____, the U.S. is stronger than Iraq.
    A. To speaking   B. Generally speaking
    C. Generally to have spoken D. Generally speak
20. With night _____, they come back home.
    A. be fell   B. fell   C. falling   D. falls
21. It is no use _____ him not to cheat in the exams.
    A. for you to have told   B. you tell
    C. your telling   D. having told
22. — It can't work.
    — Why not _____ it in another way?
    A. try to solve   B. try solving
    C. tries solving   D. try solve
23. The thief was caught with two hands _____.
    A. tied   B. to be tied
    C. being tied   D. having been tied
24. John was made _____ the truck for a week as a punishment.
    A. to wash   B. washing
    C. wash   D. to be washing
25. — The light in the room is still on.
    — I'm sorry, I forgot _____.
    A. turning it off   B. turn it off
    C. to turn it off   D. having turned it off
26. Do you know whose dog is_____ under the table?
    A. lay   B. lain   C. laying   D. lying
27. I don't allow _____ in my office.
    A. smoking   B. to smoke
    C. people to smoking   D. people smoking

28. I don't allow _____ TV.
    A. my son to watch   B. my son watching
    C. to watch   D. my son to have watched
29. It is dark. You'd better _____.
    A. to stay at home   B. staying at home
    C. stay at home   D. to have stayed at home
30. You'd better _____ your son _____.
    A. to have; to work hard   B. have; work hard
    C. have; to work hard   D. have; worked hard
31. Your hair is so long. You'd better have _____.
    A. it cut   B. it cutted   C. it cutting   D. it to cut
32. He suggested _____ with him.
    A. going shopping   B. to going shopping
    C. go shopping   D. going shop
33. When I heard from him, I couldn't help _____.
    A. jump with joy   B. jumping with joy
    C. jumping in joy   D. to jumping in joy
34. The officers narrowly escaped _____ in the hot battle.
    A. have killed   B. to kill
    C. to be killed   D. being killed
35. Peter went on _____ his homework after having a rest.
    A. with   B. to do
    C. doing   D. to have done
36. This novel is worth _____.
    A. to read   B. of reading
    C. reading   D. of to be read
37. His suggestion is worthy _____.
    A. of being considered   B. to consider
    C. considering   D. of considering
38. Their house was destroyed in the earthquake, so they have no room _____.
    A. to live   B. to live in   C. living   D. living in

39. I found the question difficult _____.
    A. to answer   B. to be answered
    C. to answer it   D. answering

40. The question is difficult _____.
    A. to answer   B. to be answered
    C. to answer it   D. answering

41. People were used to _____ clothes of cotton and wool, but now more and more other materials are used to _____ clothes as well.
    A. making; making   B. making; make
    C. making; made   D. make; make

42. I don't attend the meeting _____ in the office at present, but I'll attend the meeting _____ in the office tomorrow.
    A. held; being held   B. to be held; to be held
    C. to be held; held   D. being held; to be held

43. One learns a language by making mistakes and _____ them.
    A. correct   B. correcting
    C. corrects   D. to correct

44. When I came in, I found a cat _____ in sofa.
    A. lie   B. lying   C. to be lying   D. laying

45. Why do you have the water _____ all the time?
    A. ran   B. to be running
    C. running   D. being running

46. I'm very glad to see the question _____.
    A. answer   B. answered
    C. being answered   D. answering

47. I studied philosophy in a university _____ by many trees.
    A. surrounding   B. to surround
    C. surrounded   D. to be surrounded

48. The classroom was so noisy that the teacher couldn't make herself _____.
    A. hear   B. heard   C. hearing   D. to hear

49. I often hear both teachers and students _____ highly of him.
   A. to speak   B. spoken
   C. speak   D. to be spoken
50. The city is said _____ in a terrible earthquake a month ago.
   A. to be destroyed   B. to have been destroyed
   C. having been destroyed D. to destroy
51. The temple was found _____ empty.
   A. being   B. to be   C. is   D. was
52. I seem _____ her somewhere before.
   A. to see   B. to have seen
   C. to be seeing   D. seeing
53. They seem _____ along quite well now.
   A. to be getting   B. getting
   C. to get   D. getting
54. No one can avoid _____ by advertisements.
   A. to be influenced B. having influenced
   C. influenced   D. being influenced
55. We are looking forward to _____ fashion show next month.
   A. watch   B. watching
   C. be watching   D. have watched
56. My bike is so old that it needs _____.
   A. repair   B. repaired   C. repairing   D. to repair
57. I found the door _____ and no one was in the office.
   A. to lock   B. to be locked
   C. locking   D. locked
58. I'm sorry for keeping you _____ for two hours.
   A. waiting   B. wait   C. to wait   D. waited
59. I'm busy _____ the examination.
   A. preparing for   B. with preparing
   C. preparing with   D. to prepare
60. I regret _____ that your mother fell ill the day before yesterday.
   A. saying   B. to say   C. telling   D. to tell

61. — Your son has not attended classes for four days.
    — What? It's not likely for him _____ so many classes.
    A. missing   B. to miss
    C. having missed   D. to have missed

62. Charles Babbage is generally considered _____ the first computer.
    A. to invent   B. inventing
    C. to have invented   D. having invented

63. _____ more attention, the trees could have grown better.
    A. Given   B. To give
    C. Giving   D. Having given

64. It's no use _____ over spilt milk.
    A. cry   B. to cry   C. crying   D. be crying

65. I don't mind _____ by him.
    A. interrupted   B. to be interrupted
    C. being interrupted   D. interrupted

66. Mary was seen _____ the office.
    A. enter   B. to enter
    C. be entering   D. to entering

67. Your work requires _____ carefully.
    A. doing   B. to do   C. being done   D. done

68. The whole house requires _____.
    A. to be painted   B. to be painting
    C. being painted   D. to paint

69. I wish you'll succeed _____ him with his task.
    A. help   B. helping   C. to help   D. in helping

70. Everyone is afraid of _____.
    A. laughing   B. laughing at
    C. being laughed   D. being laughed at

71. I have difficulty _____ the walkman.
    A. repair   B. in repairing
    C. repaired   D. to repair

72. _____ from the window, I found the city was so bright.
    A. See   B. Seeing   C. Seen   D. To see
73. _____ from the window, the city was so bright.
    A. See   B. Seeing   C. Seen   D. To see
74. Reading is _____, and I'm _____ in reading.
    A. interesting; interested   B. interesting; interesting
    C. interest; interesting   D. interested; interesting
75. _____ to the wedding, Mr. Brown didn't mind it.
    A. Having not been invited   B. Not having been invited
    C. Having not invited   D. Not having invited
76. He devoted his life to _____ AIDS.
    A. study   B. studying   C. learn   D. learning
77. When the teacher came into classroom, these students stopped _____.
    A. talk   B. talking
    C. to talking   D. having talking
78. I spent three years _____ a novel.
    A. write   B. writing
    C. to write   D. writed
79. Please remember _____ these books after reading them.
    A. put away   B. to put away
    C. putting away   D. to be put away
80. My mother promised _____ me new clothes.
    A. buy   B. buying   C. to buy for   D. to buy
81. It is no good _____ other's weakness.
    A. to laugh at   B. laughing at
    C. to laugh   D. laughing
82. Could you image _____ as a doctor?
    A. yourself work   B. you to work
    C. yourself working   D. you to be working
83. I went to Canada _____ English.
    A. for learning   B. to learn
    C. learning   D. and learn

84. The chief denied _____ 1000 dollars before.
    A. to steal   B. stealing
    C. stole   D. having stolen

85. The teachers don't permit _____ in examinations.
    A. cheated   B. to cheat
    C. cheating   D. to cheating

86. I know the man _____ by John.
    A. described   B. describing
    C. describe   D. to describe

87. I often think of the _____ scene.
    A. excited   B. excite
    C. to excite   D. exciting

88. With the new year _____, the little town looks blooming.
    A. come   B. to coming   C. will come   D. coming

89. _____ there will be of great help to them.
    A. You go   B. You going
    C. Your going   D. Yours going

90. When _____, ice changes into water.
    A. heating   B. heated
    C. to heat   D. having heated

91. I object to _____.
    A. him wasting of time   B. his wasting of time
    C. him to waste of time   D. his to waste of time

92. I appreciate _____ me with so much money.
    A. you supply   B. your to supply
    C. you supplying   D. your supplying

93. I happened to _____ his address before.
    A. having known   B. have known
    C. knowing   D. known

94. It's dark now. I hoped _____ the work earlier.
    A. to finish   B. finish
    C. having finished   D. to have finished

95. My teacher took the trouble to _____ me how to learn English.

    A. telling B. tell

    C. have told D. tells

96. The woman would rather _____ than go by ship.

    A. traveled by train B. traveling

    C. to travel in train D. travel by train

97. Alex insisted _____ money.

    A. asking for B. on asking for

    C. to ask for D. on asking

98. The old lady used to _____ at the bank of the river.

    A. have a walk B. having a walk

    C. take walk D. taking walk

99. She pretended _____ me when I passed by.

    A. not to see B. not seeing

    C. to not see D. having not seen

100. He is going to start now _____ miss the film.

    A. as to B. not so as to

    C. so as not to D. not to

101. — Would you like to join my birthday party?

    — I'd _____.

    A. love B. like

    C. like to it D. love to

第九天

突破英语的虚拟语气

在英语动词的学习中,最为重要的是动词的时态、语态和语气,其中又以语气最为重要。今天就要学习英语中最难的语法现象之一——虚拟语气。实际上,大家只要按照本书中的结构学习法,相信学习虚拟语气也是很简单的。中文当中也存在很多的虚拟语气,我们一般是用"如果"或"要是"等词来表示,这一点和英语很相似,但是英语中还有很多其他的用法,让我们来看看吧!

9.1 虚拟语气

1. 语气的定义

语气是用动词的不同形式来表达说话人不同态度的一种语法现象。

2. 语气的种类

一般来说,语气可以分为以下四种。

(1) 陈述语气:表示说话的人直接陈述某种事实的语气。

- e.g.: I am a nurse.
  我是个护士。
  I have already finished this job.
  我已经完成工作了。

(2) 疑问语气:表示说话的人提出问题或对某事实产生疑问的语气。

- e.g.: What is your name?
  你叫什么名字?
  Does he like swimming?
  他喜欢游泳吗?

（3）祈使语气：表示说话的人要求、命令、请求等的语气。

✎ e.g.: Be careful!　　　　　　　Keep away from the fence!
　　　 小心!　　　　　　　　　　远离栅栏!

（4）虚拟语气：表示说话的人主观的愿望、假设和猜想等的语气，一般和事实不相符合。

✎ e.g.: If I were you, I would not marry her.
　　　 如果我是你，我不会和她结婚的。
　　　 They suggested that they (should) have more money.
　　　 他们建议应有更多的钱。

9.2　虚拟语气和条件句

条件句实际上是状语从句的一种，其功能可以说是说话人猜想、假设的一种条件。按其真实程度来分，可以分为真实条件句和非真实条件句两种。

✎ e.g.: <u>If it rains tomorrow</u>, we will put off the sports meeting.
　　　 如果明天下雨，我们就推迟运动会。（表示可能实现，真实条件句）
　　　 <u>If I were Tom</u>, I would not refuse the money.
　　　 如果我是汤姆，我就不会拒绝这些钱。（表示不可能实现，非真实条件句）

按照时间划分，虚拟条件句（非真实条件句）又可以分为现在、过去、将来三种情况（如表9-1所示）。

✎ e.g.: If I were you, I would not marry her.
　　　 如果我是你，我就不会和她结婚。（和现在情况相反）
　　　 If I had been you, I would not have married her.
　　　 如果我是你，我就不会和她结婚。（和过去情况相反）
　　　 If the fridge were broken, please call us to repair it.
　　　 如果冰箱坏了，请通知我们来修。（和将来情况相反）

表9-1 条件句

三种情况	if 条件句	结果主句
和现在情况相反	If I（其他人称）+动词的过去式（be动词用were）	I（其他人称）should/would+动词原形
和过去情况相反	If I（其他人称）+had+动词过去分词	I（其他人称）should/would+have+动词过去分词
和将来情况相反	If I（其他人称）+动词的过去式（be动词用were）	I（其他人称）should/would+动词原形

学习过程中要注意以下三点。

（1）单独条件句的使用可以表示某种感情色彩。

> e.g.: If your father had not been dead.
> 要是你爸爸没死该有多好啊！（表示某种遗憾和怜悯）

（2）凡是be动词用于一般过去时都应该使用were，而不是was。

> e.g.: If I were you, I would not promise a lot to her.
> 如果我是你的话，我不会对她承诺那么多的。

Tips 实际上根据一般的语法知识，我们认为应该使用I was而不是I were，但是在虚拟语气中就必须用I were。

（3）从句中出现had，should和were的时候，可以引起倒装。

> e.g.: If I had been you, I would not have married her.

这句话可以倒装成为：Had I been you, I would not have married her.

Tips 注意省略if，并且把助动词都放在句首。

9.3 虚拟语气和从句

1. 虚拟语气在主语从句中的使用

当主句中出现appropriate, essential, important, natural, strange, unfair, vital等时，主语从句

的动词形式要用should+动词原形，should一般省略。

> e.g.: It is unfair that they (should) get many more jobs.
> 他们得到更多的工作是不公平的。
> It is vital that we (should) finish the task.
> 我们完成任务很重要。

2. 虚拟语气在表语从句中的使用

当主句中出现decision, idea, requirement, suggestion等时，表语从句的动词形式要用should+动词原形，should一般省略。

> e.g.: Our decision is that you (should) go to hospital.
> 我们的决定是你要去医院看病。
> His suggestion is that you and I (should) kill these people.
> 他的建议是你和我要杀了这些人。

3. 虚拟语气在同位语从句中的使用

当主句中出现decision，demand，idea，requirement，resolution, suggestion等时，同位语从句的动词形式要用should+动词原形，should一般省略。

> e.g.: They had demands that president (should) resign.
> 他们要求总统辞职。
> He gave me a resolution that men (should) be punished.
> 他给我的解决方案是男人应该受到惩罚。

4. 虚拟语气在宾语从句中的使用

当主句动词出现advise，demand，propose，suggest，urge等时，宾语从句的动词形式要用should+动词原形，should一般省略。

> e.g.: She advised that our oral English (should) be improved.
> 她建议我们的口语应该提高。
> They suggested that women (should) be paid more money.
> 他们建议说女人应得到更多的报酬。

> **Tips** 在从句中使用虚拟语气，一个单词的词根引起了虚拟语气，那么它的所有衍生词和其他形式都可以引起这种虚拟语气，和它引起什么样的虚拟语气没有任何关系。

9.4 虚拟语气的特殊用法

1. 表示某种祝愿

🖋 e.g.: God bless you!
上帝保佑你！
Long live Chairman Mao!
毛主席万岁！

2. It is (about/high) time ... 后接句子应用一般过去时

🖋 e.g.: It is (high) time we went home.
我们该回家了。
It is (high) time we caught the robbers.
是该我们抓强盗了。

3. 由 to think 引导的句子，表示"没想到"

🖋 e.g.: To think that he was a girl.
真没想到他是个女孩。
To think that she was such a woman.
真没想到她是这样一个女人。

4. as it were 做插入语，表示"姑且这么说"

🖋 e.g.: I, as it were, eat like a horse.
我吃起来简直像匹马啊！
He looks like a lion as it were.
他看上去简直就像是头狮子。

5. if need be 做插入语，表示"如果有必要的话"

✏️ e.g.: I can go anywhere if need be.
如果有必要的话，我可以去任何地方。

If need be, you will have five meals a day.
如果有必要的话，你一天要吃五顿饭。

6. would have thought 表示"会想到，会以为"

✏️ e.g.: Who would have thought to meet a white elephant.
谁会想到会遇到一头白象啊！

They would have thought they might get more money.
他们会以为能拿到更多的钱。

7. 虚拟条件句的某些倒装

在某些虚拟条件句中，有时候if可以省略，这时句子要发生部分倒装。

✏️ e.g.: Were I you, I would not marry her.
如果我是你，我就不会和她结婚。

Should he be interested in learning English, he would keep in touch with me.
如果他对学习英语感兴趣，他会和我保持联系的。

8. "情态动词+have+动词过去分词"的用法

详见于情态动词一节（P124）。

9. wish后宾语从句的情况

（1）与现在和将来情况相反，宾语从句的动词形式用一般过去时。

✏️ e.g.: I wish she had a baby.
我希望她能有个孩子。

I wish they went home.
我希望他们能到家。

（2）与过去情况相反，宾语从句的动词形式用过去完成时。

✏️ e.g.: I wished that she had not been dead.
我真希望她没死啊！

He wished that he had not come.
他真希望他没来过啊!

小 结

今天学习了虚拟语气,可以看出主要有三个部分:虚拟条件句、虚拟语气在从句中的使用和虚拟语气一些特殊用法的识别。到这里,动词的学习也就结束了。本书花了很大的篇幅来介绍动词,它是英语中最重要的一部分。在学习动词时,要始终贯穿这样一条主线:定义—分类—基本形式—时态—语态—助动词和情态动词—非谓语动词—虚拟语气,动词的词尾屈折变化更加重要。学好动词可以为学好英语打下坚实的基础。还是请大家来看一看几个关于虚拟语气的问题吧!

(1) 虚拟条件句可以分为几种?时态分别是什么?
(2) 从句当中是如何使用虚拟语气的?
(3) 虚拟语气的特殊用法有哪些?

如果这几天学习的关于动词的所有问题都能回答的话,那么我们英语语法的学习就能够迈上一个新的台阶。

练 习

1. If I _____ you, I wouldn't marry her.
   A. were   B. was   C. be   D. is
2. He suggested that we _____ to the park.
   A. go   B. went   C. will go   D. gone
3. If only I _____ a very beautiful lady.
   A. have   B. has   C. were   D. have been
4. A lot of people wish that there _____ no war in the world.
   A is   B. were   C. have been   D. am
5. It is high time they _____ a delicious supper.
   A. have   B. had
   C. have been   D. has been
6. Were the trousers cheaper, she _____ it.
   A. buy   B. would buy
   C. bought   D. will buy

7. Long _____ Chairman Mao!
   A. live   B. lived
   C. will live   D. have lived
8. Without electricity, edifices _____ suitable for people to live in.
   A. wouldn't have been B. wouldn't be
   C. haven't been   D. shouldn't be
9. _____ the man been sent to hospital, his life would have been saved.
   A. Has   B. Will have   C. Had   D. Have
10. She looks as if she _____ for several months.
    A. hasn't eaten   B. haven't eaten
    C. hadn't eaten   D. didn't eat

第十天

突破英语的介词、连词和基本句型

今天我们将学习英语词法的最后两部分——介词和连词。介词是关系到名词和代词的一类词，传统的语法书是用列举的方法来说明介词，但是在这里我们用比较的方法来学习常用的介词，而连词在后面并列句的学习中还会讲解一些用法。在这之后，我们就会进入句法的学习，本章主要讲解简单句和并列句的用法。

10.1 介 词

1. 定义

介词是用于名词或代词（或相当于名词词组或从句）前，用于表示两者之间关系的一类词。

2. 分类

按照构成，介词可分为三类。

（1）简单介词。如：at，in，on，with等。
（2）合成介词。如：into，onto，within，without等。
（3）短语介词。如：as a result of，due to，in case of，in the front of等。

> **Tips** 注意短语介词和介词短语的区别。
> in front of 在……前面（短语介词只是介词）
> in front of the door 在门前（介词短语是一个短语，是一个介词和名词构成的短语）

3. 常见介词的介绍（在本章中引进比较的方法进行学习）

（1）on和about。

e.g.: He wrote a book *on* math.

他写了一本关于数学方面的书。

She often talks *about* you.

她经常谈论你。

Tips 两者都用于表示"关于"，但是前者表示具体的"关于"，特别是表示某个学科，而后者用法广泛。

（2）above, on 和 over。

e.g.: There is a fan *above* the ceiling.

房顶上有个电扇。

There is an apple *on* the desk.

桌子上有个苹果。

The plane is flying *over* the bridge.

飞机正从桥上飞过。

Tips 三者都用于表示"在……上"，但是 above 表示"在……正上方"，还可以表示"在……（温度）的上面"；on 表示"在……上面"（与面接触）；而 over 表示"在……上方"（不与任何物体接触）。

e.g.: It will be *above* 0°C tomorrow.

明天零度以上。

（3）under 和 below。

e.g.: There is a chair *under* the desk.

桌子底下有把椅子。

There are a lot of mines *below* the surface.

地表下有许多矿产。

> **Tips** 两者都用于表示"在……下面",但是前者表示"在某物下面"(不与任何物体接触),而后者表示"在……下方"(与物体接触),而且below可以表示"在……(温度)的之下"。

✐ e.g.: It will be *below* 0°C tomorrow.
　　　 明天零度以下。

(4) before, in front of和in the front of。

✐ e.g.: *Before* having breakfast, we needed to wash our hands.
　　　 我们在吃饭之前要洗手。
　　　 In front of the classroom, there is a tree.
　　　 教室的前面有一棵树。
　　　 In the front of the classroom, there is a teacher.
　　　 教室的前面有一名老师。

> **Tips** 三者都用于表示"在……前面",但是before表示"在……(时间)的前面",in front of表示"在……前面"(在范围外),而in the front of表示"在……前面"(在范围内)。

(5) across和through。

✐ e.g.: The man is coming *across* the road.
　　　 这个男人正在过马路。
　　　 A group of people dare not go *through* the forest.
　　　 这群人不敢穿过森林。

> **Tips** 两者都用于表示"穿过",但是前者表示"从平面穿过",而后者表示"从内部穿过(立体)"。

（6）after, behind和at the back of。

e.g.: *After* several days the enemies came.
过了几天，敌人来了。
Behind him there is a pretty girl.
在他后面有一个漂亮的女孩子。
A lady is sitting *at the back of* me.
一个女人正坐在我后面。

Tips 三者都用于表示"在……后面"，但是after表示"在……（时间）的后面"，且用于一般过去时，behind表示"在……（位置）后面"，而at the back of表示"在……（某人）背后"。

（7）among, in the middle of, in the center of和between。

e.g.: That is my son *among* a crowd of boys.
我儿子在一群男孩子中间。
There is a computer *in the middle of* the room.
房间中间有台电脑。
In the center of the hall stands a handsome man.
大厅中央站着个英俊的小伙子。
Between your mother and your father there is a gap.
你妈和你爸有代沟。

Tips 四者都用于表示"在……中间"，但是among表示"在……（多样事物）之间"，in the middle of表示"在……（某物）中间"，in the center of表示"在……（某物）中央"，而between表示"在……（两者）之间"，它亦可用于时间中。

e.g.: You can come here *between* 7 and 9.
你可以在七点到九点之间来。

（8）beside, besides 和 except。

e.g.: There is a broom *beside* the door.
　　　门边有一个扫把。

　　　Besides Tom we want to go to the factory.
　　　除汤姆外，我们也想去工厂。

　　　Except Tom we want to go to the factory.
　　　除汤姆外，我们想去工厂。

Tips　beside 表示"在……旁边"，besides 和 except 都表示"除……外"，但是 besides 表示"除……外，还有"，而 except 表示"除……外，其余"。

（9）in 和 into。

e.g.: The teacher is coming *in* the classroom.
　　　老师正进教室。

　　　The teacher is coming *into* the classroom.
　　　老师正进入教室。

Tips　两者都用于表示"在……里面"，但是前者表示"进入"，而后者更侧重于方向性。in 亦可表示"在……方向"或"用……（语言）"。

e.g.: You can speak *in* English.
　　　你可以说英语。

　　　I do well *in* drawing.
　　　我擅长于绘画。

（10）to 和 towards。

e.g.: He went *to* the entrance.
　　　他进了门。

He went *towards* the entrance.

他进入了门里。

Tips 两者都用于表示"到",但是前者表示一般的"到",而后者更侧重于方向性。

to 亦可表示以下的意义。

① 到。He goes *to* Shanghai every week. 他每周都去上海。

② 差(时间)。It is five *to* six. 现在六点差五分。

③ 对。You are strict *to* me. 你对我太严厉了。

(11) with 和 without。

e.g.: Miss Li came *with* a book.

李小姐带了一本书来。

Miss Li came *without* a book.

李小姐没有带书来。

Tips 前者表示"和……在一起",后者表示"除了,没有"。with 亦可表示"用……(工具)"。

e.g.: I wrote a letter *with* a blue pen.

我用蓝色的钢笔写了封信。

(12) 几个没有做比较但较重要的介词如表10-1所示。

表10-1 几个没有比较但较重要的介词

介 词	意 义	例 句
against	靠着 对着	She is sitting *against* the door. 她正对着门坐着。 He is always *against* U.S. 他一直反对美国。
along	沿着	If you go *along* this street, you can find the building. 如果你沿着这条路走,你能找到大楼。
(a)round	在……周围	There are many goats *around* the house. 房子的周边有许多羊。

续表

介 词	意 义	例 句
as	作为	*As* a chairman you can't do that. 作为一个主席你不能这样做。
at	在（几点） 在（位置）	I go to school *at* 8. 我八点上学。 We are arriving *at* the bus stop. 我们要到车站了。
by	被…… 以……为手段 在……旁边	The window is broken *by* me. 窗户被我打坏了。 We go to Peking *by* air. 我们坐飞机去北京。 There is a broom *by* the door. 门边有把扫把。
for	去……（地方） 达到，共（时间） 赞成	She wanted to leave *for* America. 她想去美国。 I have studied English *for* three years. 我学英语三年了。 Are you *for* or against? 你反对还是赞成？
from	来自……（地方） 离……（地方）	Where are you *from*? 你来自哪儿？ The railway station is far away *from* here. 火车站离这儿很远。
like	像	He is *like* his father. 他像他爸。
of	表示属格 表示数量	This is a leg *of* the desk. 这是桌子的一只腿。 This is a piece *of* paper. 这是一张纸。
till/until	直……为止	I didn't go to bed *until/till* 3 a.m. 我直到三点才睡觉。

小 结

本节的介词比较简单，要把握几组重要介词的比较，而且要认真记忆单词表中的固定短语介词，这样学好介词也就容易了。那么，来试试下面的问题：

（1）介词on和about有何区别？

（2）介词above，on和over有何区别？

（3）介词under和below有何区别？

（4）介词before，in front of和in the front of有何区别？

（5）介词across和through有何区别？

（6）介词after，behind和at the back of有何区别？

（7）介词among，in the middle of，in the center of和between有何区别？

（8）介词beside，besides和except有何区别？

（9）介词in和into有何区别？

（10）介词with和without有何区别？

（11）介词to和towards有何区别？

如果大家能把以上十一组基本介词的区别都弄懂的话，那么这节的学习就很成功了。

10.2 连　　词

1. 定义

连词是用来连接词与词、短语与短语、从句与从句、句子与句子的一类词。

2. 分类

按照连词本身的含义和连接的成分，可将连词分为并列连词和从属连词。

（1）并列连词。

并列连词是用来连接平行的词语、短语和句子的一类连词，也就是并列句的连接词。

e.g.: *Either* he *or* I am a worker.

他是工人或我是工人。（either ... or ... 是并列连词，表示"要么……要么……"）

It is hot today, *but* I insist on doing morning exercise.

今天很热，但是我还坚持做早操。（but是并列连词，表示"但是"）

（2）从属连词。

从属连词是用来连接从句和主句的连词，也就是复合句的连接词。

e.g.: *If* it rains tomorrow, we'll put off the sports meeting.

如果明天下雨，我们就延期运动会。（if是从属连词，表示"如果"）

I got up *so* late *that* I couldn't catch the first train.

我起得太晚了以至于我赶不上第一趟火车了。（so ... that是从属连词，表示"太……以至于……"）

3. 常用连词的用法

详见第十一天句法。

小　结

在这里用很少的笔墨来阐述连词的用法，这也许是和其他语法书都不一样的地方，因为在语法结构学习的指导下，我们只要分清楚什么是并列连词和从属连词就可以了。其他的内容我们可以在以后句法的学习中再慢慢涉及。

到现在为止，我们用了十天左右的时间把英语中的词法全部讲完。可能大家认为花费的时间太多，实际上任何一个句子都是由词汇构成的，而且我们在讲授词法的过程中也不只是单独地讲述，而是放在各个句子当中的，所以词法和句法是相辅相成的。下面我们专门花上几天时间来讲述句法。

10.3 基本句型知识点

现在要开始学习句法了，这是英语语法中最后一大部分的语法现象，其中最重要的是定语从句的学习，其他知识点按照本书所列的条目记下来即可。

一、简单句

英语中的句子按照结构可以分为简单句、并列句和复合句。在这里引进数学数列的办法来给大家说明一下：

简单句：$s_1+s_2+s_3+\cdots+s_n+v_1+v_2+v_3+\cdots+v_n+o_1+o_2+o_3+\cdots+o_n$

并列句：$s_1+v_1+o_1+c_1+s_2+v_2+o_2+c_2+s_3+v_3+o_3+c_3\cdots+\cdots+c_{n-1}+s_n+o_v+o_n$

复合句：　　S　　　+　　V　　+　　O　　+　　C

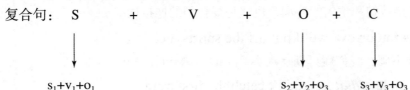

　　　　　　$s_1+v_1+o_1$　　　　　　　　$s_2+v_2+o_3$　　$s_3+v_3+o_3$

（上面的s指的是主语，v指的是动词谓语，o指的是宾语，c指的是连词，C指的是修饰成分。）

说明如下：

所谓简单句就是有n多个并列主语，n多个并列谓语和n多个并列宾语构成的一个句子。简化出来的结构就是一个大主语，一个大谓语和一个大宾语。

所谓并列句就是有n多个并列句子用n-1个连词连接起来的句子。这样的连词称之为并列连词。

所谓复合句就是在一个大句子中的某个成分上出现一个小句子，这个小句子称之为"从句",在什么位置上出现句子就称为这个位置上的从句,所以就有了所谓的主语从句、宾语从句、表语从句和同位语从句等。

那么,简单句按照用途可以分为:陈述句、疑问句、祈使句和感叹句。

1. 陈述句

陈述句一般要求主语在前、谓语在后,但有时谓语也置于主语之前(详见12.1),且要求主语的数形和谓语的数形保持一致(详见12.2),句末用降调。

e.g.: I like swimming and dancing.
我喜欢游泳和跳舞。
He has not finished this subject yet.
他还没完成这个课题。
Here is a map of China.
这是一张中国地图。
There came a bus.
车来了。

2. 疑问句

(1)一般疑问句是针对某一情况是否存在而提出的,句末用升调,常用yes或no来回答。

e.g.: Are you a doctor?
你是医生吗?
Yes, I am. / No, I am not.
是的,我是医生。/不,我不是医生。
Did you want to have a look at her?
你想去看她吗?
Yes, I did. / No, I did not.
是的,我想去看她。/不,我不想去。

(2)特殊疑问句是以疑问代词或疑问副词位于句首,引起问句,句末用降调,不能用yes或no来回答。

🔹 e.g.: What is your name?
你叫什么名字？
My name is Xiaoli.
我的名字叫肖丽。

When did you leave for Tokyo?
你什么时候到的东京？
Last night.
昨天晚上。

Why did he ask this question?
他为什么问这个问题？
Sorry, I don't know.
对不起，我不知道。

（3）选择疑问句一般由两个答案共同组成，用or连接，or之前的部分用升调，or之后的部分用降调。一般不用yes或no来回答，回答在句中选择一个。

🔹 e.g.: Did you want to go on studying or start to work?
你想继续上学还是工作？
I wanted to go on studying.
我想继续上学。

Is he from America or Australia?
他从美国来还是澳大利亚来？
He is from America.
他来自美国。

（4）反意疑问句一般用在陈述句之后，用逗号隔开，对提出的事实向对方进行证实。

🔹 e.g.: He is a nurse, *isn't he*?
他是个护士，对吗？
There isn't a pig in the box, *is there*?
盒子里没有猪，对吗？

反意疑问句的形式要遵循以下几个原则：
① 前句肯定，后句否定；前句否定，后句肯定。
② 前后动词形式一致。
③ 前后人称、数形一致。
但有几种特殊情况要区别对待：

e.g.: I am a student, *aren't I*?
　　　I am not a student, *am I*?

Tips 当前句出现I am ... 形式时，反意疑问句用aren't I。

e.g.: Everyone can do it, *can't he*?
　　　Anyone wants to be successful, *doesn't he*?
　　　Everything can be done, *cannot it*?

Tips 前句主语出现复合不定代词时，要用he或it来代替。

e.g.: They must have done this job, *didn't they*?
　　　He could have found the missing boy, *didn't he*?
　　　He must be a doctor, isn't he?

Tips 前句出现"情态动词+现在完成体"时，反意疑问句的动词形式用过去式。前句的情态动词如是表示推测的，反意疑问句的动词形式要与情态动词后的动词形式一致。

e.g.: ① ⎰ I think she is a book-seller, *isn't she*?
　　　　 ⎱ I don't think she is a book-seller, *is she*?
　　　② She thinks she is a book-seller, *doesn't she*?

Tips ①句中出现的I think, I don't think都可以认为是插入语，可以不管，直接看后面的主语和谓语动词（注意否定前移现象）。②句中出现的是宾语从句，所以可以直接看主句的情况。

3. 祈使句

祈使句是用以表示说话人的要求、命令等的一类句子，学习时要注意以下几点。

（1）祈使句始终为第二人称。

e.g.: Open the door. = *You* open the door.
（你）开门。

Shut the window. = *You* shut the window.
（你）关窗。

（2）祈使句否定时在句首加don't。

e.g.: Catch the bird.
抓住小鸟。　　（否定：Don't catch the bird.）

Be careful!
当心！　　（否定：Don't be careful!）

（3）祈使句的反意疑问句为will you。

e.g.: Let us go to the park, will you?
我们去公园，好吗？
（除了Let's go to the park, shall we? 我们去公园，好吗？）

Pass me the sugar, will you?
给我糖，好吗？

（4）祈使句以动词原形开头，常用降调。

e.g.: Close your books.　　　　Give me a pen.
合上你的书。　　　　　给我一支钢笔。

4. 感叹句

感叹句是用来表示说话人的喜怒哀乐的一类句子。句末用感叹号，用降调，常用what和how引导。

（1）用what引导的感叹句。

e.g.: What a beautiful lady she is!
多么漂亮的女士啊！

Tips 本句是倒装句，正常语序为She is what a beautiful lady。在表语中前三者都是用来修饰lady的，特别是what, a和beautiful是并列关系，所以what后接的中心词为名词或代词。

🖉 e.g.: What important information it is!
多么重要的信息呀!

Tips information是不可数名词，所以用零冠词。

（2）用how引导的感叹句。

🖉 e.g.: How beautiful the lady is!
多么漂亮的女士啊!

Tips 本句是倒装句，正常语序为The lady is how beautiful。在表语中how用来修饰beautiful，所以how后接的中心词为形容词、动词或副词。

🖉 e.g.: How fast he runs!
他跑得真快呀!

5. there be句型

在英语中我们常用"there + be + 物体 + 地点"的结构来表示"某地有某物"。

🖉 e.g.: There is a desk in front of the classroom.
教室前有一张桌子。
There is a pine tree on the hill.
山上有棵松树。

（1）它的否定式是在be动词后加not。

🖉 e.g.: There isn't a desk in front of the classroom.
教室前没有桌子。

There isn't a pine tree on the hill.

山上没有松树。

（2）它的一般疑问句是将be动词提到句首。

✏️ e.g.: Is there a desk in front of the classroom?

教室前有桌子吗？

Is there a pine tree on the hill?

山上有松树吗？

回答为：Yes, there is.

是的，有。

No, there isn't.

不是，没有。

二、并列句

并列句是由并列连词将两个或两个以上的简单句连接起来的句子。常用的并列连词有：and，but，either ... or ... ，for，neither ... nor ... ，not only ... but also ... ，or，so。

✏️ e.g.: She likes him *and* he likes her.

她喜欢他，他也喜欢她。（and表示"和"）

He was very tired, *but* he insisted on doing it.

虽然他很累，但是他还是坚持做这件事。（but表示"但是"）

Either you didn't do it *or* he didn't do it.

要么你不做，要么他不做。（either ... or ... 表示"要么……要么……"）

The flowers here are dying, *for* winter is coming.

这儿的花都死了，因为冬天到了。（for表示"因为"）

Neither he knew it *nor* everyone knew it.

他不知道，大家也不知道。（neither ... nor ... 表示"既不……也不……"）

Not only did he say it, *but also* he did it.

他不但说了而且做了。（not only ... but also ... 表示"不但……而且……"）

Work hard, *or* **you'll fail the exam.**
你要努力学习，否则考试不及格。（or表示"否则"）

It is rather urgent, *so* **everyone need know it.**
因为这件事太紧急了，所以大家想知道。（so表示"所以"）

小 结

在介绍句法时，我们讲到了两种重要的句型——简单句和并列句。希望大家记住简单句中几种重要的功能性句型的用法和并列句中连词的意义及用法。我们来看看，这些问题大家能回答出来吗？

（1）疑问句可以分为几类？
（2）一般疑问句和特殊疑问句的特点分别是什么？
（3）附加疑问句的主要用法是什么？特殊用法是什么？
（4）感叹句的两个引导词分别怎么用？
（5）祈使句的四个特点是什么？
（6）There be句型的特点是什么？

大家一定要对以上问题做到心中有数，这样就可以很好地把握住简单句和并列句的学习了。

介词练习

1. How are you getting _____ with your classmates?
   A. at   B. in   C. on   D. out
2. _____ my surprise, he failed to pass the examination.
   A. For   B. In   C. To   D. On
3. The entrance _____ the theatre is too big.
   A. for   B. to   C. at   D. into
4. Do you find the key _____ the question?
   A. to   B. for   C. on   D. with
5. We were discussing the plan that we would like to put _____ practice in the future.
   A. to   B. into   C. for   D. on

6. The fire had burnt half the forest _____ when it was put out.
   A. over B. alone C. off D. away

7. You should think _____ these questions that you are doing.
   A. about B. of C. for D. over

8. — Where is Alex?
   — He is dancing _____ the music.
   A. to B. for C. with D. on

9. The girl _____ red is my sister.
   A. on B. with C. for D. in

10. I'll leave for America _____ October 10th.
    A. in B. at C. about D. on

11. People lived badly _____ the war.
    A. during B. on C. in D. over

12. I get up early _____ the morning.
    A. on B. at C. in D. during

13. I'll get there _____ two o'clock.
    A. after B. from C. in D. for

14. I spent two days walking _____ the forest.
    A. over B. across C. out D. through

15. I waited for a long time _____ the bus stop.
    A. in B. on C. over D. at

16. My grandmother often goes _____ the street to buy apples.
    A. over B. through C. across D. cross

17. The plane is flying _____ the bridge.
    A. on B. in C. over D. with

18. I'll arrive _____ Shanghai in two days.
    A. at B. in C. on D. to

19. — Who is knocking _____ the door?
    — It must be Ricky.
    A. at B. on C. over D. with

20. I'll never give _____ my study.
    A. up B. in C. off D. at

21. We are proud _____ his courage.
    A. of   B. to   C. at   D. in
22. It is hot indoors. You'd better _____ your coat.
    A. put off   B. take off
    C. put on   D. not to take off
23. I often listen to VOA _____ radio.
    A. on   B. on the   C. through   D. by
24. Taiwan lies _____ the southeast of China.
    A. to   B. on   C. at   D. in
25. Taiwan lies _____ the east of Fujian.
    A. to   B. on   C. at   D. in
26. Japan lies _____ the east of China.
    A. to   B. on   C. at   D. in
27. Shanghai is divided _____ two parts by Huangpu River.
    A. by   B. with   C. into   D. of
28. Please wait for a moment. I'll change _____ a beautiful suit.
    A. on   B. for   C. to   D. into
29. John stayed _____ making experiments till midnight.
    A. away   B. on   C. up   D. with
30. The suit fitted him well _____ the color was a little bright.
    A. except for   B. except that
    C. expect when   D. besides
31. Put the sugar in the cupboard to prevent it safe _____ ants.
    A. for   B. with   C. of   D. from
32. Please turn _____ the radio. It's too noisy.
    A. up   B. down   C. off   D. on
33. — How can you get there?
    — I'll _____ bus or _____ foot.
    A. by; in   B. take; on
    C. by; on   D. in; on
34. He threw the ball _____ the wall and it bounced back.
    A. on   B. to   C. against   D. at

35. — Did you fly to London directly?
    — No, I traveled from Taiwan _____ Paris.
    A. through   B. by way of
    C. by the way   D. in the way
36. — How many students in your classroom?
    — Students reduce _____ forty.
    A. by   B. on   C. below   D. to
37. Paper is made _____ wood while the machine is made _____ steel.
    A. from; of   B. of; from
    C. from; into   D. out; of
38. The old lady died _____ illness.
    A. of   B. from   C. into   D. through
39. _____ the development of the economy, China is becoming stronger and stronger.
    A. For   B. With   C. On   D. Through
40. Do you agree _____ what he just now said?
    A. with   B. to   C. for   D. in
41. I spent two hundred dollars _____ my clothes.
    A. in   B. on   C. about   D. with
42. The policeman caught the robber _____ the arm and struck him _____ the head.
    A. on; in   B. on; on   C. on; by   D. by; on
43. I wish to thank him _____ helping me _____ math.
    A. for; with   B. to; with   C. for; on   D. to; about
44. He is the cleverest one _____ three of us.
    A. between   B. among   C. out   D. in
45. Mr. Smith lives _____ 118 Oxford Street.
    A. on   B. at   C. in   D. of
46. In summer, I often cool myself _____ the tree.
    A. below   B. beneath   C. under   D. in
47. I was surprised _____ how he made so much money.
    A. at   B. with   C. by   D. on

48. Apples are sold _____ pound.
    A. by   B. with   C. in   D. on
49. He was stopped by police when he was driving _____ full speed.
    A. in   B. for   C. with   D. at
50. — How do you know she loves you?
    — I could tell _____ her eyes.
    A. for   B. from   C. to   D. by

连词练习

1. Hurry up, _____ you will miss the last bus.
   A. and   B. or   C. while   D. so
2. Work hard, _____ you will be successful one day.
   A. and   B. or   C. while   D. so
3. John is thin _____ his brother is very fat.
   A. and   B. or   C. while   D. so
4. My bike is very old, _____, it was in wonderful condition.
   A. so   B. however   C. for   D. while
5. It was raining, _____ the sports meeting was put off.
   A. and   B. while   C. so   D. but
6. He learns not only Chinese _____.
   A. but also learns English   B. but also English
   C. or English   D. and English
7. He not only learns Chinese _____.
   A. but also learns English   B. but also English
   C. or English   D. and English
8. _____ your homework carefully, and some mistakes can certainly be avoided.
   A. Having done   B. As far as you do
   C. While doing   D. Do
9. It must have rained _____ there was water in the street.
   A. and   B. but   C. for   D. or

10. _____ my money back, or I'll charge you.
    A. Give   B. Giving
    C. To give   D. If you give
11. _____ your opinions are, you are welcomed to join our discussion.
    A. Whatever   B. However
    C. Whichever   D. Wherever
12. _____ Nick _____ Jenny like reading very much.
    A. Neither; nor   B. Either; or
    C. Both; and   D. Not only; but also
13. How long is it _____ you came to Shanghai?
    A. after   B. since   C. until   D. till
14. _____ breaks the law shall be punished.
    A. Those who   B. Who   C. Anyone   D. Whoever
15. Both Peter and Ricky, _____ Alex, are good at math.
    A. as well as   B. well
    C. as well   D. and as well
16. _____ she likes the skirt or not is not clear to me.
    A. If   B. What   C. Which   D. Whether
17. My problem is _____ I should blame him right now.
    A. if   B. whether   C. so   D. and
18. I'll phone you _____ I arrive in Beijing.
    A. as soon as   B. so sooner
    C. no sooner   D. no sooner than
19. _____ he got the message, he told me that.
    A. The moment   B. Moment
    C. The moment when   D. Whether
20. Hardly had I seen you _____ I recognized you.
    A. than   B. before   C. as   D. when
21. No sooner had I arrived at the station _____ the train left.
    A. before   B. as   C. than   D. when
22. The student was praised _____ helping the old.
    A. from   B. as   C. for   D. because

23. You can't get into the meeting room _____ you have a special pass.
    A. until   B. though   C. as large as   D. unless
24. We hope the laws to protect forests, _____ were taken by the government, will succeed.
    A. when   B. while   C. as   D. since
25. There was no news, _____, she did not give up hope.
    A. moreover   B. therefore
    C. but   D. nevertheless
26. It is not wise to give your child _____ he or she wants.
    A. whichever   B. whenever   C. whatever   D. however
27. It was five o'clock in the morning _____ we climbed up to the top of Mountain Tai.
    A. since   B. that   C. when   D. until
28. The weather was terrible, _____ the plane was delayed.
    A. and   B. whether   C. or   D. so
29. — What should I do about it?
    — Do it _____ I told you.
    A. because   B. when   C. as   D. while
30. They are so alike _____ they were twins.
    A. even though   B. as if
    C. as   D. as long as
31. Terrorists will be defeated _____ all the countries in the world work together.
    A. so   B. as soon as
    C. as long as   D. until
32. I'll solve the problem _____ it is very difficult to me.
    A. as if   B. even if   C. even   D. while
33. Beautiful girl _____ she is, no one likes her.
    A. as if   B. as   C. while   D. even if
34. _____ a student, he works hard.
    A. Because   B. As   C. As if   D. Except

35. Shut up and _____.
    A. you do your work   B. have your work done
    C. do your work   D. to do your work

36. — Would you like to have a dinner with me?
    — I'd like to, _____ I'm very busy.
    A. and   B. so   C. as   D. but

37. _____ you _____ I am to meet her at the railway station.
    A. Both; and   B. Either; nor
    C. Neither; or   D. Either; or

38. These houses are sold at such a low price _____ people expected.
    A. like   B. as   C. that   D. which

39. _____ you are a disabled person, what would you do?
    A. Supposing   B. As soon as
    C. Until   D. Except for

40. You should take an umbrella _____ it rains.
    A. in case of   B. as if
    C. in case   D. as far as

41. Speak loud _____ I can hear you.
    A. since   B. so as to   C. because   D. so that

42. It is _____ that I take off my coat.
    A. so warm day   B. such warm day
    C. such a warm day   D. so a warm day

43. You must do your best to solve it _____ difficult it may be.
    A. whichever   B. whatever   C. however   D. wherever

44. _____ you have been there for many years, I think you should know the environment clearly.
    A. Since   B. Because of
    C. Provided   D. Supposing

45. Seven minutes left, _____ you can caught the bus.
    A. or   B. but   C. so   D. and

第十一天

突破英语的复合句

句法中最重要的就是复合句，也就是我们经常提到的从句。实际上，从句和句子是有本质区别的，从句是句子的一个部分，在一个句子的什么位置出现句子就被称为什么从句。但是谓语的位置上是不可以有从句的。下面我们来看看主要从句的用法，特别要关注定语从句的用法，因为这是英语当中最后一个语法难点了，如果这个知识点可以突破，那么英语的语法学习就没有任何问题了！

11.1 主语从句

主语从句指在主语的位置不出现词或词组，而是出现一个句子，这样的句子称为主语从句。

- e.g.: *What he said* is true.

  他所说的是真的。

  That he did so much made everyone puzzled.

  他做得这么多让每个人都感到疑惑。

（1）引导主语从句的词有：how, that, what, when, where, whether, which, who, why 等。

- e.g.: *How we solve this problem* is very obvious.

  怎么解决这个问题很明显。

  When and where we will hold this meeting has not been decided.

  我们举行会议的地点和时间还没有决定。

  Whether he will come or not was not very clear.

  他是否来还不清楚。

Which one will be our teacher is a secret.

哪一个是我们老师是个秘密。

Who had stolen the gun has not been known.

谁偷了枪还不知道。

Why he didn't kill her has not been known.

为什么他没有杀她还不清楚。

（2）主语从句可以用it作为引导词来代替。

e.g.: *It* is very clear that where and when we have this meeting.

我们什么时间和地点举行会议很清楚了。

It is said that there are 300 people killed in the accident at least.

据说至少有300人死于这场车祸。

Tips 在主语从句中that作为引导词时不可省略，无意义；其余引导词有意义，不可省略；疑问词引导从句时，从句用陈述句语序。

11.2 宾语从句

宾语从句指在宾语的位置不出现词或词组，而出现一个句子，这样的句子称为宾语从句。

e.g.: I suppose (that) *her bag has been stolen*.

我想她的包已经被偷了。

Henry wanted to know *if she would come*.

亨利想知道她是否来。

引导宾语从句的词有：if，how，that，which，when，where，whether，who，whom，whose，why等。

e.g.: Sherry is studying *how to use this machine*.

谢丽正在学习如何使用这台机器。

Henry wants to know *when Bruce will come*.
亨利想知道布鲁斯什么时候来。

Everybody doesn't know *where the place is*.
每个人都不知道这是哪儿。

Tips 第一句是"疑问词+不定式"做宾语从句的现象。

e.g.: The teacher asked me *why I was late*.
老师问我为什么迟到。
Bruce showed *which one was better*.
布鲁斯展示哪一个更好。
Let's see *whose shirt it is*.
让我们看看这是谁的衬衫。
I know *who did it*.
我知道谁做的。

Tips 宾语从句中的that作为引导词时可省略，无意义；其余引导词有意义，不可省略；疑问词引导从句时，从句用陈述句语序。

e.g.: I think (that) *we will land on the moon one day*.
我想我们总有一天会登上月球。

过去将来时、过去完成时、过去进行时常用于宾语从句中。

e.g.: I said *I would go to Shanghai next day*.
我说我明天去上海。（过去将来时）
He told me that *he had finished this job*.
他告诉我他已经完成了这项工作。（过去完成时）

She said *she was doing the housework at the same time last day*.

她说昨天这个时候她正在做家务。（过去进行时）

11.3 表语从句

表语从句指在表语的位置不出现词或词组，而出现一个句子，这样的句子称为表语从句。

🔘 e.g.: That is *why he was late*.

那就是为什么他迟到了。

It's *how we solve this problem*.

这就是我们如何解决问题的。

引导表语从句的词有：how，that，what，when，where，whether，which，who，why 等。

🔘 e.g.: The problem is *how to solve the affair*.

问题是怎么解决这个事件。

The difficulty is that *we couldn't speak French*.

困难是我们不懂法语。

That's *what we are anxious to*.

那是我们着急的事情。

The last question is *when and where we will hold the competition*.

最后一个问题是我们何时何地举行竞赛。

The question is *whether they will come*.

问题是他们会不会来。

The suggestion is *which one goes to America should be better*.

建议是哪一个去美国更好。

The problem is *who will take over this subject*.

问题是谁来接管这个项目。

Tips 在表语从句中 that 作为引导词时不可省略，无意义；其余引导词有意义，不可省略；疑问词引导从句时，从句用陈述句语序。

11.4 同位语从句

同位语指的是前后两个名词或是名词短语相互说明，不分前后，不分主次。

- e.g.: Beijing, the capital of China, is a very beautiful city.
  北京是中国的首都，也是一个很漂亮的城市。

Tips 句中 Beijing 和 the capital of China 就是同位语关系，它们是相互说明的关系，而且前后位置可以互换。

同位语从句指在同位语的位置不出现词或词组，而出现一个句子，这样的句子称为同位语从句。它一般在（fact，idea，news，way，promise等）后面，用于解释前面的名词。

- e.g.: The fact *that he had broken the window* has been proved.
  他打破玻璃的事实已经证实了。

引导同位语从句的词有：how，that，when，where等。

- e.g.: The way *how we cope with this thing* has been not very clear.
  怎么解决这个问题的方法我们还不清楚。
  He had no idea *when and where she was dead*.
  他不知道她是何时何地死的。

Tips 在同位语从句中，that 作为引导词时不可省略，无意义；其余引导词有意义，不可省略；疑问词引导从句时，从句用陈述句语序。

以上所提到的四种从句都可以称为名词性从句，因为它们在句子中做的成分都是由名词来充当的。在英语中还有两类更加重要的从句,就是形容词性的定语从句和副词性的状语从句。

11.5 定语从句

这是英语中最重要的语法现象之一。中文中也有定语,也有定语从句,如:"美丽的祖国",这就是"定语加中心词"的用法;"我生活的祖国",这就是"定语从句加中心词"的用法。但是,中文的定语从句和英语的是不一样的,一般来说,中文的定语从句在被修饰词的前面,英语中的定语从句则在被修饰词的后面。

1. 定义

用来做定语的句子被称为定语从句。

e.g.: The man *whom you are talking with* is my brother.
你正在说话的人是我兄弟。

2. 几个重要概念

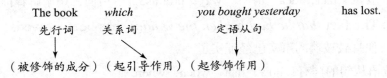

3. 关系词的用法

(1) who用于指人,在句中做主语。

e.g.: The woman *who is wearing a red coat* is my mother.
穿红外套的是我妈。
The girl *who is standing under the tree* is my daughter.
站在树下的女孩是我女儿。

(2) whom用于指人,在句中做宾语。在口语中可省略,可以用who来代替。

e.g.: That man *whom* (*who*) *you were beating* is dying.
你刚刚打的男人要死了。

The woman *whom (who) you talked to just now* was a thief.

刚刚跟你讲话的女人是个小偷。

（3） whose用于指人，在句中做定语。

e.g.: Henry *whose mother is a physician* has gone abroad.

妈妈是内科医生的亨利已经出国了。

Bruce *whose brother is a famous scientist* wanted to be a doctor.

兄弟是著名科学家的布鲁斯想成为一个医生。

（4） which用于指物，在句中做主语或宾语。

e.g.: The radio (*which*) *you wanted to buy* is sold.

你想买的收音机已经卖了。

The house (*which*) *you lived in* was destroyed by a terrible earthquake.

你住的房子在地震中毁坏了。

The element *which made you upset* was dismissed.

使你紧张的原因消失了。

Tips　当which引导物在定语从句中做宾语的时候是可以省略的，所以上面句子中带有括号的which都是可以省略的。

（5） that 用于指人，也可以指物，在句中做主语或宾语，做宾语时可省略。

e.g.: The mobile phone (*that*) *you bought* is of no use.

你买的手机没有用。

This kind of deer *that lived in China* has decreased.

生活在中国的这种鹿已经减少。

Who is that boy *that is fishing now*?

正在钓鱼的男孩是谁？

（6）when 用于指时间，在句中做状语。

试比较
① I never forget those days *when I lived here*.
我再也忘记不了住在这儿的日子。
② I never forgot those days *which I spent here*.
我再也忘记不了在这儿过的日子。

Tips 在①句中，lived 为不及物动词，所以先行词做状语，用when；而在②句中，spend为及物动词，先行词做宾语，用which。

（7）where 用于指地点，在句中做状语。

试比较
① This is a house *where I lived before*.
这是我以前住过的房子。
② This is a house *which I lived in before*.
这是我以前住过的房子。

Tips 在①句中，lived为不及物动词，所以先行词做状语，用where；而在②句中，lived in是及物动词词组，所以先行词用which，实际上in which相当于where。

（8）why用于指原因，在句中做状语，前面先行词一般为reason。

e.g.: That's the reason why *I wanted to join the army*.
那是我参军的原因。
Who told you the reason *why they didn't want to come here*?
谁告诉你他们不想来这儿的原因？

4. that（"不止最两序"）和which（非介）用法比较

Tips 这是定语从句中最重要的内容，一定要记住本书中讲到的这几种用法。

（1）which用于非限定性定语从句中。

🖊 e.g.: He said he was busy, *which was not true*.
他说他很忙，那是假的。

We don't want to enter the house, *which is very cold*.
我们不想进房间，因为太冷了。

（2）which用于介词后做句子中的各种成分。

🖊 e.g.: The room *of which windows are opposite to the sea* is large.
窗户正对着海的房间很大。

The chair *in which you are sitting* is made of iron.
你坐的椅子是用铁做的。

（3）that一定用于"不"（不定代词做先行词时）、"止"（"只是"only修饰先行词时）、"最"（形容词最高级修饰先行词时）、"两"（先行词同时出现人和物）和"序"（序数词修饰先行词时）五种情况。

🖊 e.g.: All *that you need* is help.
你所需要的是帮助。（all为不定代词）

A lot of things and children *that are full of the car* were lost in the district.
装满了东西和孩子们的车子在这个地区失踪了。（先行词既有人又有物）

That is only thing *that I want to know*.
那是我唯一想知道的事情。（先行词有only修饰）

The last book *that you bought* is that I wanted to buy.
你买的最后一本书是我想买的。（先行词有序数词修饰）

What is the size of the largest map *that you have seen before*?
你以前见过的最大尺寸的地图有多大？（先行词有形容词最高级修饰）

5. 定语从句的种类

定语从句可分为非限定性定语从句（描绘性定语从句）和限定性定语从句。

🖊 e.g.: They don't like that person *who is noisy*.
他们不喜欢那个吵闹的人。

> **Tips** 限定性定语从句和先行词关系紧密，不可省略。

✏️ e.g.: They don't like that people, *who is noisy*.
他们不喜欢那个人，因为他太吵闹了。

> **Tips** 非限定性定语从句（描绘性定语从句）和先行词关系疏松，用逗号和主句隔开，可以省略。翻译时，它相当于一个状语从句。

11.6 状语从句

状语从句指在状语的位置不出现词或词组，而出现一个句子，这样的句子称为状语从句。

1. 时间和条件状语从句（用一般时代替将来时）

✏️ e.g.: *If it rains tomorrow*, we will put off the sports meeting.
如果明天下雨，我们就延迟运动会。

> **Tips** 在if引导的条件句中，应用rains（一般现在时）代替will rain（一般将来时）。

✏️ e.g.: *As soon as she gets home*, I will ask her to call you.
她一到家，我就让她打电话给你。

> **Tips** 在as soon as引导的时间句中，应用gets（一般现在时）代替will get（一般将来时）。

When he goes to the theatre, the film will start.
当他到电影院时，电影开始了。

Unless I die I will struggle with you forever.
除非我死了，要不我会和你斗争到底。

2. 原因状语从句，它常由as, because, since来引导

> e.g.: *As he was old*, he can't lift the stone.
> 因为他年纪大了，所以他举不起这块石头。
>
> I can't go to school *because I caught a terrible cold.*
> 我不能去上学，因为我得了严重的感冒。
>
> We could do whatever we like *since they didn't care for us.*
> 既然他们不喜欢我们，我们可以做任何想做的事情。

Tips 在原因状语从句中，so不可和because同时出现，记住"有因为没有所以；有所以没有因为"。它们的使用方法与在中文中是不同的。

3. 让步状语从句，它常用although, even if和though来引导

> e.g.: *Although she was too old*, she still did well in drawing.
> 尽管她年纪很大了，但还是很擅长绘画。
>
> It is cold *although /though it is* early *fall*.
> 尽管还是秋天，但是天气很冷了。

Tips 在原因状语从句中，although/though不可和but同时出现，记住"有虽然没有但是；有但是没有虽然"。它们的使用方法与在中文中是不同的。

4. 比较状语从句

详见3.2中的"形容词和副词的比较等级"。

5. 结果状语从句和目的状语从句

> e.g.: Bruce got up *so late that he could not catch the first train.*
> 布鲁斯起得太晚了以至于没有赶上头班火车。（so ... that表示"太……以至于"，结果状语)

Bruce got up early *so that he could catch the first train*.
布鲁斯起得这么早就为了赶上头班火车。（so that表示"为了……"，目的状语）

结果状语从句的连接词还有：in order ... that, in order ... to, so ... as to等。

试比较
- His eyesight is in order bad that he couldn't see anything.
- His eyesight is so bad as not to see anything.
- 他的视力太差了以至于什么也看不见。

Tips so ... as to和in order to后接不定式，而in order ... that后接句子。

目的状语从句的连接词还有：in order that, in order to，so as to等。

试比较
- She spoke in order slowly that she can be understood.
- In order to be understood she spoke slowly.
- She spoke slowly so as to be understood.
- 她说得很慢是为了让别人听懂。

Tips so as to和in order to后接不定式，而in order that后接句子。

6. 方式状语从句，它常由as if/though来引导

   e.g.: He looks *as if he's very happy*.
   他看上去很高兴。

   It looks *as though it is going to rain*.
   看起来要下雨了。

7. 地点状语从句，它常由where和wherever来引导

   e.g.: Put it *where it was*.
   把它放在原来的地方。

   You could go *wherever you like*.
   你可以去你想去的任何地方。

Tips 用where引导定语从句的用法，详见定语从句。

Put it where it was.

Put it in which where it was.

Put it in the place where it was.

Put it in the place in which it was.

第一句正确，是地点状语从句。第二句错误，因为定语从句需要先行词，而此句中没有。第三句正确，这是用where引导的表示地点的定语从句。第四句正确，因为在定语从句在某些场合下，where和in which可以互换。

所以，要判断地点状语从句和定语从句，要看引导词前是否有名词，如果有先行词就是定语从句，没有的话就是状语从句。

小 结

在本章中，我们讨论了复合句。大家要掌握各种从句的用法，引导词的使用情况（特别是要把重点放在定语从句上）。在学完本章后，语法的学习也要进入尾声了，下面几个语法点只要了解就可以，把握住小结中所提到的要点，记住它们即可。下面还是请大家回答以下问题：

（1）什么从句中的that可以省略？

（2）主语从句用it代替的用法是怎样的？

（3）表语从句可不可以用疑问词来连接？

（4）什么是同位语？同位语从句的先行词一般有哪些？

（5）定语从句主要引导词的用法是什么？

（6）在定语从句中，that和which的用法区别是什么？

（7）非限定性定语从句和限定性定语从句的区别是什么？

（8）八大状语从句分别是什么？其区别和联系是什么？

大家一定要多花点时间把以上的问题一一弄清楚，这样就可以把复合句的所有内容都弄懂了。努力吧！

练习

1. — She is your teacher, isn't she?
   — _____.
   A. Yes, she isn't   B. Yes, she is
   C. No, she is   D. No, she wasn't

2. Let's do a game, _____?
   A. will you   B. shall I
   C. shall we   D. don't we

3. Let us do a game, _____?
   A. will you   B. shall I
   C. shall we   D. don't we

4. Don't be noisy, _____?
   A. is you   B. shall I   C. shall we   D. will you

5. Pass me the salt, _____?
   A. don't you   B. don't I   C. shall I   D. will you

6. Everything is not easy, _____?
   A. isn't it   B. is it
   C. is everything   D. isn't everything

7. Everybody wants to become white collar, _____?
   A. don't it   B. do they
   C. doesn't he   D. don't he

8. I am a teacher, _____?
   A. am I   B. am not I   C. are I   D. aren't I

9. She seldom goes shopping, _____?
   A. does she   B. doesn't she C. will she   D. shall she

10. You'd like to attend the meeting, _____?
    A. won't you   B. wouldn't you
    C. hadn't you   D. haven't you

11. I had to tell the truth, _____?
    A. haven't I   B. wouldn't I
    C. didn't I   D. shouldn't I

12. — Isn't your uncle an engineer?
    — _____.
    A. No, he isn't   B. No, he is
    C. Yes, he isn't   D. Yes, he does

13. — You're not a new member, are you?
    — _____. I joined only yesterday.
    A. No, I'm not   B. Yes, I'm not
    C. No, I am   D. Yes, I am

14. I can't speak Japanese, _____?
    A. can't I   B. can I   C. will I   D. shall I

15. He used to live in New York, _____?
    A. did he   B. used he   C. didn't he   D. doesn't he

16. The boy ought to be punished, _____?
    A. ought to he   B. shouldn't he
    C. ought not he   D. ought not to he

17. You need to study English, _____?
    A. needn't you   B. need you
    C. don't you   D. do you

18. I needn't study English, _____?
    A. need I   B. do I   C. don't I   D. needn't I

19. Nobody dares to tell him the bad news, _____?
    A. does he   B. don't he
    C. daren't he   D. dare he

20. Nobody dare tell him the bad news, _____?
    A. does he   B. don't he
    C. daren't he   D. dare he

21. You must be excited, _____?
    A. mustn't you   B. aren't you
    C. needn't you   D. will you

22. You must clean the classroom right now, _____?
    A. mustn't you   B. don't you
    C. needn't you   D. will you

23. You must have drunk too much, _____?
    A. mustn't you   B. haven't you
    C. didn't you   D. will you
24. No one was injured in the accident, _____?
    A. weren't they   B. was he
    C. won't it   D. was it
25. I don't think she is a good doctor, _____?
    A. do I   B. isn't she
    C. is she   D. do I
26. She doesn't believe she can do it by herself, _____?
    A. does she   B. can she
    C. can't she   D. do I
27. John is hardly twenty years old, _____?
    A. isn't he   B. is he   C. does he   D. doesn't he
28. She told me that Peter could manage it, _____?
    A. couldn't he   B. did she
    C. didn't she   D. could he
29. You'd better go, _____?
    A. hadn't you   B. had you
    C. wouldn't you   D. would you
30. He may bring my books, _____?
    A. mayn't he   B. mustn't he
    C. can I   D. will I
31. How beautiful the flower he gave me is, _____?
    A. did he   B. didn't he   C. is it   D. isn't it
32. I wish you to succeed, _____?
    A. may I   B. don't I   C. shall I D. will I
33. _____ from Beijing to London!
    A. How long way it is   B. What a long way is it
    C. How long way is it   D. What a long way it is
34. _____ happy life they are living!
    A. How   B. What
    C. How a   D. What a

35. _____ wonderful weather they are having!
    A. How   B. What   C. How a   D. What a
36. _____ careless he is !
    A. What   B. How   C. How a   D. How much
37. _____ beautiful the flower is!
    A. How a   B. What a   C. How   D. What
38. _____ she gave me!
    A. What good advice   B. How good advice
    C. What a good advice   D. How a good advice
39. _____ he is!
    A. How funny   B. What funny
    C. What a fun   D. How a fun
40. _____ handsome he is!
    A. What   B. How
    C. What a   D. How a
41. _____ handsome boy he is!
    A. What   B. How an
    C. What a   D. How a
42. _____ she speaks Japanese!
    A. How fluent   B. How fluently
    C. What fluent   D. What fluently
43. Look at the children over there! What _____?
    A. do they do   B. are they doing
    C. they are doing   D. is he doing
44. — How is your father?
    — _____.
    A. He's fine, thank you   B. He is only fifty
    C. He is a doctor   D. He likes football very much
45. — What does your father do?
    — _____.
    A. He's fine, thank you   B. He is only fifty
    C. He is a doctor   D. He likes football very much

46. — _____ do you go to see your father?
    — Once a week.
    A. How often   B. How long
    C. How soon   D. What about
47. — _____ have you learned English?
    — Six years.
    A. How long   B. How long time
    C. How much time   D. How much long
48. — ____ will you finish your task?
    — I'll finish it in two days.
    A. How long   B. How soon
    C. How often   D. How much
49. — What is the date today?
    — It is _____.
    A. April 17th B. Thursday
    C. a terrible day   D. the day for me to travel
50. — What's day today?
    — It is _____.
    A. April 17th   B. Thursday
    C. a terrible day   D. the day for me to travel
51. The man _____ talked to you just now is an engineer.
    A. who   B. which   C. where   D. when
52. I still remember the days _____ we studied together.
    A. that   B. which   C. where   D. when
53. The ancient people used stone to build a house in _____ they stored food.
    A. who   B. that   C. which   D. what
54. He is the cleverest boy _____ I have known.
    A. who   B. that   C. which   D. whom
55. The book, the cover of _____ is white, is mine.
    A. that   B. where   C. which   D. it
56. The book, and the cover of _____ is white, is mine.
    A. that   B. where   C. which   D. it

57. She is one of the students who _____ the examinations.
    A. passes   B. pass
    C. have passed   D. has passed
58. She is only one of the students who _____ the examinations.
    A. passes   B. pass
    C. have passed   D. has passed
59. There are fifty students in our class, _____ are girls.
    A. most of them   B. most of whom
    C. most of who   D. and most of whom
60. I live in a house _____ windows are painted red.
    A. that   B. which   C. who   D. of which
61. All _____ glitters is not gold.
    A. which   B. that   C. who   D. what
62. Hong Qi is the best car _____ is made in China.
    A. which   B. that   C. and which D. what
63. This is the first film _____ I've ever seen.
    A. that   B. which   C. and which D. what
64. _____ is well known to all, the earth is becoming warmer.
    A. That   B. Which   C. What   D. As
65. He is always late, _____ annoys me.
    A. what   B. that   C. which   D. who
66. The reason _____ America wants to disarm Iraq is for oil.
    A. that   B. which   C. why   D. on which
67. She is the only girl _____ has ever seen the chief.
    A. whom   B. that   C. which   D. she
68. The doctor _____ is leaving for Africa next month.
    A. the nurse is talking to him   B. whom the nurse is talking
    C. the nurse is talking to   D. who the nurse is talking
69. After living in Pairs for fifty years, he returns to the small town _____ he grew up as a child.
    A. which   B. where   C. that   D. when

70. They talked of the things and classmates _____ they remembered in the school.
    A. which   B. that   C. who   D. they
71. I have the same book _____ you do.
    A. that   B. which   C. who   D. as
72. Edison is one of the greatest scientists _____ ever lived.
    A. that   B. who   C. whom   D. about whom
73. Fortunately we had a compass, without _____ we would have got lost.
    A. which   B. it   C. that   D. what
74. John got high marks, _____ had been expected.
    A. who   B. what   C. that   D. as
75. David lost his money, _____ made him very sad.
    A. this   B. which   C. as   D. that
76. I still remember the day _____ I met you.
    A. on that   B. on which   C. in which   D. on when
77. I have two books, _____ is interesting.
    A. neither of them   B. neither of which
    C. none of them   D. none of which
78. World War II _____ millions of people were killed ended in 1945.
    A. that   B. which   C. during   D. in which
79. It was midnight, and there wasn't a person _____ I should turn for help.
    A. who   B. whom   C. to whom   D. what
80. The knife _____ we use to cut the apples is very sharp.
    A. what   B. with that   C. with it   D. which
81. Is there anything _____ to you?
    A. that belong   B. which belongs
    C. that belongs   D. that is belonged
82. — Why were you late yesterday?
    — The reason is _____ I was ill yesterday.
    A. because   B. as   C. that   D. why

83. This is the factory _____ I visited last year.
    A. when   B. where   C. that   D. why
84. This is the restaurant _____ I had dinner yesterday.
    A. which   B. where   C. in where   D. that
85. It was in 1991 _____ Changjiang River flooded.
    A. that   B. in which   C. when   D. in that
86. It was the teacher _____ I respected very much.
    A. who   B. that   C. which   D. with whom
87. October the first is the day _____ we Chinese people will never forget.
    A. which   B. when   C. on which   D. on that
88. The house _____ we live is new.
    A. which   B. in which   C. that   D. in that
89. There are three labs, the longest one _____ was built 20 years ago.
    A. which   B. /   C. among which D. who are
90. I, _____ your good friend, try my best to help you out.
    A. who is   B. who am   C. that am   D. who are
91. This factory is _____ you have visited before.
    A. that   B. which   C. where   D. the one
92. The Swedish people did not understand the three questions _____ were asked in French.
    A. where   B. who   C. in which   D. which
93. He didn't know which room _____.
    A. they lived   B. they lived in
    C. did they live   D. did they live in
94. The book _____ sold out in the bookstore.
    A. which you need it   B. what you needed
    C. which you needed it   D. you needed
95. Is this the shop _____ sells men's clothes?
    A. which   B. where   C. in which   D. what
96. The clothes _____ Ricky paid 100 dollars was very beautiful.
    A. that   B. which   C. for which   D. to which

97. His wife, _____ you met on the street, was a doctor.
    A. who   B. whom   C. which   D. that
98. The window _____ glass was broken faces south.
    A. whose   B. that   C. of which   D. where
99. _____ the day went on, the weather got worse.
    A. With   B. Since   C. Which   D. As
100. _____ he said is true.
    A. Whether   B. That   C. Which   D. What
101. We know the fact _____ she is a chief.
    A. that   B. which   C. of which   D. what
102. No one doubts the theory _____ light travels faster than sound.
    A. which   B. that
    C. what   D. about which
103. The problem _____ has happened is not known to me.
    A. that   B. what   C. whether   D. if
104. The question _____ there are living things in space will be found out.
    A. that   B. what   C. whether   D. if
105. I have no idea _____ I'll leave for Shanghai.
    A. that   B. whether   C. what   D. when
106. I have no idea _____ I'll go for coming vacation.
    A. that   B. whether   C. where   D. when
107. There is no doubt _____ Newton is a great scientist.
    A. that   B. which   C. what   D. why
108. My father made a promise _____ he would buy me a watch.
    A. what   B. when   C. that   D. which
109. _____ he was elected as president was beyond me.
    A. If   B. Which   C. How   D. What
110. _____ you have done might do harm to other people.
    A. That   B. What   C. Which   D. This
111. It was doubtful _____ we would make it or not.
    A. what   B. that   C. whether   D. if

112. _____ she is the most intelligent girl is known to everybody.
   A. /   B. That   C. What   D. As
113. It looks _____ it is going to rain.
   A. that   B. as if   C. what   D. whether
114. The water is _____ we want.
   A. that   B. which   C. what   D. whether
115. What she wants to tell you is _____ the meeting will begin.
   A. when   B. what   C. that   D. which
116. Everything depends on _____ you have confidence.
   A. as if   B. what   C. that   D. whether
117. Nobody believed him _____ what he said.
   A. even though   B. in spite
   C. no matter   D. contrary to
118. They want to know _____ do to help us.
   A. what can they   B. what they can
   C. how they can   D. how can they
119. _____ there is a will, there is a way.
   A. When   B. That   C. While   D. Where
120. Speak slowly and clearly _____ everyone could understand you.
   A. for   B. since   C. because of   D. so that
121. John gives me more help than _____.
   A. Tom is   B. Tom has
   C. Tom does   D. Tom gives
122. We all agreed that he was stronger than _____.
   A. I looked   B. I was looked
   C. he looked   D. he was looked
123. Bright _____ the sun is, it is very cold.
   A. if   B. because   C. as   D. since
124. He doesn't know _____ to stay or not.
   A. whether   B. if   C. either   D. if he will
125. _____ you are, I'll be missing you.
   A. Where   B. Wherever   C. Whether   D. Who

126. _____ Jack finishes his homework, he will leave at once.
   A. As soon as   B. As if
   C. Unless   D. In order that
127. Go get your coat. It's _____ you left it.
   A. there   B. where
   C. there where   D. where there
128. It was only two hours _____ I arrived in New York.
   A. after   B. that   C. when   D. till
129. It worried her a bit _____ her hair was turning gray.
   A. while   B. that   C. if   D. for
130. I didn't manage to do it _____ you had explained how.
   A. until   B. unless   C. when   D. before
131. We must get up early tomorrow, _____ we'll miss the first bus to the Great Wall.
   A. so   B. or   C. but   D. however
132. You may take an umbrella _____ it'll rain.
   A. in case   B. in case of
   C. in order to   D. in order that
133. _____ he won't go with us, let's go.
   A. For   B. Because
   C. Now that   D. That
134. _____ what will happen, I'll persist in my belief.
   A. Even if   B. Although
   C. Perhaps   D. No matter
135. Jack was a very kind man. He helped me _____ I asked him to.
   A. whatever   B. whenever
   C. only   D. however
136. Jenny is _____ girl that we all like her.
   A. a pretty so   B. so pretty a
   C. a such pretty   D. such pretty a
137. It has been six years _____ I started to learn English.
   A. before   B. after   C. since   D. that

138. _____ he worked very hard, he failed again.
   A. Whether   B. Although
   C. Because   D. Since
139. _____ you borrow the book, you must return it in two weeks.
   A. However   B. Whenever
   C. Whichever   D. Wherever
140. — How can I do it?
   — You should do _____ I told you.
   A. what   B. so   C. as   D. as if
141. There was no news, _____, she did not give up hope.
   A. moreover   B. therefore
   C. but   D. nevertheless
142. The men will have to wait all day _____ the doctor works faster.
   A. if   B. unless   C. whether   D. that
143. I shall stay in the hotel all day _____ there is some news about the missing child.
   A. in case   B. no matter
   C. in any case   D. ever since

第十二天

突破英语的语序、主谓一致和it的用法

最后一天,我要把英语中最后三个语法现象拿出来和大家一起讨论,虽然这三个语法现象并不是十分重要,但是在英语中却很常见,希望能够引起大家足够的重视。

12.1 语 序

1. 定义

语序是用来表示句子中主谓和宾语之间位置关系的一种语法现象。

Tips 　　一般来说,在讨论语序的时候,很少讨论宾语前置的情况,而只讨论主谓倒装的问题,所以我们在这里也是按照常规的方法来讲解,遇到个别宾语前置的情况也会给大家讲解。

---

2. 分类

(1) 自然语序:主语在前,谓语在后的一种语序。

> e.g.: We love peace. 　　　　That apple tree is so big.
> 　　　我们热爱和平。　　　　那棵苹果树太大了。

(2) 倒装语序:谓语提到主语前面的语序。

① 谓语部分完全置于主语之前的语序,称为完全倒装。

> e.g.: There came a bus.
> 　　　来了一辆汽车。
> 　　　Here is a map of China.
> 　　　这是一张中国地图。

第十二天 突破英语的语序、主谓一致和it的用法

Tips 在这里可以看到，当有某些词在句首的时候，会引起倒装。

② 谓语部分中的助动词提到主语之前，而实义动词的位置不变的语序，称为部分倒装。

e.g.: How did you like the show?
你觉得演出如何？
When did you come to China?
你什么时候来的中国？

3. 常见的倒装形式

（1）由引导词there引起的完全倒装。

e.g.: *There are* three desks in the classroom.
教室里有三张桌子。
There is a pear in the box.
盒子里有个梨子。

Tips 很少讲there be句型是一种倒装形式，但是在某种程度上，there be句型中的there就是一个引导词，并没有任何含义，只是引起了be动词的前置而产生的倒装。

（2）由时间状语（now和then等）或地点状语（down，here，there，up等）位于句首引起的完全倒装。

e.g.: *Now* comes your turn.
现在轮到你。
At the top of the hill stands a pine tree.
山顶上有棵松树。
Here is a dog.
这是一条狗。

（3）由 either，neither，so 位于句首引起的完全倒装。

e.g.: The first one is not good. *Neither is the last one.*

第一个不好，最后一个也不好。

I can't swim. *Nor can you.*

我不会游泳，你也不会。

You can swim. *So can I.*

你会游泳，我也会。

（4）由分词短语位于句首引起的完全倒装。

e.g.: *Standing* by the table was a beautiful lady.

桌子边站了一位漂亮的女士。

Sitting in a chair is a fox.

椅子上坐了一只狐狸。

（5）在直接引语中出现的完全倒装。

e.g.: "I love you!" *said she.*

她说："我爱你！"

"Don't you know it?" *cried your wife.*

你老婆叫道："难道你不知道吗？"

（6）某些否定副词（never, nowhere, seldom 等），否定短语（hardly...when, no sooner ... than, not only ... but also, scarcely ... when 等）位于句首引起部分倒装。

e.g.: *Never* does he realize how important the meeting is.

他根本不知道会议的重要。

Hardly had she gone out *when* it began to rain.

当她出去时开始下雨了。

Not only does she speak English very well, *but also* she speaks Japanese very fluently.

她不但英语说得很好，而且日语也说得很流利。

（7）在疑问句中引起的倒装。

① 一般疑问句引起的部分倒装。

e.g.: Did he have a cold?
他感冒了？

Have you finished your homework?
你已经完成作业了吗？

② 特殊疑问句引起的完全倒装。

e.g.: What is your name?
你的名字是什么？

How old are you?
你多大年纪了？

小 结

在本节中大家主要记忆各种倒装的情况即可。特别是要注意部分倒装，它不是直接将谓语提到主语之前，而是将谓语部分中的助动词部分提到主语之前。

请大家回答下列问题：
（1）倒装指的是什么？
（2）部分倒装和完全倒装又有什么样的不同？
（3）完全倒装一般有几种形式？
（4）部分倒装总的特点是什么？

如果这些问题都可以回答的话，就说明大家已经很好地掌握了这节的内容。

12.2 主谓一致

在这一节当中，我们主要讨论主语和谓语的数形问题。在名词一章中我们讨论过名词的数，现在已经很少看到有关名词形的说法了，大家只要记住名词的后面有s的单词都称为复形单词，就可以了。

1. 定义

主谓一致是指主语的数及形和谓语的数及形保持一致的一种语法现象。

e.g.: They are workers.
他们是工人。

He is a teacher.
他是位老师。
I have a bag.
我有一个包。

Tips bag为单数，单形；bags为复数，复形。

2. 主语的数形和谓语的数形的几种特殊情况
（1）单形词表示复数概念。
在英语中，cattle，people，police三个词的谓语部分始终用复数。

e.g.: The cattle are female.
这些牛是母的。
The people are having breakfast.
这些人正在吃早饭。
The police have already caught the thief.
警方已经抓住了小偷。

（2）复形词表示单数概念。
① 以-ics结尾的学科要用单数谓语（physics, politics, etc.）。

e.g.: Linguistics is a difficult subject.
语言学是一门很难的学科。
I like studying politics.
我喜欢学习政治。

② means和news后要用单数谓语。

e.g.: It is a quick means to get to Beijing.
这是去北京的捷径。
This is a piece of surprising news.
这是一条令人震惊的消息。

③ 货币和度量衡后要用单数谓语。

e.g.: Three hundred dollars is a large sum.

三百美元是笔大数目。

Four meters has been very high.

四米已经很高了。

（3）整体原则（以and和both ... and ... 连接的词或词组后用复数谓语）。

e.g.: You and I are teachers.

你和我都是老师。

Both his brother and his father are drivers.

他兄弟和他父亲都是司机。

（4）就近原则（以either ... or ... ，neither ... nor ... 和there be句型连接的词或词组后接谓语，要与后一个主语的数形一致）。

e.g.: Either boys or girls are doing their homework.

要么男孩正在做作业，要么女孩正在做作业。

Neither he nor you are a student.

他和你都不是学生。

There is an apple and a pear on the desk.

桌子上有一个苹果和一个梨子。

There are six pupils and a dog in the room.

房间里有六个小学生和一条狗。

（5）不管原则（以along with，as well as，together with和with连接的词或词组后接谓语，要与第一个主语的数形一致）。

e.g.: Bruce, as well as Henry, has gone to Shanghai.

布鲁斯和亨利已经去了上海。

He, with three students, attends the significant meeting.

他和三个学生参加了这次重要会议。

（6）非谓语动词做主语时，后接单数谓语。

> e.g.: Doing morning exercise is good for your health.
> 做早操有利于身体健康。
>
> To know these conditions is very useful.
> 知道这些情况很有用。

（7）集体名词的数（详见1.2中的"名词的数"）。

（8）数式做主语时，谓语既可用单数，又可用复数。

> e.g.: 1 + 1 = 2　One and one is (are) two.
>
> 　　　3×2 = 6　Three times two is (are) six.

（9）复合不定代词anybody, anyone, anything, each, everybody, everyone, everything, no one, nobody, nothing, somebody, someone, something, the other等做主语时后接单数谓语。

> e.g.: Anyone needs to have a lot of water every day.
> 任何人每天都要喝大量的水。
>
> Is everyone here?
> 每个人都在吗？
>
> The other is red.
> 另一个是红的。

小　结

本节的难点是各种主谓一致的特殊情况。大家要仔细阅读三原则（整体原则、就近原则、不管原则），这些在各种考试中出现的频率很高。

请大家回答下列问题：

（1）复形表示单数的词汇有哪些？

（2）单形表示复数的词汇有哪些？

（3）整体原则、就近原则、不管原则分别指什么？

弄清楚这几个问题将使大家对主谓一致有全面的认识，希望大家能认真回答。

12.3 it 的用法

英语中最难的两个代词分别是it和that,在本书的最后一节中,用不是很长的篇幅来说明其用法,只是将其最常见的用法罗列出来供大家参考。

1. it一般指物不指人

   e.g.: *It* is a car, *isn't it*?
   那是一辆车,不是吗?

   It has happened before.
   这事之前已经发生过了。

   但是it可以指婴儿或不明确是谁。

   e.g.: My sister has a baby. *It* is very lovely.
   我姐姐有个孩子。他很可爱。

   Who is speaking? *It's* Bruce.
   是谁?是布鲁斯。(用于打电话时)

   Who is *it*?
   是谁?(用于敲门时)

2. it起指示作用(用于回答特殊疑问句)

   e.g.: What's that? *It's* a pig.
   那是什么?那是一头猪。

   Who is *it*? *It's* Mr. Green.
   是谁?是格林先生。

3. it用于前后指代

   e.g.: I lost a book. Where is *it*?
   我丢了一本书。它在哪儿?(前指)

   The cat has already been dead. You can't forget *it*.
   那只猫已经死了。你不能忘记它。(前指)

   It is a pity that they can't come here.
   很遗憾他们不能到这儿来。(后指)

If you kill *it* — the wolf, the people won't be hurt by *it*. （前后指）

如果你杀了它——那只狼，人们就不会因为它而受伤了。

4. it指时间、距离、天气或自然现象

> e.g.: *It* is six o'clock.　　　　　　*It* is about four kilometers long.
>
> 现在六点。　　　　　　　　　　　大概有四公里长。
>
> *It* was cloudy yesterday.　　　　　*It* is going to rain.
>
> 昨天多云。　　　　　　　　　　　要下雨了。

5. it用于强调结构中，做形式主语

> e.g.: He carried the box to go upstairs.
>
> 他把箱子搬上了楼。
>
> *It* was him who carried the box to go upstairs.
>
> 是他把箱子搬上了楼。
>
> *It* was the box that he carried to go upstairs.
>
> 他把箱子搬上了楼。
>
> *It* was to go upstairs that he carried the box.
>
> 他把箱子搬上了楼。

英语中的强调句型结构为：

It + be + 强调部分 + 人（who）/物（that）+ 其他成分。

Tips 当强调谓语时，需要用助动词形式，而不是强调结构。如He did carry the box to go upstairs.

要特别注意这样一句话的强调：

> He did not go to sleep <u>until 3 o'clock last night</u>.

强调画线部分的结果是：

> It was not until 3 o'clock last night that he went to sleep.

在这里发生了形式上的否定前置，甚至要是把It was省略的话还会有倒装的情况出现，因为有否定副词在句首。

Not until 3 o'clock last night did he go to sleep.

6. it做形式主语或形式宾语

e.g.: *It* is necessary to know this point.
知道这一点很有必要。

Tips it在这里做形式主语，代替不定式to know this point。（详见"不定式"一节）

e.g.: I found that *it* is necessary to know this point.
我发现知道这一点很有必要。

Tips it在这里做形式宾语，代替不定式to know this point。（详见"不定式"一节）

试比较：I found *it* necessary to know this point.
我发现知道这一点很有必要。

Tips 在此句中，it做形式宾语，代替不定式to know this point，而后的necessary则做宾语补足语，而不是由it引导的宾语从句。

小 结

在本节中，it的用法难点包括：it用于强调结构中和it做形式主语或形式宾语。其他知识点作为一般了解即可。

请大家回答下列问题：

（1）it在什么情况下可以代替有生命的物体？
（2）it的什么结构是强调结构？
（3）it做形式主语的用法？

这几个问题都能够对答如流的话，那么对it的用法就算是完全掌握了！

语序练习

1. Not only _____ a promise, but also he kept it.
   A. he'd made   B. had he made
   C. did he make   D. he made

2. — I don't think I can finish it tonight.
   — _____. Let's stop and do it tomorrow.
   A. So can I   B. I agree
   C. Neither do I   D. Nor can I

3. _____ the teacher.
   A. There goes   B. Here comes
   C. Then follow   D. Here goes

4. He likes swimming. _____.
   A. So I do   B. Nor do I   C. Nor I do   D. So do I

5. No sooner _____ than I heard the ringing of the telephone.
   A. I had gone out   B. had I gone out
   C. did I go out   D. I did go out

6. _____ I you, I would tell her the truth.
   A. I were   B. I can   C. Were   D. Am I

7. Not until the late years of 20th century _____ WTO.
   A. China joined   B. did China join
   C. China has joined   D. has China joined

8. Seldom _____ her homework in the morning.
   A. my sister does   B. does my sister
   C. does my sister do   D. my sister do

9. Farmers had to work hard in fields, _____ in the factory.
   A. works did so   B. so do workers
   C. workers work so   D. so had workers

10. — John has been to the Great Wall.
    — _____.
    A. So he did   B. So did he
    C. So he has   D. So has he

11. Only recently _____ to deal with the environmental problem.
    A. something has done   B. has something done
    C. has something been done   D something has been done
12. Hardly _____ one problem settled _____ another appeared.
    A. have I had; than   B. have I had; when
    C. do I had; than   D. had I had; when
13. Busy _____ I am, I'll spend Sunday playing with my child.
    A. no matter how   B. because
    C. as   D. not matter how
14. — Where is Peter?
    — Oh, _____.
    A. he here comes   B. here does he come
    C. here he comes   D. here comes he
15. — I like to play football, but I don't play it every day.
    — _____.
    A. I do so   B. So I do
    C. So do I   D. So it is with me
16. _____, I would have called you.
    A. Did I know your telephone number
    B. If I knew your telephone number
    C. Had I known your telephone number
    D. If I know your telephone number
17. — It was warm yesterday.
    — _____.
    A. So it did   B. So it was
    C. So is it   D. So was it
18. He is a university student, _____.
    A. so I am   B. so am I
    C. neither am I   D. neither I am
19. I don't like philosophy, _____.
    A. either does John   B. neither does John
    C. so doesn't John   D. so does John

20. Never _____ such a terrible story.
    A. I have heard   B. have I heard
    C. did I hear   D. I heard
21. Only when you realize that how valuable water is _____ it.
    A. you can save   B. can you save
    C. that you can save   D. that can you save
22. She often goes shopping on Sunday, however, she _____ today.
    A. did it   B. does go
    C. does it   D. shopping
23. So _____ that he can't run fast.
    A. fat is he   B. fat he is   C. fat does he   D. fat he does
24. He can't solve this problem, _____.
    A. nor I can   B. nor can I   C. I either can   D. either can I
25. _____, it can't stop our advance.
    A. Wide as the river is   B. Wide the river is
    C. Wide as the river   D. As wide the river is
26. I don't enjoy this film. _____.
    A. My friend either   B. Neither my friend does
    C. My friend doesn't either   D. Either does my friend
27. Not until _____ it was totally dark.
    A. I came back home   B. came back I home
    C. come I back home   D. did I come back home
28. So little _____ about economy that I can't understand the main idea of this passage.
    A. neither I know   B. do I know
    C. I know   D. neither do I know
29. The service is so terrible in that restaurant. Never again _____ there.
    A. I'll go   B. will I go
    C. do I go   D. I do go
30. So thick _____ that you couldn't stand on.
    A. is the ice   B. the ice is
    C. the ice was   D. was the ice

31. Seldom _____ such a big diamond.
    A. will be see   B. was I looking
    C. had I seen   D. can I see
32. _____, nor does Mary.
    A. Mike planted trees today   B. Mike didn't plant trees today
    C. Mike plant trees today   D. Mike doesn't plant trees today
33. By no means _____ look down upon the disabled.
    A. we should   B. ought we to
    C. we shall   D. should we
34. No sooner _____ the airport _____ the plane flew.
    A. I had reached; than   B. I had reached; when
    C. had I reached; than   D. had I reached; when
35. The closer to the top of the mountain, _____.
    A. air is thicker   B. the thicker is air
    C. the thicker air is   D. thicker is air
36. _____ a good teacher, I would study hard in the university.
    A. Should I to become   B. Were I to become
    C. I should become   D. Had I become
37. _____, her clothes is very plain.
    A. A popular star she is   B. Popular star as she is
    C. A popular star as is she   D. Popular star as is she
38. In the old house _____ 10 years ago.
    A. an old lady live   B. had old lady lived
    C. lived an old lady   D. have old lady lived
39. Only the world works together _____ peacefully.
    A. people were able to live   B. were able to people live
    C. were people able to live   D. live people were able

主谓一致练习

1. All you have to do _____ to protect environment.
   A. have to   B. are   C. is   D. to

2. Reading novels and articles _____ what I enjoy most.
   A. is   B. has   C. have   D. are
3. Neither of us _____ to climb the mountains.
   A. dares   B. dare   C. daring   D. dare not
4. The writer and the poet _____ attending the party.
   A. will   B. is   C. are   D. would
5. The writer and poet _____ attending the party.
   A. will   B. is   C. are   D. would
6. To see _____ to believe.
   A. is   B. are   C. has   D. mean
7. The family _____ having the delicious dinner now.
   A. are   B. being   C. were   D. was
8. The police _____ patrolling on the streets at this time of yesterday.
   A. were   B. is   C. was   D. are
9. Each teacher and student _____ present.
   A. is   B. are
   C. were   D. have to be
10. Many a soldier _____ in Gulf war already.
    A. had died   B. were died
    C. is died   D. has been dead
11. The whole class _____ to the Great Wall.
    A. has been   B. have been
    C. has gone   D. have gone
12. A number of people _____ in 9.11 attack already.
    A. has died   B. is died
    C. were died   D. have been killed
13. The number of articles published on pollution _____ amazing.
    A. are   B. is   C. have been   D. be
14. Both bread and milk _____.
    A. is on sale   B. are on sale
    C. is sale   D. are sale

15. Bread and milk _____ my favorite food for breakfast.
    A. is   B. will be
    C. are   D. should be
16. A series of lectures on philosophy _____ by Professor Wang yesterday.
    A. is given   B. are given
    C. were given   D. was given
17. Not only you but also I _____ in trouble.
    A. am   B. were   C. is   D. are
18. Neither Jane nor her classmate _____ go abroad for studying.
    A. are going to   B. is going to
    C. have gone to   D. have been to
19. Either the principal or the teachers _____ the meeting.
    A. attends   B. is attending
    C. has attended   D. attend
20. Ten minutes _____ too short for me to prepare the presentation.
    A. is   B. are   C. being   D. were
21. Parents as well as Peter _____ football very much.
    A. likes to play   B. like
    C. likes   D. likes playing
22. Three sevenths of ice _____.
    A. have melted   B. melt
    C. are melting   D. has been melted
23. Jerry is one of the students who _____ England.
    A. have been to   B. has been to
    C. have gone to   D. has gone for
24. George is the only one of the students who _____ England.
    A. have been to   B. has been to
    C. have gone to   D. has gone for
25. Ten percent of the apples _____.
    A. goes bad   B. go bad
    C. turn bad   D. turned bad

26. Two thirds of the forest _____.
    A. have been destroyed   B. has been destroyed
    C. have destroyed   D. has destroyed
27. The Smiths have gone to Beijing, _____?
    A. haven't they   B. do they
    C. don't they   D. hasn't they
28. Every man and every woman _____ the right of voting.
    A. has   B. is
    C. will have   D. would have
29. Politics _____ more difficult than history.
    A. are   B. is   C. have been   D. was
30. All _____ and all _____.
    A. have left; are quiet   B. has left; is quiet
    C. have left; is quiet   D. has left; are quiet
31. To know something about the Iraq War _____ easy.
    A. is   B. are
    C. were   D. have been
32. The poor _____.
    A. have no house to live   B. has no house to live
    C. have no house to live in D. has no house to live in
33. More than one child _____ dead in the big fire last year.
    A. was   B. were   C. is   D. are
34. One or two months _____ enough for you to prepare the examination.
    A. are   B. is   C. have   D. has
35. If anyone calls me, please take _____ name and address.
    A. her   B. their   C. his   D. theirs
36. I don't think he is honest, _____?
    A. do I   B. don't I   C. isn't he   D. is he
37. The teacher, with her students, _____ discussing the environmental problem.
    A. is   B. are   C. were   D. who is

38. Not all children will get _____ presents on Christmas day.
    A. his　　　　　B. her　　　　　C. their　　　　　D. theirs
39. Where to go and how to go _____ yet.
    A. have not been decided　　　B. has not been decided
    C. have not decided　　　　　　D. has not decided
40. What you said just now _____ me.
    A. has nothing to do with　　　B. have nothing to do with
    C. had nothing to do with　　　D. has been nothing to do with
41. More than one people _____ in the accident yesterday.
    A. were killed　　　　　　　　B. killed
    C. has killed　　　　　　　　　D. was killed
42. More friends than one _____ to his party.
    A. has been invited　　　　　　B. have been invited
    C. has invited　　　　　　　　　D. have invited

it的用法练习

1. She thought _____ necessary that she should practice her spoken English.
    A. that　　　　B. him　　　　C. it　　　　D. this
2. — What's the day today?
   — _____ Monday.
    A. Its　　　　B. It's　　　　C. It was　　　　D. It were
3. _____ Peter who broke the windows.
    A. It is　　　　B. It　　　　C. It was　　　　D. It were
4. _____ of you to tell lies.
    A. It is right　　　　　　　　B. It is wrong
    C. It right　　　　　　　　　D. It wrong
5. _____ was reported that U.S. wanted to disarm Iraq.
    A. It　　　　B. He　　　　C. She　　　　D. they
6. Food and service in this restaurant are better than _____ used to be.
    A. they　　　　B. it　　　　C. we　　　　D. then

7. The color of my pen is different from _____ of yours.
   A. this   B. it   C. one   D. that
8. _____ between 1830 and 1835 that the modern newspaper was born.
   A. It is   B. It was
   C. There was   D. What was
9. _____ cost me three Pounds to buy fruit yesterday.
   A. It   B. That   C. Which   D. What
10. — What is time now?
    — _____ 7 o'clock.
    A. It   B. It is   C. It was   D. That was
11. The baby was about to cry when _____ heard noise.
    A. he   B. she   C. it   D. they
12. — Do you see the bird singing in the tree?
    — Yes, I see _____.
    A. one   B. it   C. that   D. this
13. We often take _____ for granted that the tiger should be killed.
    A. that   B. it   C. what   D. which
14. Mary speaks in a low voice; _____ is difficult to know what she is saying.
    A. that   B. it   C. so   D. she
15. Hasn't _____ been discussed if we will visit Pairs?
    A. that   B. which   C. what   D. it
16. _____ seems that she is not a university student.
    A. That   B. She   C. That's   D. It
17. — Can you tell me where my book is?
    — _____ is over there.
    A. It   B. That   C. This   D. Its
18. _____ the year of 1949 _____ People's Republic of China was founded.
    A. It was until; that   B. It was until; when
    C. It was not until; that   D. It was not until; when

19. _____ I will come back home.
    A. That is before long that
    B. When is before long that
    C. It is before long that
    D. This is before long that
20. — How long was the Long March?
    — _____ was twenty-five thousand Li.
    A. It   B. That   C. What   D. There
21. I felt _____ would be silly to tell him what had happened.
    A. that   B. it   C. its   D. it is
22. _____ was useless to forbid people to smoke cigarettes.
    A. That   B. What   C. Its   D. It
23. My watch is so old. I want to _____.
    A. change one for it
    B. change it for a new one
    C. change it with a new one
    D. change one for that
24. _____ surprised us very much that Mary should have left without a word.
    A. What   B. It   C. Its   D. That
25. — _____ that she is looking for?
    — She is looking for her English book.
    A. What is it
    B. What was it
    C. What are they
    D. What were they

附录　参考答案与解析

第一天　突破英语语法的基本知识和名词

1. C。解析：brain表示"头脑、智慧"时，常用brains，he has brains表示"他很有头脑"。

2. D。解析：advice是不可数名词，表示"建议、忠告"，"一条建议"为a piece of advice，"一些建议"为some advice。

3. D。解析：homework是不可数名词，表示"家庭作业"，用much修饰，"许多家庭作业"为much homework。

4. B。解析：traffic是不可数名词，表示"交通"，heavy traffic表示"拥挤的交通"。

5. C。解析：of + 's 的形式为双重属格，an old friend of my father's表示"我父亲的一个老朋友"，强调父亲的老朋友不止一个。

6. B。解析：shoe是集合名词，表示"鞋"，名词做定语用单数，shoe store表示"鞋店"。

7. D。解析：men teachers是复合名词，由man，woman构成的词在变复数时两部分都发生变化；由who引导的定语从句先行词是he，表语中有only修饰，所以come用单数，即comes。

8. A。解析：hour表示"小时"，是可数名词，复数的所有格为hours'，two hours' walk表示"走路两小时"。

9. C。解析：thirty-foot-high是"数词+名词单数+形容词"构成的合成形容词，中间只能用单数，表示"三十英尺高的"。

10. C。解析：man表示"男人"时，是可数名词，变复数用men，所有格表示类别用men's，做名词shoes的前置修饰语，men's shoes表示"男鞋"。

11. D。解析：life表示"生活"时，是可数名词，what a happy life是感叹小村庄的人过着如此快乐的生活。

12. A。解析：goose是可数名词，表示"鹅"，farmers raise geese表示"农民养了许多鹅"。

13. C。解析：所有格的用法表示共同拥有的关系时，'s加在最后一个词上，Ricky and Bruce's表示"新车是两人共有的"。

14. D。解析：passer-by是可数名词，表示"过路人"，复合名词变复数是主要部分发生变化，passers-by表示"许多过路人"。

15. B。解析：potato是可数名词，表示"土豆"，some修饰可数名词复数，potato是以字母"o"结尾，变复数是potatoes，bread表示"面包"，是不可数名词。

16. B。解析：Frenchman是可数名词，表示"法国人"，German是可数名词，表示"德国人"，民族词变复数时遵循"中日不变，英法变，其余复数加后面"的原则，因此，Frenchman变成Frenchmen，German变成Germans。

17. A。解析：sheep表示"羊"时，其复数也用sheep，表示种类时用many sheeps，grass表示"草"时是不可数名词。

18. C。解析：children's是名词所有格表示类别，做名词books的前置修饰语，children's books表示"儿童图书"。

19. A。解析：manner表示"礼貌"时，常用manners，it is bad manners to do something表示"做某事是坏习惯"。

20. B。解析：congratulation表示"祝贺"时，常用congratulations，是一种固定的祝贺语，congratulations to sb. on sth. 表示"向某人祝贺……"。

21. C。解析：women doctors是复合名词，由man，woman构成的词在变复数时两部分都发生变化；由who引导的定语从句先行词是doctors，表语中没有only修饰，所以come不变单数。

22. D。解析：stomach表示"胃"，虽然以"ch"结尾，但是stomach的"ch"读/k/不读/ch/，所以变复数时加s。

23. A。解析：chemistry表示"化学"，chemistry teacher表示"教化学的老师"，而chemical teacher表示"具有化学性质的老师"，chemistry teacher是名词修饰名词，表示名词的属性或性质。

24. B。解析：society表示"社会"，是抽象名词，前面不加the，表示团体时加the，harm to society表示"对社会有害"。

25. B。解析：a表示"某（一）个/位"，用在姓氏前表示不认识的人，a Mr. Smith表示"一位叫史密斯的先生"。

26. B。解析：else做形容词，表示"其他的"时，和不定代词在一起表示所有格时用anyone else's，表示"其他任何人的"。

27. D。解析：moment是可数名词，a moment表示"片刻"，用所有格时加's，a moment's rest表示"片刻休息"。

28. D。解析：cattle是表示复数意义的集体名词，谓语动词用are，根据"at that time"可知此题用过去进行时。

29. D。解析：hour是可数名词，超过一就要用复数，在表示时间的名词上加所有格，one and a half hours' ride表示"一个半小时的车程"。

30. D。解析：tooth是可数名词，变为复数是teeth，Tom的牙不止一颗，应用teeth，Tom's teeth表示"汤姆的牙"。

31. B。解析：pain表示"疼痛感"，是可数名词，用a pain表示"一处疼痛"。

32. C。解析：the East表示"东方国家、亚洲国家"，the east表示"东方"，East表示"东部，东边"。

33. C。解析：homework是不可数名词，修饰homework的much变为比较级用more，any other加可数名词单数表示"除……以外的人或物"，本题中表示"露西和班里除她以外的学生比"。

34. D。解析：politics表示"政治学"这一学科时，谓语动词只能用单数。

35. B。解析：数字后加连接符号，形成复合短语，词性为形容词，所以不能加s，ten-dollar表示"十美元的"。

36. A。解析：money表示"钱"时是不可数名词，many和a number of修饰可数名词，a great deal of修饰不可数名词，a plenty of这个词组不存在。

37. A。解析：cloth表示"布料"时，是不可数名词，表示用作某种特殊用途的布（如：桌布、台布）时，是可数名词；clothes和clothing均可表示衣服，但clothes是没有单数形式的复数名词；clothing是不可数名词。this piece of cloth表示"这块布料"。

38. B。解析：a fool of a girl相当于a fool-like girl，表示"像傻瓜一样的女孩"，是转移修辞格的特殊形式。

39. B。解析：hair表示"头发"，用作不可数名词时，表示整体地指一个人的头发；用作可数名词，表示几根头发时需要加s。a few表示"少许、一点点"，可修饰可数名词，a few gray hairs切合题意，表示"有些许白发"。

40. C。解析：the是定冠词，用以特指人或物，本题中特指"我上个月拜访的那个学校"，school是定语从句的先行词，在定语从句中

做宾语，因此关系代词that可以省略，本句陈述句语序为This is the school I visited last month。

第二天　突破英语的代词和冠词

代词练习

1. D。解析：money是不可数名词，a large number of相当于many，只能修饰可数名词，a great deal of 可以修饰不可数名词，a great deal of money表示"一大笔钱"。

2. C。解析：选C。one...the other 指的是两者之间一个和另一个；one...another一般指的是三者或三者以上的另一个（第三个使用still another）；this和that是指示代词，用于近指和远指。

3. A。解析：many和few都修饰可数名词，little修饰不可数名词，在这里表示"做了很少的事来帮助他们"。

4. D。解析：当两个或两个以上的人称代词并列使用时，单数人称顺序为"二三一"，复数人称顺序"一二三"。当承认错误或承担责任时，常把I放在前面，即"一二三"。I, you and Jim made a mistake表示"你，我和吉姆犯了个错误"。

5. D。解析：both一般与and连用，表示"两者都"，谓语动词用复数，either表示"两者其中一个"，谓语动词用单数，either of lectures表示"两个演讲中的一个"。

6. D。解析：one...the other表示"一个……另一个"，some...the others表示"一些，另一

些",other是一个形容词,the other two表示"另外两个儿子"。

7. A。解析:many和much表示"许多",little表示"几乎没有",a little表示"一些",little left表示"剩下的墨水几乎没有了"。

8. C。解析:both指的是"两者都",neither指的是"两者都不",either指的是"两个中其中一个",all指的是全都(三者或三者以上),either在这里表示"苹果和梨哪个都行"。

9. A。解析:of是介词,后面接代词的宾格,us boys是同位语,a few of us boys表示"我们男孩中的一些"。

10. B。解析:one...the other表示"一个……另一个",是固定搭配。

11. A。解析:not all of 为部分否定,表示"不是所有的都"。

12. D。解析:too many接可数名词复数,表示"太多";much too常用作副词,后接副词、形容词或动词;too much常用作副词或代词,修饰不可数名词,too much food表示"太多食物了"。

13. B。解析:all和each都可以单独使用,也可以接of短语;every既不能单独使用,又不能接of短语;each用于两者或两者以上强调"每个",表示逐个地考虑总体,all是整体地考虑总体,all of the students表示"班级里的所有同学"。

14. D。解析:either后面接of表示"两个中的另一个";all后面接of表示"所有",放在这

个句子中不通顺;everyone后不可以接of;every one后面接of在句中表示"教室中的每一个人都吃饱了"。

15. A。解析:none既可以指人,又可以指物;no one只能指人,不能指物;nothing只能指物,不能指人;nobody只能指人,不能指物;none在句中表示"一张电影票也没买"。

16. D。解析:this和that是指示代词,分别表示近指"这个"和远指"那个";it指代go swimming with you这件事,is it OK with you表示询问对方意见。

17. C。解析:other是特指;another是泛指;another+基数词+名词复数=基数词+more+名词复数,表示"另外/多加",two more people表示"再来两个人"。

18. C。解析:none可以指人或物;nothing只能指物而不能指人;用who问人称,只能用nobody回答,nobody表示"一个人也没有"。

19. B。解析:做who是"谁"的意思,做主语和表语;whom是"谁"的意思,做宾语;whose是"谁的"意思,做定语,whose the book is表示"这本书是谁的"。

20. D。解析:此题考查定语从句关系代词的用法,who用于指代人;what不能作为关系代词;in which用于指代地点;that用于指代人或物,做主语或宾语。

21. A。解析:as引导的非限定性定语从句表示积极意义,先行词是整个主句,与主句有顺理

成章的关系，as had been expected表示"就像所期待的那样"。

22. C。解析：定语从句中先行词被序数词或形容词最高级修饰时，关系代词只用that，that has been praised by the government表示"被政府嘉奖"。

23. C。解析：定语从句中先行词被序数词或形容词最高级修饰时，关系代词只用that，且先行词是countries，是复数。

24. D。解析：many more后加可数名词复数；much more后加不可数名词，many more interesting novels than I have表示"她所拥有的好看的小说比我的多"。

25. D。解析：a few和few修饰可数名词；a little和little修饰不可数名词。little含否定意思，表示几乎没有；a little表示有一些，only a little表示"只会一点点"。

26. D。解析：'s是属格，who else's表示"字典属于其他哪个人的"。

27. A。解析：any other表示"其他任何一个"，指同一范围内一个与其他剩余的比较，但是上海不属于非洲；any表示"任何一个"，any city in Africa表示"非洲的任何一个城市"。

28. D。解析：any other表示"其他任何一个"，指同一范围内一个与其他剩余的比较，上海属于中国的一个城市。

29. A。解析：定语从句中先行词是不定代词或被不定代词修饰时只用that，anything that you said表示"你所说的一切"。

30. C。解析：As is known to all表示"众所周知的是"，是固定搭配。

31. D。解析：why在定语从句中做原因状语，the reason why表示"某事的原因是……"。

32. D。解析：some用于疑问句，表示一种客气的请求，would you like some表示"你想要什么吗"。

33. D。解析：every other day表示"每隔一天"，没有every other days这个短语；every few days表示"每隔几天"。

34. C。解析：its既是名词性物主代词，又是形容词性物主代词，表示"它的"，its指代中国。

35. A。解析：everyone表示"每个人"，谓语动词用单数，这句表示"大家都走了，不是吗"。

36. B。解析：which在非限定性定语从句中做宾语，指代前面的homework。

37. A。解析：that是指示代词，指代前面提到的population，that of America表示"美国的人口"。

38. C。解析：every和none都是指至少三者或者三个以上，both强调两个人或物，因此谓语动词用复数，neither of the side has trees表示"路两旁都没有树"。

39. D。解析：a pair of trousers表示"一条裤子"。

40. C。解析：此题两句之间有逗号，且没有连词，所以可以判断为主从复合句，which在定语从句中做主语，both of which代指前面的two watches，表示"两块手表都"。

41. D。解析：time表示"次数"时是可数名词，three times one/a day表示"一/每天三次"。

42. D。解析：此题两句之间有逗号，且有连词连接，所以可以判断为并列句，题意为"虽然我有很多朋友，但困难时没有一个人帮我"。

43. A。解析：himself是反身代词，表示"他自己"，his own表示"他自己的"。

44. B。解析：any用在肯定句中表示"任何"，any sort of job表示"随便什么工作都行"。

45. D。解析：it是指示代词，must be表示一种可能性，因为敲门的人不一定是男还是女。

46. D。解析：something用于疑问句表示一种客气的请求，anything表示"任何东西"。

47. C。解析：一般疑问句用anything，不定代词的修饰成分要放在不定代词后面，anything important表示"重要的事"。

48. C。解析：everyone是复合不定代词，在形式上是单数，在意思上既可以表示单数，也可以表示复数，everyone took off their hats表示"大家都脱帽"。

49. C。解析：none和all都表示全部，前者是否定，后者是肯定；both和neither都表示两者，前者是肯定，后者是否定，前者谓语动词用复数，后者谓语动词用单数，表示"这两个都不"。

50. C。解析：the other指的是"另一个"，一般指的是两者当中的另一个；another指的是"另一个"，一般指三者或三者以上的另一个，another cake表示"再来一个块糕"。

51. B。解析：plenty of表示"大量、许多"，后面接可数名词复数，plenty of apples表示"许多苹果"；a plenty of和lot of这两个短语都不存在；much表示"大量、许多"，后面接不可数名词复数。

52. B。解析：mine是名词性物主代词，表示"我的"，题中的mine指代"我的裙子"。

53. C。解析：it指代前面提到的一模一样的东西；one指代前面提到的可数名词的单数；that通常指代抽象名词或是句子；this用作代词，可用以指叙述中的人或事物，即指前面提到过的人或事物或下文提及的事物；此题中的one指代break。

54. B。解析：第一个it是形式宾语，真正的宾语是to后面的不定式；第二个it是固定用法，take it for granted that表示"想当然地……"；it is very difficult to do中的it是形式主语，真正的主语是to learn a foreign language。

55. C。解析：which在非限定性定语从句中做主语，指代前面整个句子。

56. B。解析：both表示"两者都"；any表示"任何的"；all表示"所有的"，不符合题意；most of the houses表示"这些房子中的大部分"。

57. A。解析：整句是由that引导的主语从句，从句做主语时，谓语动词用单数。

冠词练习

1. A。解析：第一个定冠词the表示特指；第二个metal and wood前不用冠词，表示类指。

2. A。解析：man前面不使用冠词，或称为零冠词表示"人类"。

3. A。解析：序数词前一般使用定冠词the，但是在second前使用不定冠词在本句中表示"两次获得"。

4. A。解析：the是定冠词，用于特指，the right girl we are waiting for表示"我们等的那个女孩"。

5. B。解析：定冠词the用于复数名词前表示一类人，the Smiths表示"史密斯一家人"，是集体名词，谓语动词用复数。

6. D。解析：a是不定冠词，用于单数名词前表示"一个"，a satellite表示"一颗卫星"；send into space表示"送上太空"，space是物质名词，前面不加冠词。

7. C。解析：不定冠词a用于姓氏前，表示讲话者不认识这位格林先生，a Mr. Green表示"一位名叫格林的先生"。

8. A。解析：live in peace表示"和平相处"，是固定搭配。

9. B。解析：对人口提问，用large，不用many，have/has a population of表示"人口有……"，此题应选B。

10. B。解析：sell by weight表示"按/论重量卖"；sell by the dozen表示"按打卖"。

11. C。解析：这是由as引导的让步状语从句，正确语序是As he is a child，让步状语从句中必须将表语提前，并且当句首表语是名词时不加任何冠词，Child as he is表示"尽管他是一个孩子"。

12. B。解析：a waste of 是固定搭配，表示"浪费……"，industry是物质名词，前面不用冠词。

13. D。解析：fun是抽象名词，前面不加冠词，what fun it is to do表示"做某事多有趣啊"。

14. B。解析：trade是抽象名词，一般不用冠词。

15. A。解析：the same as表示"和……一样"，是固定搭配，a pen the same as mine表示"和我有一样的钢笔"。

16. C。解析：fire前使用不定冠词，表示"一场火，一堆火"；a fire break out表示"发生一场火灾"；put out the fire特指"扑灭那场火灾"。

17. B。解析：in the habit of表示"有着……习惯"；place表示"地方"，没有特指，不用代词，in the habit of smoking in places表示"有到处抽烟的习惯"。

18. D。解析：what is the matter with sb. 是固定搭配，表示询问某人状况；pain是可数名词，have a pain in+身体部位，表示"……疼"。

19. B。解析：pay attention to the main idea是固定搭配，表示"注意中心思想"；一本英文小

说不是特指，English是元音音素开头，因此用不定冠词an，an English novel表示"一本英文小说"。

20. A。解析：中国传统节日前采用定冠词用法，the Middle Autumn表示"中秋节"。这是一个传统节日，是泛指，不是特指，因此后一个空填不定冠词a。

21. D。解析：tea和milk都是不可数名词，且是物质名词，因此不用冠词。

22. A。解析：乐器前面用定冠词the，球类前面不用冠词，play the piano表示"演奏钢琴"，play football表示"踢足球"。

23. D。解析：两个都不是特指，a hat表示"一顶帽子"，a red one表示"一顶红色的帽子"。

24. C。解析：职务、职位和头衔前采用零冠词用法，the man who is talking with president表示"正在和总统讲话的那个男人"，其中the man是特指"那个男人"。

25. B。解析：in the washroom是固定搭配，表示"在洗手间"；in bed表示"卧床"；in the bed表示"在床上躺着"。

26. D。解析：information是不可数名词，前面不用冠词；what用于对名词表示感叹，what bad information I have got表示"我得到的消息多坏啊"。

27. D。解析：look at sb. in the eye表示"直视/正视某人"。

28. B。解析：the next day表示的是参考当时的时间的第二天，next day就表示参考现在的时间的第二天。

29. A。解析：work in the field表示"在田地里干活"，日月星辰前面用定冠词the。

30. B。解析：形容词最高级前面用定冠词the，the tallest boy表示"最高的男孩"。

31. B。解析：the+过去分词表示"一类人"，the injured表示"受伤的人"，后面接复数形式；hospital没有特指哪家医院，在这里表示"送去医院治疗"。

32. C。解析：Leifeng是专有名词，前面若加不定冠词，表示"像这样的一类人"，这是专有名词具体化的使用。

33. C。解析：church表示"教堂"，教堂和星期前采用零冠词用法，go to church on Sundays表示"在星期天去教堂做礼拜"。

34. A。解析：the Pacific Ocean是世界上独一无二的，前面用the；形容词最高级前面用the修饰。

35. D。解析：means表示"方法、手段"，a quick means表示"一种快速的方法"，means虽然是复形名词，但是表示单数概念；交通工具前不加冠词，by plane表示"坐飞机"。

36. A。解析：lunch表示"午餐"，前面不加冠词，一日三餐前不用冠词，若三餐前有形容词修饰时需加冠词，a wonderful supper表示"一顿丰盛的晚餐"。

37. A。解析：in front of表示在一个整体的前面，in the front of表示在一个整体的前排部分，in front of our classroom表示"在我们教室前"。

38. A。解析：at night表示"在夜间"，是固定搭配。

39. C。解析：have a holiday表示"去度假"，go on business表示"出差"。

40. A。解析：the second是序数词前用the，表示"第二名"；学科前不用冠词，in physics examinations表示"在物理考试中"。

第三天 突破英语的数词、形容词和副词

数词练习

1. D。解析：how soon是对频率提问，every+基数词（大于或等于2）+复数名词表示"每隔……"，every five minutes表示"每隔五分钟"。

2. C。解析：倍数+as+形容词/副词原级+as表示"……是……的几倍"，twice his age表示"David兄弟的年龄是David的两倍"。

3. C。解析：two-head表示"双头的"，two-head baby表示"双头的婴儿"，数词+量词形成定语时需要在中间加连字符，且量词需要用单数。

4. B。解析：two修饰的是名词egg，dozen前有具体数字修饰时不加s，也不后接介词of，two dozen eggs表示"两打鸡蛋"。

5. B。解析：thousands of表示"成千的"，thousand前无具体数字时后面必须与of连用，tens是数词表达约数，一般与of连用，tens of thousands of表示"成千上万的"。

6. A。解析：thousand表示"千"，前面有具体数字时，后不与of连用，也不加s，five thousand表示"五千"。

7. C。解析：in one's+基数词复数，表示"在某人……岁时"，in his twenties表示"在他二十多岁的时候"。

8. C。解析：6700 meters long表示"6700米长"，meter前有具体数字时要用复数形式。

9. A。解析：page+基数词=the+序数词+page，表示"……页"，page ten表示"第十页"。

10. C。解析：in the 1980's表示"20世纪80年代"。

11. C。解析：在分数表达法中，当分子基数词大于一时，分母序数词用复数，three sevenths表示"3/7"。

12. B。解析：score表示"二十"，three score and ten people表示"七十人"，scores of表示不确切的数量，表示"大量的"。

13. B。解析：hundred表示"百"，基数词+hundred表示"……百"，hundred后不加s。

14. D。解析：first of all表示"首先"，是固定搭配。

15. A。解析：ten years表示"十年"，是一个时间段，谓语动词用单数，ten years is a long time 表示"十年很长"。

16. A。解析：A+be+基数词+times+as+形容词/副词原级+as+B表示"A是B的n倍"，five times as many as表示"A是B的5倍"或"A比B大4倍"。

17. B。解析：百分数+of+ the total表示"是总数的百分之几"，10% of the total表示"是总额的百分之十"。

18. D。解析：超过一小时，hour后加s，one and a half hours表示"一个半小时"。

19. C。解析：a hundred-dollar表示"面值一百美元"，同第三道题的原理。

形容词和副词练习

1. D。解析：picnic表示"野餐"，是名词，前面用形容词修饰，wonderful picnic表示"美妙的野餐"。

2. B。解析：good是形容词，well是副词，as good as 和as well as都表示"和……一样好"，但performance是名词，表示"表演"，需要用形容词修饰。

3. C。解析：very interesting表示"很有意思"，做表语；much是副词，用于形容词比较级前；quite是副词，用于形容词原级前。

4. C。解析：all是形容词，表示"所有的"，当有多个形容词修饰名词时，遵循"数词/冠词+描绘性形容词、大小、形状、新旧、颜色、国别、材料和中心词"的顺序，all the poor little babies表示"所有可怜的小孩"。

5. A。解析：当有多个形容词修饰名词时，遵循"描绘性形容词、大小、形状、新旧、颜色、国别、材料和中心词"的顺序，two-storied big red 表示"两层的大红房子"。

6. D。解析："the+形容词比较级，the+形容词比较级"表示"越……越……"，the easier it is to look after it表示"越容易照看"。

7. C。解析：should have done本应该（实际没有），是虚拟语气，smart trick表示"精妙的戏法"。

8. B。解析：other than表示"除了……"，nothing you can do other than wait表示"只能等了"。

9. A。解析：such为形容词，一般修饰名词或代词，后接的中心词为名词或代词；so为副词，修饰形容词、副词或动词，后接的中心词为形容词、副词或动词，两者都可表示程度，表示"如此/那么"，so small a car that 表示"车实在太小了"。

10. A。解析：some other time表示"改天吧、下次吧"。

11. D。解析：当形容词修饰复合不定代词时，要放在它后面，something interesting表示"有趣的事"。

12. C。解析：exactly是副词，修饰形容词或副词；look为系动词，后接形容词做表语，look exactly alike表示"看起来完全一样"。

13. A。解析：两个名词相比较时用形容词比较级，which do you like better表示"你更喜欢哪个"。

14. B。解析：三者或三者以上比较，用形容词或副词最高级，who do like best表示"你最喜欢哪个"。

15. C。解析：fall asleep表示"睡着了"，是固定搭配。

16. B。解析：three-hundred-year-old做定语，用连字符连接时，每个单词都不加s，是形容词，表示"三百岁的"。

17. B。解析：some time表示"一段时间"；sometimes表示"常常"，用于一般现在时或是一般过去时；some times表示"几次"；sometime作为副词词组，表示"某个时候"。

18. A。解析：place表示"地方"，是可数名词；what用于对名词的感叹，what a lively place表示"这个多么有趣的地方啊"。

19. B。解析：speak是动词，后面用副词，speak highly of sb. 表示"夸奖某人"，high和highly都可以作为副词，但是前者一般修饰具体含义的单词，而后者修饰抽象含义的单词。

20. D。解析：very much做程度副词时一般位于被修饰词之后；so much做程度副词时一般位于被修饰词之后；too much是形容词短语，一般位于被修饰的不可数名词之前；much too是副词短语，一般位于被修饰的形容词或副词词之前。

21. D。解析：A+be+倍数+as+名词+as+B表示"A是B的几倍"。

22. D。解析：still是形容词，表示"不动的，静止的"；quite是形容词，表示"安静"，一般指声音；silent是形容词，表示"安静"，一般指环境；calm是形容词，表示"平静"。

23. A。解析：some用于一般疑问句表示客气地询问与请求（希望得到肯定回答），may I have some coffee表示"我能喝点咖啡吗"。

24. A。解析：多个形容词修饰名词时，遵循"数词/冠词+描绘性形容词、大小、形状、新旧、颜色、国别、材料和中心词"的顺序，the two beautiful young girls表示"那两个年轻漂亮的女孩"。

25. C。解析：be worthy of doing就是worth doing，表示"值得做某事"。

26. A。解析：handwriting是不可数名词，表示"字迹、笔迹"，谓语动词用单数，as good as表示"和……一样好"，否定时用not so (as) good as。

27. B。解析：两者比较用形容词的比较级，但是只有两者之间的范围时又是最高级，所以在比较级前使用定冠词the，表示这两个之中的最高级，实际上是"一个比另一个……"，the cleverer of my two sisters表示"两姐妹中最聪明的那个"，也就是"一个比另一个聪明"。

28. A。解析：much是副词，修饰late，he went to school much late yesterday表示"他昨天去学校很晚"。

29. C。解析：next to the door做后置定语修饰the family，表示"挨着门的那户人"。

30. A。解析：mostly表示"大多数"；most表示"最多或最……"，My friends are mostly teachers表示"我的朋友大部分都是老师"。

31. C。解析：poet表示"诗人"，是可数名词；alive表示"活着的"，做表语；one of+ the+形容词最高级+可数名词复数，表示"最……

之一",one of the greatest poets who are still alive表示"在世的最伟大的诗人之一"。

32. A。解析：最高级前可以用序数词，the second longest river 表示"第二长的河流"。

33. B。解析：pleasing和pleased表示"令人高兴的"和"感到高兴的"，前者形容物，后者形容人，we were rather pleased表示"我们相当高兴"。

34. B。解析：perfect是形容词，表示"完美的"，he is perfect表示"他是完美的"。

35. C。解析：successful表示"成功的"，be动词后接形容词，success是名词，successfully是副词，succeed是动词，you'll be successful表示"你将来会成功的"。

36. D。解析：beautiful表示"美丽的、美好的"，是形容词，make the earth more beautiful表示"让地球更美好"，make后面接名词再接形容词。

37. D。解析：further是形容词，在程度上表示"进一步的、更深一层的"；farther表示距离上或时间上的"更远的"。further information表示"更详尽的信息"。

38. B。解析：handsome是形容词，表示"英俊的"，beautiful是形容词，表示"美丽的"，handsome boy表示"英俊的男孩"，beautiful girl表示"漂亮的女孩"。

39. D。解析：boring和bored都是形容词，bored表示"使人感到厌烦的"，boring表示"事物本身无趣的"，boring lecture表示"无趣的讲座"，make students bored表示"使学生感到无聊"。

40. C。解析：as soon as possible相当于as soon as you can表示"尽快地"。

41. C。解析：serious是形容词，表示"认真的"。are you serious表示"你是当真的吗"。

42. D。解析：be quite able to do sth. 表示"做某事毫无问题"，是固定搭配。

43. B。解析：fun是不可数名词，前面不用冠词；so...that...表示"太……以至于……"；Peter是人，用such修饰，Peter is such fun 表示"彼得是一个特别幽默的人"。

44. D。解析：possible是形容词，probably是副词，possible for sth. 表示"……是有可能的"，the only boy possible for the monitor position表示"适合班长这个职位的唯一男孩"。

45. A。解析：far away 用作表语或状语时，away可以省去，因此，far away表示far；far away from表示far from， far（away）后不接宾语；far（away）from后一定要接宾语，three hundred meters away from here表示"离这有300米远"，far后面一般不接数字。

46. B。解析：straight是形容词，表示"直的"；go straight表示"一直走"，在这里straight是副词；left是形容词，表示方向"左"，前不加冠词。Go straight and turn left at the first turning表示"直走，第一个路口左转"。

47. C。解析：present用作形容词，表示"出席的"，用在students后，做后置定语，用在

situation前，表示"目前的状况"。

48. A。解析：still可以用作副词，表示"仍然"，可以用来修饰动词，students are still doing their homework表示"学生仍然在做作业"。

49. D。解析：形容词和副词的比较级前面可以用much来形容，much faster than表示"比……快多了"。

50. C。解析：四个选项均为副词，都表示"相当"，但是pretty和fairly一般用在褒义的形容词前，而rather一般用于贬义的形容词前。

51. C。解析：fairly表示对事物的赞赏，含褒义，修饰表示"好"的形容词或副词，而rather往往表示对事物的不赞赏，有令人不悦之感，修饰表示"不好"的形容词或副词，fairly well表示"很好"，rather badly表示"很糟糕"。

52. A。解析：enough只能放在形容词后，表示"足够……"，he is old enough to go to school by himself表示"他年龄足够大，可以自己上学了"。

53. C。解析：be good at和do well in表示"很擅长……"，都是固定搭配。

54. B。解析：exciting是形容词，表示"令人兴奋的"，主语一般用物，excited的主语一般用人。very exciting在句中表示"大学生活非常令人兴奋"。

55. B。解析：can not be too careful表示"再小心也不为过"。

56. A。解析：strange是形容词，表示"陌生的"，

the town was so strange表示"这个镇子好陌生"。

57. C。解析：anywhere是副词，表示"任何地方、无论何处"，can't put this big television anywhere表示"这个大电视机哪也放不了"。

58. D。解析：much是副词，用在形容词比较级前，look much younger 表示"看起来年轻了"。

59. B。解析：much是副词，用在形容词比较级前，much fatter than me表示"比我胖多了"。

60. A。解析：alone可作为形容词，也可作为副词，表示"单独、独自"，只能做表语，不能做定语，没有感情色彩，只表示客观状态；lonely是形容词，表示"孤独、孤寂"，一般指人，带有浓厚的主观色彩。live alone表示"独自居住"，feel lonely表示"感到孤独"。

61. B。解析：much表示"很"，既可以做形容词，也可做副词；pretty表示"十分、相当"，是副词，但语气上更重，a pretty tall building表示"一座相当高的建筑物"。

62. A。解析：lively可以做形容词，表示"活泼的"，也可以做副词，表示"轻快地"；alive和living都表示"活着的"，living主要指在某个时候是活着的，而alive指本来有死的可能，但仍活着的。was the dog alive or dead表示"这只狗是活着还是死了"。

63. B。解析：badly是副词，可以用来修饰动

词，表示"严重地"；dark是形容词，表示"漆黑的"。hurt badly in a dark night表示"在一个漆黑的夜里伤得很严重"。

64. C。解析：money是不可数名词，用little的比较级less修饰；people是可数名词，用few的比较级fewer修饰。with less money and fewer people表示"用更少的钱和更少的人"。

65. D。解析：priceless表示"无价的、天价的"，valuable表示"贵重的、值钱的在"，valueless表示"无价值的、没有用处的"，it is priceless表示"这幅画是无价的"。

66. D。解析：be ashamed of...表示"对……感到羞愧"，主语应该用人；shameful是形容词，表示"令人羞愧的"，be ashamed of his shameful behavior表示"对他令人羞愧的行为感到羞愧"。

67. A。解析：many表示"许多的"，修饰可数名词复数，A+is+倍数+as+many/much+as+B表示"A是B的几倍"，twice as many as表示"……是……的两倍"。

68. B。解析：calm是形容词，表示"冷静的"。

69. D。解析：heavily是副词，rain heavily表示"雨下得很大"；almost 可用于 any 以及 no, none, nobody, nothing, never 等否定词之前，但 nearly 一般不用在这些词汇之前，almost no one表示"几乎没人"。

70. D。解析：sure和certain的根本区别在于，sure的主语可以用人，不可以用物或是it，但是certain的主语可以用人、用物和it，it is certain that表示"毫无疑问的……"。

71. A。解析：never/not+a/an+形容词比较级，相当于最高级，I have never spent a more worrying day表示最高级，表示"这是我度过的最担忧的一天"。

72. C。解析：golden是形容词，表示"金色的"；gold是形容词，表示"金子做的"；the golden sun表示"金色的太阳"。

73. C。解析：to be honest是口语化的表达，用于说话的人想对某人讲自己的真实想法，表示"老实讲……"。

74. D。解析：never better是否定词+比较级的结构，此结构表示最高级。

75. B。解析：any time表示"任何时间"，any time you like表示"你方便什么时间都行"。

76. D。解析：either表示"也"，用于否定句，I didn't go, either表示"我也没去"。

77. D。解析：English-spoken表示"英语口语的"，English-speaking country表示"讲英语的国家"。

78. D。解析：be proud of表示"以……为骄傲"，be afraid of表示"害怕……"，be popular with表示"在……流行"，be content with 表示"对……满意"。

79. D。解析：likely是在所有表示"可能的"词中唯一一个可以用人做主语的，be likely to do sth. 表示"有可能做某事"；possible的主语一般用物或是it。

80. D。解析：older和elder都old的比较级，older是指年龄上的，而elder是指年长的、资格老、辈分上的，elder后面不能加than，all older than me表示"所有人都比我岁数大"，the eldest表示"最年长的"。

第四天　突破英语的动词及其两种时态

1. D。解析：look sth. up in the dictionary表示"在字典里查……"，是固定搭配。

2. C。解析：drive sb. mad表示"把某人逼疯"，是固定搭配。

3. C。解析：turn up表示"（声音）调高"，turn down表示"（声音）调低"，turn on表示"打开"，turn off表示"关闭"。

4. D。解析：hold表示"容纳"；manage表示"能解决、能应付"，一般用manage to do表示"成功地做到了"。this hall can hold 1000 people表示"这个大堂能容纳1000人"。

5. C。解析：recognize表示"识别、承认"；search表示"搜查"，search for表示"寻找"；learn表示"学习"；study表示"研究"，study the tiger表示"研究老虎"。

6. D。解析：wash out 表示"淘汰、洗净内部"；wash off表示"清除掉"；wash up表示"洗餐具"；wash away表示"冲走"，washed away by the flood表示"被洪水冲走"。

7. B。解析：clothes后谓语动词一般用复数，take主语是物，use和spend主语是人，the clothes took me one thousand Yuan表示"这件衣服花费我一千元"。

8. C。解析：learn by heart表示"用心学"，know by heart这个短语不存在，think of表示"想到"，keep in mind表示"记住"。

9. D。解析：spend表示"花费"，save表示"节省、保存"，share表示"分享"，spare表示"空出（时间/空间）"。had not a minute to spare表示"一分钟空闲都没有"。

10. D。解析：keep up表示"保持、跟上"，lay up表示"储存、储蓄"，look up表示"查找"，pick up表示"举起、拾起"。help me pick up my book表示"帮我捡起书"。

11. D。解析：think表示"想、思考"；say表示"说"；hope后不能直接跟名词做宾语，可跟for +名词，表示可实现的"希望"；wish后也可以跟for +名词，但表示难实现的"愿望"，wish可以接双宾语，wish me to become a teacher表示"希望我做一名老师"。

12. A。解析：depend on表示"依赖、依靠"，carry on表示"继续、持续"，keep on表示"继续（持续不断做某事）"，go on表示"进行、继续"。depend on the sun表示"靠太阳赖以生存"。

13. B。解析：get down to do和get down to doing都表示"开始做某事"，get down to doing表示开始"认真做某事"，get used to doing表示"习惯于做某事"，look forward to doing表示"希望做某事"。get down to preparing the dinner表示"开始专心为晚餐做准备"。

14. A。解析：borrow和lend都表示"借"，borrow是"借进"，lend是"借出"。

15. C。解析：look for和search for都表示"寻找"，look for强调的是找的动作和过程，search for强调"竭力搜查"；find表示"找到"，强调找的结果，其宾语往往是某个丢失的东西或人；find out着重表示通过理解、分析、思考、询问等"查明"一件事情，其后的宾语常常是某个情况、事实，find out what is right before making a decision表示"在下决定前寻找出真相"。

16. D。解析：get along with表示"和……相处"，cut down表示"削减、砍倒"，cut up表示"切碎、谴责、扮小丑"，get in表示"收割、到达、当选、插话"，the farmers get in rice表示"农民收割大米"。

17. D。解析：have sb. do sth.和let sb. do sth. 都表示"让某人做某事"，allow sb. to do sth. 表示"允许某人做某事"。allow us to use his recorder表示"允许我们用他的录音机"。

18. A。解析：bring in表示"带来、提出"，make up表示"编造（故事）"，take in表示"吸收、领会、欺骗、接待"，give in表示"屈服、投降"。bring in some new points表示"提出一些新想法"。

19. B。解析：try to do sth. 表示"尝试做某事"，manage to do sth. 表示"成功做成某事"，he tried to make it表示"他很努力地尝试去做"。

20. B。解析：beat是动词，表示"（心脏）跳动"，强调动作的连续和反复；strike表示"敲打、击打"；hit表示"撞击。my heart would beat fast表示"我的心脏快速跳动"。

21. C。解析：make up表示"编造（故事）"，be made of表示看得出的"由……组成"（物理变化），be made from表示看不出的"由……组成"（化学变化），be made into表示"被制成为……"，made of iron表示"由铁制成的"。

22. D。解析：waste表示"浪费"；spend表示"花费"；cost主语用物，表示"花费"；afford表示"承受"，couldn't afford表示"承受不了……"。

23. D。解析：put on表示"穿上"，put up表示"举起、提供、建造、推荐"，put off表示"推迟"，put out表示"放出、生产、消除、打扰、扑灭（火）"。put out the fire表示"灭火"。

24. B。解析：talk表示"谈论"，一般后面+to/with+sb.；tell表示"告诉、挑出（两者不同）"；speak表示"讲（一种语言）"；say表示"说（具体内容）"，其后一般加that从句。tell the difference表示"指出两者的不同"。

25. D。解析：set about表示"散布（谣言）"，set off表示"动身、出发、爆炸"，set up表示"开办、建立"，set out表示"动身、开始、装饰"。set out to carry out your plan表示"开始执行你的计划"。

26. C。解析：prepare是动词，prepare表示"准

备、预备（有能力而且愿意）"，后面接宾语为准备的对象；prepare for是"为……而准备"，后接宾语，并不是准备的对象，而是目的。preparing the big meal表示"正在准备大餐"。

27. C。解析：cover是动词，与page连用表示"看了多少页书"。

28. B。解析：look sth. up in the dictionary表示"查字典"，是固定搭配。

29. C。解析：add是及物动词，表示"增、增加"；add to表示"把……加到……"；add up表示"加起来，总计"；add up to表示"总计达、总的来说"。add to my taste表示"提高我的品位"。

30. A。解析：break out表示"（战争）爆发、突然发生"，break up表示"结束、（使）破碎、（使）散开"，break in表示"打断、闯入、开始（工作）"，break表示"打破"。World War One broke out in 1914表示"第一次世界大战爆发于1914年"。

31. C。解析：sth. belongs to sb. 表示"某事物属于某人"，the book belongs to me表示"这本书是我的"。

32. A。解析：fit sb. 表示"适合某人，配某人"，red suit doesn't fit me表示"红色的衣服不适合我"。

33. C。解析：have表示"拥有"；put on表示"穿上"；wear表示"穿着……"，后面接服装类；dress后面接人，be dressed in可以表示"穿着……（服装）"。wearing a black jacket表示"穿着黑色夹克"。

34. A。解析：put away表示"放好、储存、打消"，put aside表示"节省（钱、时间）"，put on表示"穿上"，put up表示"张贴、举起、建造、提高"。put away my things表示"把我的东西放好"。

35. D。解析：give up表示"放弃"，give in表示"屈服"，give away表示"赠送、泄露、失去"，give off表示"散发、放射出"。give off a lot of smoke表示"散发出许多烟"。

36. C。解析：bring out表示"发表、拿出"，bring through表示"挽救生命"，bring up表示"抚养、呕吐"，bring about表示"带来、造成"。be brought up to having manners表示"被教导有礼貌"。

37. D。解析：suggest sth. to sb. 表示"向某人建议某事"，suggest sb. doing sth. 表示"建议某人做某事"，suggest + that从句表示"暗示、表明"，beg sb. to do sth. 表示"请求某人做某事"。I beg president表示"我请求总统……"。

38. D。解析：get off表示"下车"，do away表示"处理"，get on表示"上车"，get rid of表示"摆脱、戒掉"。get rid of smoking表示"戒烟"。

39. D。解析：marry表示"结婚"，既可以做及物动词，又可以做不及物动词，marry sb. 表示"嫁给某人、与某人结婚"，一般用来描述瞬时动作；be/get married to sb. 表示"与某人结婚"，一般用来描述持续性的动作；marry一般不与with搭配。has been married to Henry for two years表示"已经和亨利结婚两年了"。

40. B。解析：receive表示"收到"，accept表示"接受"。receive but not accept表示"收到了但没接受"。

41. B。解析：lie表示"躺"时，过去式是lay，过去分词是lain，现在分词是lying；lie表示"说谎"时，过去式是lied，过去分词是lied，现在分词是lying；lay表示"安放"，过去式是laid，过去分词是laid，现在分词是laying。my son lying on the table表示"我的儿子正躺在桌子上"。

42. C。解析：look for表示"寻找"，look through表示"看穿（某事）、仔细检查"，look around表示"环顾"，look forward to (doing)表示"期待做……"。looked around in the crowded street表示"环顾拥挤的街道"。

43. C。解析：take away表示"带走、拿走"，take out表示"取出、拔掉"，take off表示"起飞、动身离开"，take up表示"开始从事、接受（提议）"。the plane was just taking off表示"飞机刚要起飞"。

44. B。解析：spend表示"花费"，主语用人；cost和take表示"花费"，主语用物；pay表示"为……付款"。cost me 100 dollars表示"花了我100美元"。

45. B。解析：shot是动词，表示"射中"，shot强调射击的动作；shot at表示"瞄准"。I shot at a bird表示"我瞄准了一只鸟"。

46. B。解析：arrive in是指到达比较大的地方，例如城市；arrive at是指到达比较小的地方，例如车站和个人住宅；reach是及物动词，后面不用加介词；get to后面直接加地点，表示"去/到"某地点。I am arriving in Beijing表示"我将要到北京"。

47. A。解析：pay for sth. 表示"为……支付"，pay off表示"付清、解雇"，pay back表示"偿还、报复"，pay out 表示"付出（款项）等"。pay for the radio表示"为录音机花费（钱）"。

48. B。解析：cut out表示"裁剪、取代"，cut off表示"切断"，cut down表示"减少、裁短"，cut away表示"去掉、迅速离开"。water supply has been cut off表示"水的供应已经被切断"。

49. B。解析：bring表示"带来"，carry表示"搬运、携带"，take表示"拿走"，fetch表示"拿来"。help you carry it表示"帮你拿"。

50. B。解析：ask for表示"请求、要求"，send for表示"申请、召唤"，call for表示"需要、（某人）去接"，look for表示"寻找"。he's always been sent for表示"他经常被召唤"。

51. D。解析：get away表示"脱身"，get off表示"下车"，get out表示"出来、出版"，get over表示"克服、度过"。get over his cancer表示"战胜他的癌症"。

第六天　突破英语的时态（二）

1. C。解析：by the end of this year表示"将来"，by后接过去时间，主句用过去完成时，by后接现在或是将来时间，主句用将来完成时。I will have taught English for three years表示"到那时我将已经教三年英语了"。

2. A。解析："一般过去时+while+过去进行时"的结构表示"……时候正……"。he stepped on a nail while he was running in the yard表示"他正在院子里跑的时候踩到了钉子"。

3. A。解析：we promise是主句，that引导宾语从句，we will meet again是宾语从句的主句，after we finish our college education in three years是宾语从句的时间状语；由when, as soon as, before, after, as, until等引导的时间状语从句以及由if, unless, as long as, in case等引导的条件状语从句不能直接用将来时态，习惯上用一般现在时代替一般将来时，又称为"主将从现"。

4. D。解析：often用于一般现在时，she是第三人称，谓语动词用单数，she often goes to see her grandparents表示"她经常去看她的祖父母"。

5. C。解析：it is the first（second，third…）time +从句结构，从句用现在完成时；如果是it will…，其从句用将来完成时；如果是it was…，其从句用过去完成时。It is the first time I have visited the Great Wall表示"这是我第一次游长城"。

6. B。解析：同上一题。

7. C。解析：位移动词表示将来时态时，常用现在进行时或一般现在时代替，所以is arriving in two hours表示"将在两小时内到达"。

8. B。解析：the moment引导的时间状语从句，符合"主将从现"的标准，所以在从句中用一般现在时态，the moment I see him表示"我一看见他"。

9. B。解析：as soon as表示"一……就"，指未发生的动作，规律是主句用一般将来时，从句用一般现在时代替一般将来时，as soon as I get to New York表示"我一到纽约，就……"。

10. B。解析：if引导的时间状语从句，符合"主将从现"的标准，所以在从句中用一般现在时态，If it rains tomorrow表示"如果明天下雨"。

11. A。解析：lie表示"躺着、平放"时，过去式是lay，过去分词是lain，"约翰的兄弟卧床"是动作发生在过去，用一般过去时。

12. B。解析：提问用what were you doing是过去进行时，回答也用过去进行时，I was reading newspaper表示"那时我正在读报"。

13. C。解析：这是由when引导的时间状语从句，主句用过去进行时，从句用when引导，用一般过去时，I was doing my homework when the telephone rang表示"电话响的时候我正在做作业"。

14. B。解析：that引导的定语从句，read在其中表示"写着"。

15. B。解析：can you tell me（that）后接宾语从

句，"你回来"是将来发生的事情，因此用一般将来时，when you will come back表示"你什么时候回来"。

16. B。解析：时间状语从句的主句用一般将来时，从句用一般现在时，when spring comes表示"春天来临时"。

17. C。解析：现在完成时表示发生在过去的动作或状态对现在的影响，I have met him once before表示"我之前见过他一次"，所以有了"认识他"的结果。

18. B。解析：现在进行时表示主语正在发生的动作或存在的状态，位移动词可以用现在进行时态代替一般将来时态，the car is coming表示"正有车过来"。

19. C。解析：现在进行时的特殊用法，位移动词可以用现在进行时代替一般将来时，they are dying soon表示"它们快死了"。

20. D。解析：一般过去时表示事情发生在过去，不强调对现在的某种影响，I didn't know you were in London表示"我不知道你在伦敦"。

21. A。解析：until引导的条件状语从句，主句用一般现在时，从句用现在完成时，Don't get off the bus until it has stopped表示"等公交车停了再下车"。

22. D。解析：过去完成时表示说话人在过去的过去所发生的动作对于过去的影响，supper发生在过去，因此用过去完成时表示发生在supper之前的事，That supper was the most delicious dinner I had ever had表示"在那顿饭

之前，我从未吃过那么好吃的饭"。

23. C。解析：before引导时间状语从句，主语是the sun，谓语动词用单数，Let's set off before the sun sets表示"让我们在太阳落山之前出发"。

24. D。解析：it's about time+一般过去时，表示"到……的时候了"，It's about time I considered it表示"我该考虑了"。

25. D。解析：Dick sat in the back发生在过去，而"我认为他坐在前面"发生在过去的过去，应该用过去完成时，I thought he had sat in the front表示"我以为他坐在前面了"。

26. C。解析：the last time相当于when的意义，主句用过去进行时，从句用一般过去时，The last time I visited her, she was studying at a medical college表示"我上次拜访她时候，她在医科大学学习"。

27. D。解析：现在完成时强调过去动作对现在的影响，have you seen my pen表示"你看见我的钢笔了吗"。

28. C。解析：until引导的条件状语从句，从句用现在完成时，主句用一般现在时，You can't watch TV until you have done your homework表示"你做完作业才能看电视"。

29. C。解析：be to do是一般将来时态的表达法，表示将来极有可能发生某事，is to become a teacher表示"一定会成为老师"。

30. C。解析：现在完成进行时表示说话人从过去发生一个动作持续到现在，并有可能持续

下去，强调动作的持续性和影响性，I have been painting the living room all day表示"我一整天都在刷客厅的墙"。

31. C。解析：insist表示"坚决主张、坚决要求"时需用虚拟语气，insist that sb. (should) do sth.，动词用原形，He insists that he manage it by himself表示"他坚决要求自己做"。

32. C。解析：look表示"看起来"，是系动词，you look upset表示"你看起来很沮丧"。

33. C。解析：he came here是过去发生的事，用一般过去时；these days是一段时间，对一段时间提问用完成时或完成进行时，what has he been doing表示"他都做什么了"。

34. B。解析：be going to do相当于will do，"我给他打电话"发生在过去，因此"我下周去"是当时时间点的将来，用过去将来时，I was going to be there表示"（过去那一刻算起）我将要去那儿"。

35. A。解析：unless引导的条件状语从句，可以用一般现在时代替一般将来时，表示"除非……"，You can't catch up with your classmates unless you work hard表示"除非你努力学习，要不然你就赶不上其他同学"。

36. C。解析：过去完成时是发生在过去动作的过去，他是在想起之前把钥匙落在家里的；把某物丢在某处用leave，而不是forget。

37. C。解析：for years表示"很多年了"用于完成时，The temple hasn't been repaired for years表示"这个庙已经多年没有整修了"。

38. C。解析：由while引导的时间状语从句，主句用一般过去时，从句可以用过去进行时，He fell while he was riding his motorbike表示"他正骑摩托车的时候摔倒了"。

39. C。解析：before引导的时间状语从句，用一般现在时代替一般将来时，before guests arrive表示"在客人到之前"。

40. D。解析："it is+一段时间+since引导的时间状语从句"相当于"it has been +一段时间+since引导的时间状语从句"，表示"自从……以来已经多久时间了"，since引导的从句用现在完成时，主句就用一般现在时；从句用过去完成时，主句就用一般过去时，It was two years since I had been here表示"自从我上次来这已经两年了"。

41. A。解析：解析同上题，It is two years since I have been away here表示"我离开这里已经两年了"。

42. A。解析：第一个if表示"是否"，引导宾语从句，后接表示将来发生的事，用一般将来时；第二个if引导条件状语从句，从句用一般现在时代替一般将来时。

43. B。解析：be going to do，will do和be to do都表示将来要发生的事，be going to表示近期"将要发生的"，will do表示客观上"势必会发生"，be to do表示"一定会发生"，come是位移动词，用现在进行时和一般现在时代替一般将来时。

44. B。解析：do you think是插入语，本句是一般现在时态，用第三人称单数。

45. B。解析：前面的问句是现在完成时的特殊疑问句，回答也用现在完成时，I have been to New York表示"我曾经去过纽约"，而I have gone to New York表示"我去过纽约（现在还没回来）"。

46. C。解析：表示陈述发生在过去的一件事，不强调动作的影响性和持续性，用一般过去时；last year作为时间状语，主句用一般过去时；He went to New York three times last year表示"他去年去了三次纽约"。

47. B。解析：他从过去开始找（这个动作）一直持续到现在（有可能持续下去），用现在完成进行时，for several days表示一段时间，表示"好多天了"，用完成时。

48. A。解析：莎士比亚是否写了这些剧发生在过去，用一般过去时。

49. A。解析：always一般用于进行时态时表示某种感情色彩，表示"总是"，Nancy is always saying "Hello"，表示"Nancy总是和人打招呼"。

50. B。解析：as做连词引导时间状语从句时，着重强调主句和从句中的动作同时发生，并且从句通常在主句前，当状语从句的谓语动词是持续性动词，从句时态常用进行时态；当状语从句的谓语动词是短暂性动词，从句时态常用一般时态，As she was reading the newspaper, Granny fell asleep表示"当她读报时，奶奶睡着了"。

51. D。解析：when引导的时间状语从句，主句用过去进行时，从句用一般过去时，本句表示"没人照顾他的时候，Tom正偷偷溜进那个房子里"。

52. C。解析："我认为你已经去美国了"是发生在过去的一件事，用一般过去时，而"你去美国"发生在过去的过去，用过去完成时。

53. D。解析：下周完工说明现在还正在建，因此用现在进行时，is being built表示"正在被建设中"。

54. C。解析：下雨是从过去开始一直持续到现在还在进行的，因此用现在完成进行时，It has been raining heavily for two days表示"雨已经下了两天了"。

55. D。解析：it/there is likely to be表示"有……可能"，Is there likely to be anyone to meet us表示"有没有可能有人会接我们呢"。

56. D。解析：出现yet时一般用完成时态，表示"还没有"，没有具体的过去时间点比较，因此用现在完成时。

57. A。解析："我和布莱克先生的对话"发生在过去，"希望"发生在过去，"给回复"是在过去表示将来发生的事，所以用过去将来时，would give us an early reply表示"尽早给我们回复"。

58. D。解析："我问他"发生在"他告诉我"这一过去时间点的动作之前，"他告诉我"发生在过去，因此用过去完成时。

59. C。解析：so far表示"到现在为止"，一般用完成时态，hear from sb. 表示"收到某人的来信"，发生在John说话之后，对现在有某种影响，因此用现在完成时，I haven't heard from him so far表示"目前为止，我还没收到他的来信"。

60. C。解析：by the time表示"到……时"，by the time+一般过去时的句子，主句用过去完成时；by the time+一般现在时或一般将来时的句子，主句用将来完成时，the train will have started表示"那时火车就已经开走了"。

61. D。解析：what do you suppose表示询问某人看法，刚刚发生了什么（导致了现在很多人在广场），因此用现在完成时表示对于现在的影响。

62. B。解析：强调说话者在过去的某一时刻没注意，用过去进行时，I wasn't noticing表示"我刚刚没注意"。

63. C。解析：表示现在进行的事情，用现在进行时，what are they doing表示"他们在做什么"。

64. C。解析：I don't think he will come相当于I think he won't come表示"我以为他要下个月才回来呢"。

65. A。解析：since表示"自……以来"接时间状语从句时，主句用现在完成时，必须是延续性动词，从句用一般过去时，必须是终止性动词，本句表示"Joan自从大学毕业就已经在医院工作了"。

66. D。解析：once用作连词时表示"一旦……就"，连接时间状语从句时相当于as，从句用一般现在时代替一般将来时，be settled表示"安顿下来"，本句表示"我一安顿下来就会立刻交朋友"。

67. C。解析：发生在过去的一件事，不强调动作的延续性和影响，用一般过去时，I forgot all about it表示"我全忘了"。

68. C。解析：not...until表示"直到……才"，本句表示"Mary外出了，直到8点才能回来"。

69. C。解析：表示某事正在进行，用现在进行时，本句表示"多国的健康专家仍在测试食物与健康的关系"。

70. A。解析：陈述客观事实用一般现在时，无论在何种从句中，本句表示"老人们说地球绕着太阳转"。

71. C。解析：位移动词用一般现在时态和现在进行时态代替一般将来时态，所以用leaves代替will leave。

72. A。解析：unless表示"除非"，引导条件状语从句，主句用一般将来时，从句用一般现在时代替一般将来时，本句表示"除非你戒烟，否则你不会健康"。

73. C。解析：just now表示"刚刚"，用于一般过去时，he went out just now表示"他刚走"。

74. B。解析：it has been+一段时间+since+一般过去时表示"距离……已经……"，本句表示"他已经戒烟五年了"。

75. B。解析：used to do表示"过去常常做某事"，本句表示"我小时候经常在河里游泳"。

76. C。解析：表示陈述过去发生的一件事，没有强调动作的持续性和影响性，用一般过去时，本句表示"他比我想象的康复得快"。

77. B。解析：made it clear表示"很明确地表示了……"，it是形式宾语，真正的宾语是由that引导的宾语从句，用过去将来时，本句表示"我们都很惊讶，他明确表示很快要离开办公室"。

78. A。解析：we could have walked to the station是虚拟语气，could have done表示"本能干……而没干"，题中"我们本可以走路去车站"（实际上是乘出租车去的），事实已经发生了，用一般过去时。

79. C。解析：when后用一般过去时，主句用过去进行时，本句表示"当我去看他的时候他正在弹吉他"。

80. D。解析：my father said这一动作发生在过去，截止到说话的时候"我的父亲已经拥有这辆车十年了"，过去完成时用持续性动词have的过去分词had，而buy是短暂性动词，本句表示"我爸爸说他这车买了有十年了"。

81. B。解析：what引导的宾语从句，其中的疑问句用陈述语序，接下来表示将来要发生的事，用一般将来时，本句表示"你能告诉我我们接下来做什么吗"。

82. A。解析：by the time引导时间状语从句，从句用一般过去时，主句用过去完成时，本句表示"当我进来的时候，她已经走了"。

83. D。解析：we found that表示"我们发现"，发生在过去，而她英语进步发生在这事之前，因此用过去完成时，本句表示"我们发现她的英语得到了迅速的提高"。

84. D。解析：be going to do表示"打算、计划、决定很有可能发生的事"，询问Nancy发生在过去，因此用was，本句表示"你问南希她明天去不去了吗"。

85. D。解析：failed表示"不及格"发生在过去，David希望通过考试发生在他不及格之前，因此用过去完成时，本句表示"David希望通过考试，可是他没及格"。

86. B。解析：she told me发生在过去，在她说话那个时间点后的两个小时，用过去将来时，本句表示"她告诉我她将在两小时内到"。

87. C。解析：in the past twenty years表示"在过去的二十年内"，包含in the past+时间的主句用现在完成时，本句表示"在过去的二十年内，我的家乡发生了很大的变化"。

88. C。解析：when引导时间状语从句，主句用一般将来时，从句用一般现在时代替一般将来时，本句表示"你们准备好了，我就开始听写"。

89. D。解析：本句表示"我们到达车站时，正下着雪"，when引导的时间状语从句，主句用过去进行时，从句用一般过去时。

90. A。解析：before用作连词引导时间状语从句，主句用一般将来时，从句用一般现在时代替一般将来时。

91. B。解析：mean to do表示"有意做……"，"伤害她"是发生在过去的一个动作，本句表示"我不是故意的"。

92. C。解析：表示说话人在将来某个时刻发生的动作，用一般将来时，本句表示"我会帮你寄出这封信的"。

93. B。解析：imagine是过去发生的动作，that引导的从句中可以用过去将来时，本句表示"Peter可能会是一个好学生"。

94. D。解析：have/had been to表示"曾经到某地去过"，have/had gone表示"去了某地"（还在那个地方）；and后面用一般过去时，表示过去发生的动作。Human beings have been to the moon and came back the earth again表示"人类曾经登月并且回来了"。

95. B。解析：by the end of last year表示"截止到去年年底"，by后接过去的时间，主句要用过去完成时，I had learnt 表示"我已经学了"。

96. B。解析：hardly/scarcely...when/before...表示"一……就……"，hardly/scarcely引出主句；when/before引出从句，主句的动作与从句的动作是一前一后紧接着发生，主句用过去完成时，从句用一般过去时；hardly/scarcely是否定副词，要引起部分倒装，部分倒装语序为hardly+助动词+主语+谓语+其他，本句表示"我刚一离开家就下雨了"。

97. C。解析：meeting was over表示"会议是在过去的一个时间点结束"，I had hoped to say my opinion表示"我本想表达我的看法"，发生在过去的过去，用过去完成时。

98. D。解析：when引导的时间状语从句，从句用一般过去时，主句用过去进行时，We were taking a walk when it started to rain表示"我们正走路呢就开始下雨了"。

99. C。解析：by the time引导的时间状语从句，从句用一般现在时或是一般将来时，主句用将来完成时；从句用一般过去时，主句用过去完成时。By the time I get to the airport, the plane will have left for Shanghai表示"等我到机场的时候，去上海的飞机就已经起飞了"。

100. C。解析：not until+状语从句位于句首，主句倒装，从句不倒装。钱包丢在我发现之前，因此用过去完成时，此句表示"没等我回家呢我就发现钱包丢了"。

101. D。解析：be to do表示将来必然要发生的事，will do表示势必要发生的事，is going to be表示近期将要发生。There is going to be a storm next week表示"下周将有风暴"。

102. B。解析：take sb. for a relative表示"把……当作亲人"，陈述一件发生在过去的事用一般过去时，I took him for a relative表示"我曾把他当作亲人"。

103. A。解析：in the past ten years表示"过去的十年里"，是一段时间，in the past+时间主句用现在完成时，I have traveled all mountains in China表示"我去过了中国所有山"。

第七天　突破英语的被动语态和助动词以及情态动词

被动语态练习

1. B。解析：prove to do表示"证明……"，是固定搭配，prove一般不用被动语态，proved to be fit for this job表示"很合适这份工作"。

2. B。解析：be made to do是make sb./sth. do的被动语态，space前面一般不用冠词，be made to go into space表示"被造出来进入太空"。

3. A。解析：be told to do表示"被告知做某事"，be told to continue my study表示"被告知去学习"。

4. B。解析：taste是系动词，表示"尝起来"，系动词一般不用被动变语态，tastes delicious表示"尝起来很美味"。

5. D。解析：be deprived of表示"被剥夺了……权利"，是固定搭配。

6. A。解析：本句是由that引导的定语从句，the best books是"被写"，所以用被动语态，而且one of +名词复数后接定语从句，谓语动词用复数，而且主句为一般现在时态，所以从句用现在完成时态，the best books that have ever been written by O. Henry表示"O. Henry写过的最好的书"。

7. B。解析：本题考查了现在进行时的被动语态，房子是"正在被刷"，所以用be+being+done的结构。

8. D。解析：同上一题，同样考查现在进行时的被动语态，is being taken care of by his aunt表示"被他的姨妈照顾"。

9. A。解析：be worth doing sth. 表示"值得做某事"，是固定搭配。

10. C。解析：本句考查不定式做宾语补足语，French hard to learn表示"法语很难学"。

11. B。解析：be fit to do sth. 表示"适合做某事"，是固定搭配。

12. B。解析：本句的主句时态是一般过去时，that引导的宾语从句应当是表示在过去发生之前的，所以动词用过去完成时，而且tickets是"被卖"，应该用被动语态，four-fifths of the tickets had been booked表示"五分之四的票已经被卖出去了"。

13. D。解析：ask for表示"要求、请求"，wait for表示"等待"，look for表示"寻找"，send for表示"召唤、申请"。

14. B。解析：本题考查不定式做形容词修饰复合不定代词，to be typed是用来修饰anything more的，而且是被动语态。

15. A。解析：本题考查sell out的被动语态形式，而且before引导的从句是一般过去时，所以主句应当用过去完成时，All the books had been sold out表示"所有书已经卖完了"。

16. A。解析：本题考查感官动词see的用法，一般来说，see sb. do/doing sth. 表示"看见某人做/正在做某事"，而这两个词组变成被动语态时，便成为了sb. be seen to do/be doing sth. 的结构，Peter is often seen to read Chinese表示"Peter经常被看见在读中文"。

17. C。解析：本题考查感官动词smell的用法，一般来说，感官动词都不用被动语态。

18. C。解析：本句是由that引导的定语从句，主句使用一般过去时，从句可以使用过去完成时，而且ship是"被建造"，所以用被动语态。

19. B。解析：本题考查现在进行时的被动语态，基本结构为be+being+done，getting在这里相当于being，My radio is getting repaired now表示"我的收音机正在被修"。

20. C。解析：marry是及物动词，后面直接接人，表示"嫁、娶"，若用被动语态，结构为be married to，Jenny married a man表示"Jenny嫁给了一个男人"。

21. B。解析：blame是不及物动词，一般来说不用被动语态，None of them should blame for the accident表示"没有人应当为这场事故负责"。

22. C。解析：belong to表示"属于"，是固定搭配，the dictionary belongs to me表示"字典属于我"。

23. C。解析：本题考查不定式做定语修饰名词的用法，do you have any clothes to be washed表示"你有没有要被洗的衣服"，是被动语态。

24. C。解析：interesting和interested的区别在于前者的主语一般用物，后者的主语一般用人，carry out表示"执行、开展"，句中的试验是"被做"，所以用被动语态。

25. C。解析：本题考查不定式做定语修饰名词的用法，a speech on history to be given next week表示"下周将要被发表的历史演讲"，是被动语态。

26. A。解析：本题考查过去分词做定语修饰名词的用法，the teacher invited to the party last week表示"上周被邀请去参加聚会的老师"。

27. B。解析：本题考查不定式做目的状语的用法，enough room to seat all of us表示"有足够的空间让我们所有人坐下来"。

28. C。解析：本题考查不定式的复合结构for sb. to do sth的用法，send for是固定搭配，表示"召唤、申请"；因为"你召唤"，所以是主动语态。

29. B。解析：本题考查"主将从现"的知识点，if引导的条件状语中使用一般现在时，主句使用一般将来时，工作"被"失去，所以用被动语态。

30. A。解析：本题考查一般过去时的被动语态，联合国（在过去）被建立，所以用被动语态，which was set up in 1945表示"在1945年被建立"。

31. D。解析：本题考查if引导的虚拟条件句，从句使用过去完成时，主句使用过去将来完成时，而且everything would have been destroyed表示"所以东西已经被烧毁"，是被动语态。

32. A。解析：本题考查不定式做定语修饰名词的用法，the right road to take表示"要走的正确的路"，因为句中road的逻辑主语是you，所以是主动语态。

33. D。解析：marry是及物动词，后面直接接人，表示"嫁、娶"，若用被动语态结构为be/get married to，My daughter got married to a doctor表示"我女儿嫁给了一个医生"。

34. A。解析：clean后加easily等副词时，句中不能使用被动语态，these dishes don't clean easily表示"这些盘子不容易洗干净"。

35. B。解析：本题考查have sth. done的用法，you should have your hair cut表示"你应该剪头发了"。

36. C。解析：yesterday evening是一般过去时的时间状语，The homework I got down to do was finished yesterday evening表示"我准备开始做的家庭作业昨天晚上就做完了"。

37. D。解析：be robbed of表示"被抢了……"，是固定搭配，he was robbed of his money表示"他被抢了钱"。

38. C。解析：be expected to do表示"被希望做某事"，he is expected to return soon表示"他被希望很快就回来"。

39. B。解析：本题考查情态动词被动语态的形式should+be+done，The money should be paid at once表示"钱马上就要付"。

40. B。解析：be required to do表示"被要求做某事"，be admitted into表示"被允许进入某地"，be supposed to do表示"应该做某

事"，be intended to do表示"打算做某事"。Only scientists are admitted into the lab表示"只有科学家才被允许进入实验室"。

助动词和情态动词练习

1. C。解析：本题考查情态动词表示推测的用法，must be David表示"肯定是David"，表示一种肯定的语气。

2. B。解析：本题考查情态动词must和have to的区别，must表示主观上的"必须"，而have to表示客观上的"必须"，本句中提到雨下得很大，所以后面填have to表示客观上的"必须"。

3. B。解析：本题考查情态动词must的否定形式，一般来说，must的否定形式为needn't，mustn't do表示"禁止做某事"。

4. D。解析：本题考查情态动词ought to的用法，ought to相当于should，而且句中的法律是应该被遵守的，所以用被动语态。

5. D。解析：本题考查情态动词+现在完成体表示对过去情况推测的用法，此用法后面的附加疑问句的谓语动词要用一般过去式，而不是用must或have。

6. A。解析：本题考查情态动词+现在完成体表示对过去情况推测的用法，should have done表示"原本（有义务）做某事，实际上没有做"，must have done表示"过去肯定做了某事"，She should have passed yesterday's examination表示"她原本应该通过昨天的考试"。

7. A。解析：be to do sth.是一般将来时的表达法，

表示将来一定会做某事，I am to go abroad next week表示"我下周一定会出国"。

8. B。解析：mean to do sth. 表示"打算做某事"，在省略时，需要将不定式后的动词省略，而保留不定式符号to，I didn't mean to表示"我没有这么打算"。

9. A。解析：be to do是一般将来时的表达法，表示将来一定会做某事，因为是在过去时间（was）提出将来（next month）会做某事，所以应当用过去将来时。

10. D。解析：as much as he could表示"尽他所能"，是固定搭配，spend time doing sth. 表示"花费（时间）做某事"。

11. D。解析：本题考查情态动词表示推测的用法，this little girl must be your daughter表示"这个小姑娘一定是你女儿"。

12. D。解析：本题考查"主将从现"的用法，if引导的条件状语从句用一般现在时，主句用一般将来时。

13. B。解析：本题考查may的否定形式，may在表示"允许"时，其否定形式为mustn't，而不是may not。

14. B。解析：本题考查can和may之间的区别，can表示"能力"，may表示"允许"，而且when引导的时间状语是一般过去时，所以主句应当用can的过去式could。

15. A。解析：本题考查祈使句的附加疑问句，let's后的附加疑问句为shall we，let us后的附加疑问句为will you。

16. B。解析：解析同上一题。

17. D。解析：本题考查情态动词can的用法，could是can的过去式，也是can的委婉说法，提问时可以用could，回答时可以用can。

18. A。解析：would rather表示"宁愿"，后接动词原形；had better表示"最好"，后接动词原形；prefer表示"更倾向于"，后接不定式。I would rather eat apples表示"我宁愿吃苹果"。

19. C。解析：本题考查must后附加疑问句的用法，句中must是情态动词，表示肯定的推测，所以在附加疑问句中不能用must这个动词，而要用must后的动词形式，句中是be动词，you是第二人称，所以使用aren't you。

20. B。解析：本题考查will的否定形式，will not可以缩写为won't。

21. D。解析：本题考查情态动词must和have to的区别，must表示主观上的"必须"，而have to表示客观上的"必须"，句中提到missed the first bus属于客观情况，所以应当使用had to。

22. D。解析：本题考查情态动词+现在完成体表示对过去情况推测的用法，should have done表示"原本（有义务）做某事，实际上没有做"，must have done表示"过去肯定做了某事"，The room is dark; Ricky must have gone to bed表示"天黑了，Ricky肯定已经睡觉了"。

23. D。解析：本题考查情态动词+现在完成体表示对过去情况推测的用法，should have done 表示"原本（有义务）做某事，实际上没有做"，must have done 表示"过去肯定做了某事"，The football match was wonderful! You should have gone to see it 表示"足球比赛特别精彩，你原本应该去看看（实际上没有去）"。

24. B。解析：had better 表示"最好"，后接动词原形，其他选项不常用。

25. B。解析：本题考查 have 的用法，Have you had a good time in America 表示"你在美国过得愉快吗"，句中 have 是助动词，和实义动词 had 形成现在完成时。

26. A。解析：have sb. do 表示"让某人做某事"。

27. C。解析：此题考查以 be 动词开头的祈使句如何进行否定，在全句前加 don't 即可，Don't be so stupid as to repeat your mistakes 表示"不要傻得总是重犯你的错误"。

28. D。解析：本题考查实义动词的强调形式，一般来说，实义动词的强调形式是在动词前加 do 动词，do 动词在这里是助动词。

29. A。解析：此题考查 do 动词后的省略情况，一般来说，第二句重复第一句的动作时，省略动词的宾语，用 do 动词进行代替即可。

30. B。解析：本题考查"主将从现"的用法，if 引导的条件状语从句一般用现在时，主句用一般将来时，you will be successful 表示"你一定会成功"。

31. D。解析：一般来说，对 would like to do sth. 的回答有两种，一种是肯定 yes, please，另一种是否定 no, thanks。

32. A。解析：本题考查 used to 的使用方法，used to do 表示"过去常常做某事"，He used to visit Beijing 表示"他过去常常去北京"。

33. C。解析：本题考查情态动词 can 的用法，could 是 can 的过去式，也是 can 的委婉说法，提问时可以用 could，回答时可以用 can。

34. B。解析：本题考查情态动词 must 的用法，must 既可以表示"必须"，也可以表示"肯定"，you must be too careful 表示"你一定要小心"，本句中 must 表示"肯定"。

35. D。解析：can't help doing 表示"不禁做某事"，是固定搭配，I can't help remembering 表示"我不禁想起"。

36. A。解析：本题考查情态动词表示推测的用法，can 表示"可能"；must 表示"肯定"；should 表示"肯定"，语气比 must 强；would 表示"愿意"。John can be wrong 表示"John 可能错了"。

37. C。解析：本题考查 may 的否定形式，may 在表示"允许"时，否定形式为 mustn't，而不是 may not。

38. A。解析：本题考查情态动词 dare 的用法，在疑问句和否定句中使用 dare 时必须遵守"有 to 有 do，无 to 无 do"，本题由 that 引导的宾语从句是一般现在时，所以主句也应当用现在时。

39. A。解析：本题考查情态动词need的用法，need to do sth. 表示"需要做某事"。

40. B。解析：本题考查情态动词+现在完成体表示对过去情况推测的用法，should have done 表示"原本（有义务）做某事，实际上没有做"，would have done表示"原本（有意愿）做某事，而未做"，I wouldn't have been late表示"我原本不想迟到的"。

41. A。解析：本题考查情态动词need的用法，need在疑问句和否定句的使用时必须是"有to有do，无to无do"。

第八天　突破英语的非谓语动词

1. A。解析：本题考查remember后接不定式和动名词做宾语的区别，remember doing表示记住做过某事，而remember to do表示记住去做某事。Don't you remember seeing the man before表示"你不记得曾经见过这个男的吗"。

2. C。解析：practice doing表示"训练做某事"，practice后接动名词做宾语，而不是不定式。

3. A。解析：本题考查不定式的否定式，不定式的否定形式是在完整结构（to do sth.）前进行否定，所以decide not to do sth. 表示"决定不去做某事"。

4. C。解析：本题考查不定式的被动式，不定式的被动式结构是to be done，I'm glad to be given an opportunity表示"我很高兴被给一个机会"。

5. B。解析：本题考查分词的独立主格结构，分词的独立主格结构是由"名词（代词）+分词"构成，It being a windy day表示"今天风很大"。

6. A。解析：have sth. done表示"让某事被做"，是固定搭配。

7. A。解析：prefer to do rather than do表示"宁愿做某事而不去做某事"，是固定搭配。

8. B。解析：prefer doing sth. to doing sth. 表示"宁愿做某事而不去做某事"，是固定搭配。

9. B。解析：本题考查分词做状语的逻辑主语问题，句子中主句的主语为this old house，分词应当选择过去分词，因为this old house是"被看"，所以用过去分词seen，主句中need后接动名词表示"某事需要被做"。

10. A。解析：本题考查分词做伴随状语的用法，由于moon让everything看上去很浪漫，所以是主动，have用现在分词形式，have sth. do表示"让某事怎么样"，The moon was shining brightly having everything there look more romantic表示"月亮照得很亮，让那里的一切都看上去很浪漫"。

11. C。解析：本题考查keep on后接不定式和动名词做宾语的区别，keep on doing表示"继续做某事"，keep on to do表示"继续做另一件事"，The girl kept on dancing to the music表示"女孩继续跟着音乐跳舞"。

12. D。解析：本题考查分词做伴随状语的用法，leaving his friend表示"让他的朋友"，是前一句话的伴随状语，leave sb. doing表示"让某人一直保持某种状态"，leave是使役动词。

13. A。解析：本题考查不定式的省略情况，不定式在省略时需要将动词省略，保留to，but his mother told him not to表示"他的妈妈告诉他不要这么做"。

14. C。解析：enjoy doing表示"喜欢做某事"，是固定搭配，由于句中出现last year表示过去时间，所以应该用enjoy having done表示过去已经发生的事，I'm enjoying having spent the vacation in Qingdao with my parents表示"我喜欢和父母在青岛度过假期"。

15. C。解析：feel like doing表示"想要做某事"，是固定搭配，I feel like going swimming in the sea表示"我想要在海里游泳"。

16. C。解析：do nothing but do表示"除了某事而不做其他事"，是固定搭配。

17. C。解析：本题考查感官动词hear变被动语态后接不定式的用法，hear sb. do表示"听见某人做某事"，be heard to do表示"某人被听见做某事"。

18. A。解析：judging from位于句首形成插入语，是固定搭配，表示"从……来判断"。

19. B。解析：generally speaking位于句首形成插入语，是固定搭配，表示"总体上来说"。

20. C。解析：本题考查with的独立主格结构，with+名词（代词）+分词构成with的独立主格结构，由于night是主动fall，所以使用现在分词。

21. C。解析：it is no use/good doing表示"做某事是无用的/不好的"，是固定搭配，而在doing前使用属格形式，应当首选物主代词your。

22. B。解析：why not do表示"为什么不做某事"，是固定搭配，try to do表示"尽力做某事"，try doing表示"尝试（用另一种方法）做某事"。

23. A。解析：本题考查with的独立主格结构，with+名词（代词）+分词构成with的独立主格结构，由于hands是被绑住，所以应当用过去分词tied。

24. A。解析：本题考查使役动词make变被动语态后接不定式的情况，make sb. do表示"让某人做某事"，be made to do表示"某人被要求去做某事"，John was made to wash the truck表示"John被要求去洗卡车"。

25. C。解析：本题考查forget后接不定式和动名词做宾语的区别，forget doing表示忘记做过某事，而forget to do表示忘记去做某事，I forget to turn it off表示"我忘记把它关掉了"。

26. D。解析：本题考查lie现在进行时的表达，whose dog is lying under the table表示"谁的狗正躺在桌子下面"。

27. A。解析：本题考查allow后用不定式或是动名词的情况，allow doing表示"允许做某事"，allow sb. to do表示"允许某人做某事"。

28. A。解析：解析同上一题，allow my son to

watch TV表示"允许我儿子看电视"。

29. C。解析：had better do表示"最好做某事"，had better stay at home表示"最好待在家里"。

30. B。解析：had better do表示"最好做某事"，have sb. do表示"让某人做某事"，had better have your son work hard表示"最好让你儿子努力工作"。

31. A。解析：have sth. done表示"让某事被做"，have it cut表示"让它被剪"。

32. A。解析：suggest doing表示"建议做某事"，suggest going shopping with him表示"建议和他一起去购物"。

33. B。解析：couldn't help doing表示"忍不住做某事"，couldn't help jumping with joy表示"忍不住高兴地跳起来"。

34. D。解析：escape doing表示"避免做某事"，escape being killed表示"避免被杀"。

35. B。解析：本题考查go on后接不定式和动名词做宾语的区别，go on doing表示"继续做某事"，go on to do表示"继续做另一件事"，Peter went on to do his homework after having a rest表示"Peter在休息完之后继续去做作业了"。

36. C。解析：be worth doing表示"值得做某事"，是固定搭配。

37. A。解析：be worthy of doing表示"值得做某事"，be worthy of being considered表示"值得被考虑"。

38. B。解析：本题考查不定式做定语修饰名词的用法，no room to live in表示"没有地方去住"，切记不要把动词live后介词in省略。

39. B。解析：本题考查不定式做定语修饰名词的用法，因为the question是被回答，所以用to be answered。

40. A。解析：本题考查不定式做状语修饰表语的情况，不定式需要用主动式代替被动式，所以be difficult to answer表示"回答起来很困难"。

41. B。解析：be used to doing表示"习惯做某事"，be used to do表示"被用来做某事"。

42. D。解析：本题考查不定式和分词的被动式，being done表示"正在被"，to be done表示"将要被"。

43. B。解析：本题考查动名词短语的并列结构，making mistakes and correcting them表示"犯错误和纠正错误"。

44. B。解析：本题考查lie现在进行时的表达，I found a cat lying in sofa表示"我看见一只猫正躺在沙发上"。

45. C。解析：have sth./sb. doing表示"让某事/某人保持某种状态"，是固定搭配，have the water running all the time表示"让水一直在流"。

46. B。解析：see sth. done表示"看见某事被做"，是固定搭配。

47. C。解析：本题考查过去分词做定语的用法，surrounded by many trees用来修饰a university,

而a university是被many trees所环绕的，所以用过去分词。

48. B。解析：make sb. done表示"让某人被做某事"，make herself heard表示"让她自己被（别人）听见"。

49. C。解析：hear sb. do表示"听见某人做某事"，hear sb. doing表示"听见某人正在做某事"。

50. B。解析：be said to do表示"被认为是"，a month ago是一般过去时的时间状语，所以要用不定式的完成体to have done，而且the city是被earthquake所destroy，所以要用不定式的完成被动体to have been done。

51. B。解析：本题考查find被动语态后接不定式的用法，be found to be表示"被发现是怎么样的"，be found to be empty表示"被发现是空的"。

52. B。解析：seem to do表示"好像做了某事"，本题用before作为时间状语，所以应该使用不定式的完成体to have done，seem to have seen her somewhere before表示"好像以前在某地见过她"。

53. A。解析：seem to do表示"好像做了某事"，本题用now作为时间状语，所以应该使用不定式的进行式to be doing，seem to be getting along quite well now表示"好像现在相处得很好"。

54. D。解析：avoid doing表示"避免做某事"，avoid being done表示"避免某事被做"，avoid being influenced by advertisements表示"避免受到广告的影响"。

55. B。解析：look forward to doing表示"期望、希望做某事"，looking forward to watching fashion show表示"希望看到服装秀"。

56. C。解析：need doing表示"某事需要被做"，是固定搭配，it needs repairing表示"它需要被修理"。

57. D。解析：find sth. done表示"发现某事被做"，是固定搭配，found the door locked表示"发现门是锁着的"。

58. A。解析：keep sb. doing表示"让某人一直保持某种状态"，keeping you waiting for two hours表示"让你一直等了两个小时"。

59. A。解析：be busy doing/with sth. 表示"忙于做某事"，prepare for sth. 表示"为某事做准备"，busy preparing for the examination表示"忙于准备考试"。

60. A。解析：regret doing表示"后悔做过某事"，regret to do表示"遗憾去做某事（未发生）"，say后面一般接说话的内容，而tell后面一般接人做宾语。

61. D。解析：be likely to do表示"有可能做某事"，根据上句not attended classes for four days是一般过去时，所以be likely to后接不定式的完成体表示已经发生，not likely for him to have missed so many classes表示"他不可能缺这么多课"。

62. C。解析：be considered to do表示"被认为做

了某事",因为invent computer是在过去发生的,所以be considered to后接不定式的完成体,表示已经发生。

63. A。解析:本题考查分词做状语的用法,the trees是主句主语,同时也是分词的逻辑主语,因为the trees是被得到照顾,所以应当用过去分词given表示被动。

64. C。解析:be no use doing表示"做某事是无用的",是固定搭配。

65. C。解析:mind doing表示"介意做某事",是固定搭配,mind being interrupted by him表示"介意被他打扰"。

66. B。解析:be seen to do表示"被看见做某事",是固定搭配,was seen to enter the office表示"被看见进了办公室"。

67. A。解析:require doing表示"要求某事被做",是被动语态的表达法。

68. A。解析:require doing相当于require to be done,都表示"要求某事被做",是被动语态的表达法。

69. D。解析:succeed in doing表示"成功地做了某事",succeed in helping him with his task表示"成功地帮助他完成任务"。

70. D。解析:be afraid of表示"害怕某事",be afraid of being laughed at表示"害怕被嘲笑",特别注意使用现在分词的被动式,而且动词词组laugh at中的介词at不能省略。

71. B。解析:have difficulty in doing表示"做某事有困难",是固定搭配。

72. B。解析:本题考查分词做状语的用法,I是主句的主语,同时也是分词的逻辑主语,因为I是从窗户那里看,所以应当用现在分词seeing表示主动。

73. C。解析:本题考查分词做状语的用法,the city是主句的主语,同时也是分词的逻辑主语,因为the city是从窗户那里"被"看,所以应当用过去分词seen表示被动。

74. A。解析:本题考查以-ed和以-ing结尾的形容词的区别,前者的主语一般是人,后者的主语一般是物,Reading is interesting, and I am interested in reading表示"阅读很有趣,我对阅读很有兴趣"。

75. B。解析:本题考查分词做状语的用法,Mr. Brown是主句的主语,同时也是分词的逻辑主语,Mr. Brown是没有"被"邀请参加婚礼,所以应用现在分词的现在完成体的被动式,而且根据句意应使用否定形式,not having been invited表示"没有被邀请参加婚礼"。

76. B。解析:devote oneself to doing表示"献身于某事",是固定搭配。

77. B。解析:stop to do表示"停下来做另一件事",stop doing表示"停下来正在做的事",根据题意,these students在老师进入教室时停止了说话。

78. B。解析:spend time (in) doing表示"花费时间做某事",是固定搭配。

79. B。解析:remember doing表示"记得做过某

事",remember to do表示"记住去做某事",remember to put away these books表示"记得把这些书放回原位"。

80. D。解析:promise to do表示"承诺做某事",是固定搭配。

81. B。解析:no good doing表示"做某事没好处",是固定搭配。

82. C。解析:imagine doing表示"想象做某事",是固定搭配。

83. B。解析:本题考查不定式做目的状语的用法,went to Canada to learn English表示"去加拿大学英语"。

84. D。解析:deny doing表示"否认做某事",是固定搭配,本题使用before作为时间状语,所以应当用分词的完成体。

85. C。解析:permit doing表示"允许做某事",是固定搭配。

86. A。解析:本题考查分词做定语的用法,the man是被John所描述的,所以应当用过去分词described表示被动。

87. D。解析:本题考查以-ed和以-ing结尾的形容词的区别,前者的主语一般是人,后者的主语一般是物,exciting scene表示"令人激动的场景"。

88. D。解析:本题考查with的分词独立主格结构,一般来说构成方式是with+名词(代词)+分词,由于new year是主动come,所以应用现在分词coming表示主动。

89. C。解析:本题考查分词的独立主格结构,一般来说其构成方式是名词(代词)+分词,代词一般用物主代词,your going there will be of great help表示"你去那里将是很大的帮助"。

90. B。解析:本题考查分词做状语的用法,ice是主句的主语,也是分词的逻辑主语,ice是被加热的,所以应用过去分词heated表示被动。

91. B。解析:object to doing表示"反对做某事",是固定搭配,doing前若出现人,应该用其物主代词的形式。

92. D。解析:appreciate doing sth. 表示"感谢做某事",doing前若出现人,应该用其物主代词的形式。

93. B。解析:happen to do表示"碰巧做某事",本题用before作为时间状语,所以应用不定式的完成体,happened to have known his address before表示"碰巧以前知道他的地址"。

94. A。解析:hope to do表示"希望做某事",是固定搭配。

95. B。解析:take the trouble to do表示"不辞辛劳地做某事",是固定搭配。

96. D。解析:would rather do表示"宁愿做某事",是固定搭配,by train表示"坐火车"。

97. B。解析:insist on doing表示"坚持做某事",ask for sth.表示"索要某物",两个都是固定搭配。

98. A。解析:used to do表示"过去常常做某事",

used to have a walk at the bank of the river表示"过去常常在河边散步"。

99. A。解析：pretend to do表示"假装做某事"，pretend not to do表示"假装没有做某事"。

100. C。解析：so as to表示"为了"，其否定形式是so as not to，是固定搭配。

101. D。解析：本题考查Would you like to...的回答形式，一般用I'd like to或I'd love to比较常见。

第九天　突破英语的虚拟语气

1. A。解析：本题考查if条件句的用法，在if引导的虚拟条件句中，主句用过去将来时，从句应当使用一般过去时，而且出现be动词时应当使用were。

2. A。解析：本句考查宾语从句中使用的虚拟语气，suggest出现在主句中表示"建议"，后接宾语从句，从句中应当使用should+动词原形，且should可以省略。

3. C。解析：本题考查if only引导的条件句单独构成虚拟语气，条件句用一般过去时表示与现在或将来事实相反。

4. B。解析：本题考查wish引导的虚拟语气，wish表示现在，后面宾语从句应与现在或将来事实相反，用一般过去时。

5. B。解析：it+is+high+time+从句，从句中始终用一般过去时，表示"该是做某事的时候了"，是固定搭配。

6. B。解析：本题考查if条件句的用法，在if引导的虚拟条件句中，主句用过去将来时，从句应当使用一般过去时，从句中有were，引起了从句的部分倒装，原来结构为if the trousers were cheap。

7. A。解析：long live sb. 表示"某人万岁"，是固定搭配。

8. B。解析：本题考查without引导的虚拟条件句与主句之间的关系，without相当于if not，从句表示"如果没有电"，与现在和将来事实相反，所以主句应当使用过去将来时。

9. C。解析：本题考查if条件句的用法，在if引导的虚拟条件句中，主句用过去将来完成时，从句应当使用过去完成时，从句原来结构为if the man had been sent to hospital，由于有had出现，所以将if省略，引起部分倒装。

10. C。解析：本题考查look as if引导的虚拟语气，for several months表示"几个月以来"，是表示过去的时间状语，应当是与过去事实相反，所以从句使用过去完成时。

第十天　突破英语的介词、连词和基本句型

介词练习

1. C。解析：get on with sb. 表示"与某人相处"，是固定搭配。

2. C。解析：to one's surprise表示"让某人很惊讶的是"，是固定搭配。

3. B。解析：entrance后接to表示"到某地的门"，是固定搭配。

4. A。解析：key后接to表示"是……的钥匙（答

案）"，是固定搭配。

5. B。解析：put into practice表示"付诸于实践"，是固定搭配。

6. D。解析：burn sth. away表示"把某物烧毁"，是固定搭配。

7. D。解析：think about表示"思考"；think of表示"想到"；think over表示"反复考虑"。

8. A。解析：dance to the music表示"随着音乐起舞"，是固定搭配。

9. D。解析：in+颜色表示"穿某颜色的衣服"，是固定搭配。

10. D。解析：on+时间表示"在某个具体日子"，是固定搭配。

11. A。解析：during the war表示"战争期间"。

12. C。解析：in the morning表示"在上午"，是固定搭配。

13. A。解析：after two o'clock表示"在两点钟之后"，"in+时间段"在一般将来时中表示某时间之内。

14. D。解析：through the forest表示"穿过森林"，因为森林是"立体的"，所以用介词through，而不是across，后者表示"穿过平面"。

15. D。解析：at一般用于小地点前，in一般用于大地点前。

16. C。解析：across the street表示"穿过街道"，因为街道是平面的，所以用介词across，而不是through，后者表示"穿过立体"。

17. C。解析：fly over the bridge表示"从桥上飞过"，over表示"在某物的上方（不与某物接触）"。

18. B。解析：arrive in表示"到达（大地点）"，是固定搭配。

19. A。解析：knock at the door表示"敲门"，是固定搭配。

20. A。解析：give up表示"放弃"，是固定搭配，give in表示"屈服"，give off表示"发出"。

21. A。解析：be proud of表示"因……感到自豪"，是固定搭配。

22. B。解析：put up表示"张贴"，take off表示"脱下（衣服），put on表示"穿上（衣服）"。

23. B。解析：on the radio表示"通过电台"，是固定搭配。

24. D。解析：本题考查lie后接不同介词的用法，lie in表示"位于（范围）内"，lie to表示"位于（同一范围内）"，lie on表示"位于（不同范围）"。根据题意，台湾是在中国的东南，在中国境内。

25. A。解析：本题考查lie后接不同介词的用法，lie in表示"位于（范围）内"，lie to表示"位于（同一范围内）"，lie on表示"位于（不同范围）"。根据题意，台湾是在福建省的东部，在中国境内。

26. 解析：选 B。本题考查lie后接不同介词的用法，lie in表示"位于（范围）内"，lie to表示"位于（同一范围内）"，lie on表示"位于（不同范围）"。根据题意，日本是在中国的东部，日本不在中国的范围内。

27. C。解析：be divided into表示"被分割"，是固定搭配。

28. D。解析：change into表示"换成"，change into a beautiful suit表示"换上一套好看的西装"。

29. C。解析：stay up表示"熬夜"，是固定搭配。

30. B。解析：except that表示"除了（后接句子）"，是固定搭配。

31. D。解析：prevent sb./sth. from sth./doing sth.表示"阻止某人/某物做某事"，是固定搭配。

32. B。解析：turn up表示"调大"，turn down表示"调小"，turn off表示"关掉"，turn on表示"打开"。

33. C。解析：by+交通工具表示"用某种交通工具"，on foot表示"步行"，是固定搭配。

34. C。解析：against the wall表示"对着墙"。

35. B。解析：by way of表示"经由"，by the way表示"顺道"，in the way表示"挡在路中间"。

36. D。解析：reduce by表示"减少了"，reduce to表示"减少到"。

37. A。解析：be made from表示"由……构成（看不出材料）"，be made of表示"由……构成（看得出材料）"。

38. A。解析：die of表示"死于（某种疾病）"，die from表示"死于（外部的因素）"。

39. B。解析：with the development of the economy表示"随着经济的发展"，是固定用法，with位于句首一般表示"随着"。

40. A。解析：agree with sb./sth. 表示"同意某人/某事"，是固定用法。

41. B。解析：spend+时间/金钱+on+事情表示"在某事上花费了金钱或时间"，是固定用法。

42. D。解析：by the arm表示"用手"，strike on the head表示"攻击到头部"。

43. A。解析：thank sb. for doing表示"感谢某人做某事"，help sb. with sth. 表示"在某事上帮助某人"。

44. B。解析：本题考查形容词最高级后接范围所使用的介词，among three of us表示"我们三个当中"。

45. B。解析：live in/at表示"住在（大地点/小地点）"，是固定用法。

46. C。解析：cool myself under the tree表示"在树底下乘凉"。

47. A。解析：be surprised at表示"因为某事而感到惊讶"，是固定搭配。

48. 解析：选A。by pound表示"按照磅来卖"，by表示通过的方式。

49. D。解析：at full speed表示"（按照）全速"，

是固定搭配。

50. D。解析：tell by her eyes表示"通过她的眼睛知道"，by表示方式。

连词练习

1. B。解析：本题考查or表示"否则"的用法，Hurry up, or you will miss the last bus表示"赶紧，否则你就会错过最后一趟车"。

2. A。解析：本题考查and做并列连词的用法，Work hard, and you will be successful one day表示"努力工作，有一天你就会成功"。

3. C。解析：本题考查while表示对照关系，John is thin while his brother is very fat表示"John很瘦，而他的兄弟很胖"。

4. B。解析：本题考查however表示对比关系，而且一般用于两个标点中间，My bike is very old, however, it was in wonderful condition表示"我的自行车很旧，但是性能非常好"。

5. C。解析：本题考查so表示结果的用法，It was raining, so the sports meeting was put off示"下雨了，所以运动会推迟了"。

6. B。解析：本题考查not only...but also...的用法，是固定搭配，表示"不仅……而且……"。

7. A。解析：本题考查not only...but also...的用法，是固定搭配，表示"不仅……而且……"，和上一题不同之处在于not only放在了动词之前，所以but also之后的动词也不能省略。

8. 解析：D。本题考查句子与句子之间的关系，由于两个句子之间有and连接，所以可以认为是并列句结构，若选择A、B、C，则构成了复合句结构，只有D才可以构成两个句子的并列形式。

9. C。解析：本题考查for表示原因的用法。It must have rained for there was water in the street表示"肯定是下雨了，因为街道上有水"。

10. A。解析：本题考查句子与句子之间的关系，由于两个句子之间有or连接，所以可以认为是并列句结构，若选择B、D则是复合句结构，根据题意A才符合本句的意思。

11. A。解析：本题考查缩合连词的用法，your opinions are后缺少表语，在四个选项中只有A和C可以做表语，但是C是用来询问"哪一个的"，所以选A。

12. C。解析：本题考查连词的用法，neither...nor...表示"既不……也不……"，谓语动词是就近原则；either...or...表示"要么……要么……"，谓语动词是就近原则；not only...but also表示"不仅……而且……"，谓语动词是就近原则；both...and...表示"……和……"，谓语动词是整体原则。本题谓语动词like是复数形式，所以选C。

13. B。解析：本题考查since的用法，How long is it since you came to Shanghai表示"你来上海多久了"。

14. D。解析：本题考查缩合连词的用法，who表示"谁"，而whoever是anyone who的缩合形式，表示"任何一个人"，范围比who要广泛。

15. A。解析：本题考查as well as的用法，表示

"和"，是固定搭配；as well表示"也"。

16. D。解析：本题考查if和whether引导从句的不同，if位于句首一般引导的是条件状语从句，而whether位于句首引导的是主语从句，更重要的是whether后可以接not形成固定搭配。

17. B。解析：本题考查if和whether引导从句的不同，if位于句中一般不能引导表语从句，只能引导宾语从句，但是whether两者都可以引导。

18. A。解析：本题考查as soon as的用法，表示"一……就……"，是固定搭配，也是时间状语的引导词，一般使用主将从现的用法。

19. A。解析：本题考查the moment的用法，表示"一……就……"，是固定搭配，也是时间状语的引导词。

20. D。解析：本题考查hardly...when...的用法，表示"一……就……"，是固定搭配，也是时间状语的引导词。

21. C。解析：本题考查no sooner...than...的用法，表示"一……就……"，是固定搭配，也是时间状语的引导词。

22. C。解析：本题考查be praised for doing，表示"被表扬做某事"，是固定搭配。

23. D。解析：本题考查否定句后接条件状语unless或是时间状语until的用法，You can't get into the meeting room unless you have a special pass 表示"你有了通行证才可以进入会议室"，unless引导的条件状语。

24. C。解析：本题考查as引导的定语从句，定语从句的先行词是the laws to protect forests，在定语从句中做主语。

25. D。解析：本题考查nevertheless的用法，一般来说，nevertheless用于连接并列句，表示强烈转折，且用于两个标点之间。

26. C。解析：本题考查缩合连词的用法，he or she wants后缺少宾语，选项中只有A和C可以做宾语，而A只能表示选择的含义，所以选C。

27. C。解析：本题考查时间状语从句引导词的用法，since引导的从句中使用一般过去时，主句用现在完成时；when引导的从句和主句中的时态较为随意；until表示"直到……才……"，一般由否定词not和until联合使用。

28. D。解析：本题考查并列句连接词的用法，The weather was terrible, so the plane was delayed 表示"天气很糟糕，所以飞机就延误了"。

29. C。解析：本题考查as引导的方式状语从句，Do it as I told you表示"就按照我告诉你的那样做"。

30. B。解析：even though表示"即使"，as if表示"好像"，as long as表示"只要"。

31. C。解析：as soon as表示"一……就……"，as long as表示"只要"。

32. B。解析：as if表示"好像"，even if表示"即使"。

33. B。解析：本题考查as做让步状语引导词的用法，as引导的让步状语从句一定要引起宾语或表语前置，且宾语或表语前的冠词需要省略，beautiful girl as she is原本的结构是as she is a beautiful girl。

34. B。解析：本题考查as引导的方式状语，as a student表示"作为一个学生"。

35. C。解析：本题考查并列句的用法，Shut up and do your work表示"别逼逼，干活去"。

36. D。解析：本题考查并列连词的用法，I'd like to, but I'm very busy表示"我很愿意，但是我很忙"。

37. D。解析：本题考查连词的用法，either...or...表示"要么……要么……"，谓语动词遵照就近原则；both...and...表示"……和……"，谓语动词遵照整体原则。本题谓语动词是am，所以是就近原则，选D。

38. B。解析：as sb. expected表示"正如某人所料"，是固定搭配。

39. A。解析：supposing表示"假设"，as soon as表示"一……就……"，except for表示"除了"。

40. C。解析：in case of表示"就……而言"，as if表示"好像"，in case表示"万一"。

41. D。解析：since表示"自从"，so as to表示"为了"，because表示"因为"，so that表示"结果"。

42. C。解析：本题考查so (such) ...that的用法，表示"太……以至于……"，so后面中心词接动词、副词或形容词，而such后面接名词或代词。

43. C。解析：本题考查缩合代词的用法，difficult it may be前缺少修饰形容词的部分，四个选项中只有however表示程度，表示"无论如何"。

44. A。解析：since表示"自从、既然"，because of表示"由于（后接短语）"，provided表示"如果"，supposing表示"假设"。

45. D。解析：本题考查并列句连词的用法，Seven minutes left, and you can caught the bus表示"还有七分钟，你能赶上那趟车"。

第十一天　突破英语的复合句

1. B。解析：本题考查附加疑问句（反意疑问句）的回答，一般来说，附加疑问句的回答需要前后一致，也就是说，要么是yes, she is，要么是no, she isn't。

2. C。解析：本题考查以let's开头的句型之后的附加疑问句，应当用shall we，是固定搭配。

3. A。解析：本题考查以let us开头的句型之后的附加疑问句，应当用will you，是固定搭配。

4. D。解析：本题考查祈使句的反意疑问句，应当用will you，是固定搭配。

5. D。解析：本题考查祈使句的反意疑问句，应当用will you，是固定搭配。

6. B。解析：本题考查everything开头的句型之后的附加疑问句，应当用it指代everything。

7. C。解析：本题考查everybody开头的句型之后的附加疑问句，应当用he指代everybody。

8. D。解析：本题考查I am开头的句型之后的附加疑问句，应当用aren't I来指代，是固定搭配。

9. A。解析：seldom在句中表示否定，句子之后附加疑问句应用肯定形式。

10. B。解析：would like to do表示"想要做某事"，句子之后的附加疑问句应用would进行提问。

11. C。解析：have to表示"必须"，是情态动词，句子之后的附加疑问句应用实义动词提问。

12. A。解析：本题考查否定疑问句的回答形式，一般来说，附加疑问句的回答需要前后一致，也就是说，要么是yes, he is，要么是no, he isn't。

13. D。解析：本题考查附加疑问句的回答形式，一般来说，附加疑问句的回答需要前后一致，也就是说，要么是yes, I am，要么是no, I am not，因为后面有I joined only yesterday表示肯定，所以选D。

14. B。解析：主句是否定句，所以附加疑问句为肯定句。

15. C。解析：主句是肯定句，是由used to做谓语的句子，附加疑问句要用实义动词来进行提问。

16. B。解析：主句是ought to做谓语的句子，附加疑问句要用should来进行提问，因为should和ought to表示相同含义。

17. C。解析：主句是need to做谓语的句子，need在句中是实义动词，附加疑问句要用do动词来进行提问。

18. A。解析：主句是need做谓语的句子，need在句子中是情态动词，附加疑问句要用情态动词来进行提问。

19. A。解析：主句是dare做谓语的句子，dare在句子是实义动词，附加疑问句要用do动词来进行提问，nobody表示否定含义，附加疑问句要用肯定句。

20. D。解析：主句是dare做谓语的句子，dare在句子是情态动词，附加疑问句要用情态动词来进行提问，nobody表示否定含义，附加疑问句要用肯定句。

21. B。解析：主句是must做谓语的句子，must be是情态动词表示对现在情况的推测，附加疑问句要用do动词来进行提问。

22. C。解析：主句是must做谓语的句子，must是情态动词，表示"必须"，附加疑问句要用must的否定形式needn't来进行提问。

23. C。解析：主句是must做谓语的句子，must have done是情态动词+现在完成体表示对过去情况的推测，附加疑问句要用do动词来进行提问。

24. B。解析：no one在句中表示否定，附加疑问句应该用肯定，而且no one表示单数。

25. C。解析：I don't think是插入语，所以在后面的附加疑问句中不用考虑，但是要考虑否定转移，所以在附加疑问句中应该使用肯定句。

26. A。解析：本句是以she引导的宾语从句，前面的she doesn't并不是插入语，所以附加疑问句应用肯定句。

27. B。解析：hardly在句中表示否定，所以在后面的附加疑问句中应用肯定句。

28. C。解析：附加疑问句的动词形式应与主句的动词形式一致，told是实义动词，所以附加疑问句要用do动词来进行提问。

29. A。解析：本题考查had better后附加疑问句的用法，hadn't you是固定搭配。

30. B。解析：may在句中做谓语，是情态动词，后面的附加疑问句应用否定形式mustn't来进行提问。

31. D。解析：本题考查以how引导的感叹句后附加疑问句的形式，感叹句中的谓语动词是is，所以附加疑问句应用isn't it。

32. A。解析：本题考查wish做谓语动词后附加疑问句的用法，一般来说，wish后常用may来进行提问。

33. D。解析：本题考查感叹句的语序问题，what开头的感叹句后接中心词为代词或名词，how开头的感叹句后接中心词为动词、形容词或副词，本句正常语序为it is what a long way from Beijing to London，表示"从北京到伦敦真是一段长路啊"。

34. D。解析：本题考查感叹句的语序问题，what开头的感叹句后接中心词为代词或名词，how开头的感叹句后接中心词为动词、形容词或副词，本句正常语序为they are living what a happy life，表示"他们正在过着幸福的生活"，life是可数名词，所以要用冠词。

35. B。解析：本题考查感叹句的语序问题，what开头的感叹句后接中心词为代词或名词，how开头的感叹句后接中心词为动词、形容词或副词，本句正常语序为they are having wonderful weather，表示"他们这里的天气真好"，weather是不可数名词，所以要用零冠词。

36. B。解析：本题考查感叹句的语序问题，what开头的感叹句后接中心词为代词或名词，how开头的感叹句后接中心词为动词、形容词或副词，本句正常语序为he is how careless，表示"他是多么不小心啊"。

37. C。解析：本题考查感叹句的语序问题，what开头的感叹句后接中心词为代词或名词，how开头的感叹句后接中心词为动词、形容词或副词，本句正常语序为the flower is how beautiful，表示"花朵多么漂亮啊"。

38. A。解析：本题考查感叹句的语序问题，what开头的感叹句后接中心词为代词或名词，how开头的感叹句后接中心词为动词、形容词或副词，本句正常语序为she gave me what good advice，表示"她给我多好的意见啊"，advice是不可数名词，所以要用零冠词。

39. A。解析：本题考查感叹句的语序问题，what开头的感叹句后接中心词为代词或名词，how开头的感叹句后接中心词为动词、形容词或副词，本句正常语序为he is how funny，表示"他是多么有趣啊"。

40. B。解析：本题考查感叹句的语序问题，what开头的感叹句后接中心词为代词或名词，how开头的感叹句后接中心词为动词、形容词或副词，本句正常语序为he is how handsom，表示"他是多么帅啊"。

41. C。解析：本题考查感叹句的语序问题，what开头的感叹句后接中心词为代词或名词，how开头的感叹句后接中心词为动词、形容词或副词，本句正常语序为he is what a handsome boy，表示"他是多么帅的一个男孩啊"，boy是可数名词，所以前面要用冠词。

42. B。解析：本题考查感叹句的语序问题，what开头的感叹句后接中心词为代词或名词，how开头的感叹句后接中心词为动词、形容词或副词，本句正常语序为she speaks Japanese how fluently，表示"她说日语多么流利啊"。

43. B。解析：本题考查现在进行时的用法，Look at the children over there是正在发生的时间状语。

44. A。解析：本题考查how提问的用法，how表示"方式、程度等"，所以How is your father表示"你父亲身体怎么样"。

45. C。解析：本题考查what提问的用法，what表示"性质、工作等"，所以What does you father do表示"你父亲是做什么工作的"。

46. A。解析：本题考查用何种频率副词进行提问，How often do you go to see your father表示"你多久才去看你父亲一次"。

47. A。解析：本题考查对时间状语的提问，how long表示"多久"，是时间状语。

48. B。解析：本题考查对时间状语的提问，how long表示"多久"，一般用于过去时或是完成时；how soon表示"多久"，一般用于将来时；how often表示"多久"，一般表示频率；how much表示"多少钱"。

49. A。解析：本题考查具体日期的回答，It's April 17th表示"今天是四月十七日"。

50. B。解析：本题考查对周几的提问，It's Thursday表示"今天是周四"。

51. A。解析：本题考查定语从句关系词的用法，who在定语从句中做主语，替代the man。

52. D。解析：本题考查定语从句关系词的用法，when在定语从句中做时间状语，替代the days。

53. C。解析：本题考查定语从句关系词的用法，which在定语从句中做宾语，替代a house，定语从句的正常语序是they stored food in a house，由于有介词in，所以可以将in放在关系词之前。

54. B。解析：本题考查定语从句关系词的用法，that在定语从句中做宾语，替代the cleverest boy，先行词boy有形容词最高级修饰，所以只能用that，而不能用which。

55. C。解析：本题考查定语从句关系词的用法，which在定语从句中做主语，替代the book，由于是非限定性定语从句，所以只能用which，不能用that。

56. D。解析：本题考查并列句之间的关系，和上

附 录 **练习答案与解析** 275

一题不一样，本句中间出现and连接的句子，所以直接用it替代前句中的the book即可。

57. C。解析：本题考查定语从句中的单复数，定语从句的先行词为复数时，从句需要使用复数形式。

58. D。解析：本题考查定语从句的单复数，定语从句先行词有only修饰时，从句需要使用单数形式。

59. B。解析：本题考查定语从句关系词的用法，若选择most of them则成为前后两个句子，但是句子与句子之间没有连接词；whom在定语从句中做宾语；who在定语从句中做主语。

60. D。解析：本题考查定语从句关系词的用法，of which在定语从句中做定语，a house of which windows are painted red表示"房子的窗户都是刷成红色的"。

61. B。解析：本题考查定语从句关系词的用法，that在定语从句中做主语，替代all，由于all是不定代词，只能用that替代，而不能用which替代。

62. B。解析：本题考查定语从句关系词的用法，that在定语从句中做主语，替代the best car，由于car有形容词最高级the best修饰，只能用that替代，而不能用which替代。

63. A。解析：本题考查定语从句关系词的用法，that在定语从句中做宾语，替代the first film，由于film有序数词the first修饰，只能用that替代，而不能用which替代。

64. D。解析：本题考查as引导的定语从句，as is

well known to all表示"众所周知"，是固定搭配。

65. C。解析：本题考查定语从句关系词的用法，which在定语从句中做主语，替代前面整句话，由于是非限定性定语从句，只能用which替代，而不能用that替代。

66. C。解析：本题考查定语从句关系词的用法，why在定语从句中做原因状语，the reason why表示"是……的原因"，是固定搭配。

67. B。解析：本题考查定语从句关系词的用法，that在定语从句中做主语，替代the only girl，由于girl有形容词only修饰，只能用that替代，而不能用which替代。

68. C。解析：本题考查定语从句关系词的用法，that/which在定语从句the nurse is talking to中做宾语，可以省略。

69. B。解析：本题考查定语从句关系词的用法，where在定语从句中做地点状语，where he grew up相当于he grew up in the small town。

70. B。解析：本题考查定语从句关系词的用法，that在定语从句中做宾语，替代the things and classmates，由于the things and classmates既出现了人又出现了物，只能用that替代，而不能用which替代。

71. D。解析：本题考查定语从句关系词的用法，the same book as you do表示"和你有一样的书"，the same as表示"和……一样"，是固定搭配。

72. A。解析：本题考查定语从句关系词的用法，

that在定语从句中做主语，替代the greatest scientists，由于scientists有形容词最高级greatest修饰，只能用that替代，而不能用who替代。

73. A。解析：本题考查定语从句关系词的用法，without which在定语从句中做状语，由于是非限定性定语从句，只能用which替代，而不能用that替代。

74. D。解析：本题考查定语从句关系词的用法，as had been expected是as引导的定语从句，表示"正如所料"，是固定搭配。

75. B。解析：本题考查定语从句关系词的用法，which在定语从句中做主语，替代前面整句，由于是非限定性定语从句，只能用which替代，而不能用that替代。

76. B。解析：本题考查定语从句关系词的用法，which在定语从句中做时间状语，替代前面的时间the day，定语从句的正常语序为I met you on the day。

77. B。解析：本题考查定语从句关系词的用法，neither of which中的which替代前面two books，表示"两本书都不"。由于两句之间没有连词，所以应当是主从复合句，所以A、C不正确，而none指的是三者或三者以上的否定，所以D也不正确。

78. D。解析：本题考查定语从句关系词的用法，in which在定语从句中做时间状语，which用于替代World War Ⅱ。

79. C。解析：本题考查定语从句关系词的用法，to whom在定语从句中做宾语，定语从句的正常语序为I should turn to whom for help，whom用于替代a person。

80. D。解析：本题考查定语从句关系词的用法，which在定语从句中做宾语，替代the knife。

81. C。解析：本题考查定语从句关系词的用法，that在定语从句中做主语，替代anything，由于anything是不定代词，只能用that替代，而不能用which替代。

82. C。解析：本题考查表语从句连接词的用法，the reason is后接表语从句，只能用that，不能用because，why等。

83. C。解析：本题考查定语从句关系词的用法，that在定语从句中做宾语，替代the factory，因为visited是及物动词，缺少宾语，所以只能用that替代。

84. B。解析：本题考查定语从句关系词的用法，where在定语从句中做地点状语，相当于in which，which替代the restaurant。

85. A。解析：本题考查强调结构的用法，强调结构一般构成是it+be动词+强调部分+that（指物）/who（指人）+其他成分。

86. A。解析：本题考查强调结构的用法，强调结构一般构成是it+be动词+强调部分+that（指物）/who（指人）+其他成分。

87. A。解析：本题考查定语从句关系词的用法，which在定语从句中做宾语，替代the day。

88. 解析：B。选本题考查定语从句关系词的用法，in which在定语从句中做地点状语，which替代the house，定语从句的正常语序为we live

in which (the house)。

89. C。解析：本题考查定语从句关系词的用法，本句中两个句子之间没有连词，那么一定是主从复合句的结构，the longest one among which中的which替代three labs。

90. B。解析：本题考查定语从句关系词的用法，本句中有非限定性定语从句，所以只能用who引导，而不能用that，而且I之后的动词需用am。

91. D。解析：本题考查定语从句的用法，the one在句中做先行词，you have visited before做定语从句，the one在定语从句中做宾语，所以可以用that或which进行替代，并且that或which做宾语时可以省略。

92. D。解析：本题考查定语从句关系词的用法，which在定语从句中做主语，替代three questions。

93. B。解析：本题考查宾语从句中疑问句的用法，疑问句在宾语从句中应当使用陈述句语序，所以排除C和D，而且live是不及物动词，所以介词in不能省略。

94. D。解析：本题考查定语从句的用法，the book是先行词，you needed是定语从句，the book在定语从句中做宾语，所以可以用that或which进行替代，并且that或which做宾语时可以省略。

95. A。解析：本题考查定语从句关系词的用法，which在定语从句中做主语，替代the shop。

96. C。解析：本题考查定语从句关系词的用法，for which在定语从句中做宾语补足语，which替代the clothes，定语从句的正常语序为Ricky paid for 100 dollars for which (the clothes)。

97. B。解析：本题考查定语从句关系词的用法，本句中出现了非限定性定语从句，由于his wife是人，所以用whom进行替代更合适。

98. C。解析：本题考查定语从句关系词的用法，of which在定语从句中做定语，which替代the window，the window of which glass was broken表示"玻璃坏了的窗户"。

99. D。解析：as the day went on表示"随着时间的流逝"，是固定搭配。

100. D。解析：本题考查what引导的主语从句，what he said表示"他所说的话"，由于said是及物动词，所以缺少宾语，而what刚好可以做宾语。

101. A。解析：本题考查以that引导的同位语从句，she is a chief是用于解释说明the fact的。

102. B。解析：本题考查同位语从句关系词的用法，that后同位语从句用来说明解释the theory。

103. A。解析：本题考查定语从句关系词的用法，that在定语从句中做主语，替代the problem。

104. A。解析：本题考查同位语从句关系词的用法，that后同位语从句用来说明解释the question。

105. D。解析：本题考查宾语从句关系词的用法，when之后引导的是宾语从句，表示时间；whether也可以引导宾语从句，表示"是否",但是一般在从句末接or not；that之后一般引导陈述句。

106. C。解析：本题考查宾语从句关系词的用法，where之后引导的是宾语从句，表示地点；whether也可以引导宾语从句，表示"是否",但是一般在从句末接or not；that之后一般引导陈述句。

107. A。解析：there is no doubt that表示"毫无疑问的是",是固定搭配。

108. C。解析：本题考查同位语从句关系词的用法，that后同位语从句用来说明解释a promise。

109. C。解析：本题考查主语从句关系词的用法，主语从句he was elected as president缺少状语，所以B和D错误；if在句首很少引导主语从句，一般是条件状语从句。

110. B。解析：本题考查主语从句关系词的用法，主语从句you have done缺少宾语，所以用what作为宾语。

111. C。解析：本题考查主语从句关系词的用法，主语从句末尾有or not，所以只有用whether进行搭配较为合适。

112. B。解析：本题考查主语从句关系词的用法，主语从句she is the most intelligent girl是陈述句，所以用that引导较为合适。

113. B。解析：本题考查方式状语关系词的用法，looks as if表示"看上去如何",是固定搭配。

114. C。解析：本题考查表语从句关系词的用法，表语从句we want缺少宾语，what可以做宾语。

115. A。解析：本题考查表语从句关系词的用法，表语从句the meeting will begin缺少时间状语，when可以做时间状语。

116. D。解析：本题考查宾语从句关系词的用法，depend on后接宾语从句，从句中缺少状语，whether可以做状语，表示"是否"。

117. C。解析：本题考查让步状语从句关系词的用法，no matter what等同于whatever，表示"无论是什么"。

118. B。解析：本题考查宾语从句关系词的用法，know后面接宾语从句，what they can do是宾语从句，to help us是目的状语。

119. D。解析：本题考查条件状语从句关系词的用法，where表示"只要、只有",是条件状语的引导，Where there is a will, there is a way表示"有志者事竟成"。

120. D。解析：本题考查结果状语从句关系词的用法，so that表示"结果是",是固定搭配。

121. C。解析：本题考查比较状语从句的用法，本句的完整结构为John gives me more help than Tom gives me，重复动词省略时，用同类动词进行替代，用do动词替代give。

122. C。解析：本题考查比较状语从句的用法，look是系动词中的感官动词，一般不用被动语态，而且根据整句意思是指"他"和"他自己"比较。

123. C。解析：本题考查以as引导的让步状语从句的用法，在as引导的让步状语从句中，需要将从句中的表语或是宾语置于句首，且不用任何冠词，从句正常语序为as the sun is bright。

124. A。解析：本题考查宾语从句关系词的用法，宾语从句句末出现or not，所以只能用whether进行搭配，形成whether or not的固定搭配。

125. B。解析：本题考查地点让步状语的用法，wherever等同于no matter where，表示"无论在哪里"，是固定搭配；where引导的是地点状语从句，不能单独成句。

126. A。解析：本题考查时间状语从句关系词的用法，as soon as表示"一……就"，as if表示"好像"，unless表示"除非"，in order that表示"为了"。

127. B。解析：本题考查表语从句的用法，where you left it是where引导的表示地点的表语从句。

128. B。解析：本题考查强调结构的用法，强调结构一般构成是it+be动词+强调部分+that（指物）/who（指人）+其他成分。

129. B。解析：本题考查主语从句的用法，that引导的陈述句her hair was turning gray是真正的主语，而it是形式主语。

130. B。解析：本题考查条件状语从句的用法，unless表示"除非"，I didn't manage to do it unless you had explained how表示"除非你解释了，要不我还不会处理这件事"。

131. B。解析：本题考查并列句的用法，or在句中表示"否则"。

132. A。解析：本题考查条件状语从句关系词的用法，in case和in case of都表示"万一"，前者后接句子表示条件，后者接词或词组表示条件；in order to/that表示结果。

133. C。解析：本题考查条件状语从句关系词的用法，for和because都表示原因；now that表示"既然"。

134. D。解析：本题考查让步状语从句关系词的用法，even if表示"即使"；although表示"尽管"；no matter what表示"无论是什么"，是固定搭配。

135. B。解析：本题考查让步状语从句关系词的用法，whenever I asked him to等同于no matter when I asked him to，若选择A，从句结构必须是whatever I asked him to do，do后面缺少宾语，whatever做宾语。根据题意，应选B。

136. B。解析：so (such)...that表示"太……以至于"，so后面接动词、形容词或副词作为中心词，而such后面只接名词或代词作为中心词，so pretty a girl that表示"太漂亮的姑娘以至于"。

137. C。解析：本题考查since引导的时间状语从句，从句用一般过去时，主句用现在完成时。

138. B。解析：本题考查让步状语从句关系词的用法，whether表示"是否"，although表示

"尽管"，because表示"原因"，since表示"因为"。

139. B。解析：本题考查让步状语从句关系词的用法，因为在主句中有in two weeks的时间状语，所以从句应当用时间来提问。

140. C。解析：本题考查方式状语从句关系词的用法，as I told you表示"正如我所告诉你的那样"。

141. D。解析：本题考查并列句连接词的用法，在两个标点之间，且是表示转折关系，只有nonetheless合适，表示"尽管如此"。

142. B。解析：本题考查条件状语从句关系词的用法，unless等同于if not，The men will have to wait all day unless the doctor works faster表示"除非医生工作得很快，要不这些人不得不等一整天"。

143. A。解析：in case表示"万一"，no matter表示"无论"，in any case表示"无论如何"，ever since表示"自从"。

第十二天 突破英语的语序、主谓一致和it的用法

语序练习

1. C。解析：本题考查否定副词not位于句首引起的部分倒装，部分倒装是将谓语部分中的did提到主语he之前。

2. D。解析：本题考查否定副词nor位于句首引起的部分倒装，表示和上一句话中否定的情况相同，nor can I表示"我也不能"。

3. B。解析：本题考查地点状语位于句首引起的句子完全倒装，Here comes the teacher表示"老师来了"，come和here连用，go和there连用。

4. D。解析：so+助动词+人称代词表示对上一句情况的重复。

5. B。解析：本题考查no sooner...than的用法，表示"一……就"，是固定搭配，no是否定副词，位于句首引起部分倒装，由于从句heard是一般过去时，主句应当使用过去完成时，had I gone out的正常语序为I had gone out。

6. C。解析：本题考查if条件句中出现had，were和should所引导的省略和倒装，were I you的正常语序为if I were you。

7. B。解析：本题考查否定副词词组not until位于句首引起的部分倒装，the late years of 20th century是表示过去的时间状语，主语应用一般过去时。

8. C。解析：本题考查否定词seldom位于句首引起的部分倒装，in the morning是一般现在时的时间状语。

9. D。解析：so+助动词+人称代词表示对上一句情况的重复，so had workers in the factory表示"工人们在工厂也是一样的"。

10. C。解析：so+助动词+人称代词表示对上一句情况的重复，so+人称代词+助动词表示对上一句情况的肯定，so he has表示"他确实去了"。

11. C。解析：本题考查only位于句首引起的部分倒装，only recently has something been done

with的正常语序是only recently something has been done with。

12. D。解析：本题考查hardly...when的用法，表示"一……就"，是固定搭配，hardly是否定副词，位于句首引起部分倒装，由于从句中appeared是一般过去时，主句应当使用过去完成时，had I had one problem settled的正常语序为I had had one problem settled。

13. C。解析：本题考查as引导的让步状语从句引起的部分倒装，从句中出现宾语或表语，需要提到句首，且省略它们之前的冠词，busy as I am的正常语序是as I am busy。

14. C。解析：本题考查地点状语位于句首引起的完全倒装，here he comes表示"他来了"，正常语序为he comes here。

15. D。解析：So it is with me表示"和我的情况一样"，是固定搭配，如果前句表述的某人或某物情况复杂，无法使用so或neither（nor）引导的倒装句型表达另一人或物的情况，则用It is/was the same with sb.。

16. C。解析：本题考查虚拟语气if条件句的倒装情况，if条件句中若出现had，should，were时，可以将if省略，had，should，were可以提到句首形成部分倒装，本题中主句是过去将来完成时，if引导的从句用过去完成时，had I known your telephone number的正常语序是if I had known your telephone number。

17. B。解析：so+助动词+人称代词表示对上一句情况的重复，so+人称代词+助动词表示对上

一句情况的肯定，so it was表示"确实是"。

18. B。解析：so+助动词+人称代词表示对上一句情况的重复，so+人称代词+助动词表示对上一句情况的肯定，本题中用逗号隔开，表示重复上句的情况。

19. B。解析：neither+助动词+人称代词表示对上一句情况（否定）的重复，neither+人称代词+助动词表示对上一句情况（否定）的肯定，本题中用逗号隔开，表示重复上句的情况。

20. B。解析：本题考查否定副词never位于句首引起的部分倒装，Never have I heard such a terrible story的正常语序为I have never heard such a terrible story。

21. B。解析：本题考查only位于句首引起的部分倒装，only后句子不倒装，主句部分倒装，can you save it的正常语序为you can save it。

22. C。解析：however后的句子和前句情况一致，所以可以用助动词进行替代，she does it today表示"她今天去购物了"，it替代goes shopping。

23. A。解析：本题考查so位于句首引起的完全倒装，so fat is he的正常语序为he is so fat。

24. B。解析：nor+助动词+人称代词表示对上一句情况（否定）的重复，nor+人称代词+助动词表示对上一句情况（否定）的肯定，本题中用逗号隔开，表示重复上句的情况。

25. A。解析：本题考查as引导的让步状语从句引

起的宾语（表语）前置，wide as the river is的正常语序为as the river is wide。

26. C。解析：本题考查either表示"也"（否定）的用法，一般用于句末。

27. D。解析：本题考查not until位于句首引起的部分倒装，Not until did I come back home it was totally dark的正常语序为I did not come back home until it was totally dark。

28. C。解析：本题考查so位于句首引起的完全倒装，so little I know about economy的正常语序为I know so little about economy。

29. B。解析：本题考查否定副词never位于句首引起的部分倒装，本题第一句表示"这个饭店的服务太差"，所以后面一句用将来时表示"将来再也不会"，Never again will I go there的正常语序为I will never go there again。

30. D。解析：本题考查so位于句首引起的完全倒装，so thick was the ice的正常语序为the ice was so thick；that引导的句子是一般过去时，前面的句子也应该是一般过去时。

31. D。解析：本题考查否定副词seldom位于句首引起的部分倒装，Seldom can I see such a big diamond的正常语序为I can seldom see such a big diamond。

32. D。解析：本题考查否定副词nor前主句的形式，nor句中为一般现在时，所以前句为一般现在时，而且为否定。

33. D。解析：本题考查否定副词by no means位于句首引起的部分倒装，should和ought to都表示"一定"，by no means should we look down的正常语序为we should by no means look down。

34. C。解析：本题考查no sooner...than的用法，表示"一……就"，是固定搭配，no是否定副词，位于句首引起部分倒装，由于从句中heard是一般过去时，主句应当使用过去完成时，had I reached的正常语序为I had reached。

35. C。解析："the+比较级，the+比较级"表示"越……越"，句中全部用正常语序。

36. B。解析：本题考查虚拟语气if条件句的倒装情况，if条件句中若出现had，should，were时，可以将if省略，had，should，were可以提到句首形成部分倒装，本题中主句是过去将来时，if引导的从句用一般过去时或过去将来时，were I to become a good teacher的正常语序是if I were to become a good teacher。

37. B。解析：本题考查as引导的让步状语从句引起的部分倒装，可以将宾语（表语）置于句首，且将冠词省略，popular star as she is的正常语序为as she is a popular star。

38. C。解析：本题考查地点状语位于句首引起的完全倒装，in the old house lived an old lady的正常语序为an old lady lived in the old house。

39. C。解析：本题考查only位于句首引起的部分倒装，only后的句子不倒装，主句部分倒装，were people able to live peacefully的正常语序为people were able to live peacefully。

主谓一致练习

1. C。解析：all you have to do中的all是主语，且是不定代词，谓语动词用单数。

2. A。解析：reading novels and articles是动名词做本句的主语，谓语动词用单数。

3. A。解析：neither做主语时谓语动词用单数。

4. C。解析：the writer and the poet做主语，表示"作家和诗人"，谓语动词用复数。

5. B。解析：the writer and poet做主语，表示"一个具有作家和诗人身份的人"，谓语动词用单数。

6. A。解析：to see做主语，不定式做主语时谓语动词用单数。

7. A。解析：本题考查集体名词的数，family表示"家族"时谓语动词用单数，表示"家里所有人"时谓语动词用复数，句子中有now，所以用现在进行时。

8. A。解析：the police做主语时谓语动词用复数，at this time of yesterday是过去时间状语。

9. A。解析：each修饰主语时谓语动词用单数。

10. D。解析：many+不定冠词+可数名词表示"许多像这样的……"，谓语动词用单数。

11. B。解析：本题考查集体名词的数，class表示"班级"时谓语动词用单数，表示"班上所有成员"时谓语动词用复数，has been to表示"曾经去过"，has gone to表示"已经去了"。

12. D。解析：a number of+可数名词谓语动词用复数，句中有already，是现在完成时的时间状语。

13. B。解析：the number of+名词谓语动词用单数。

14. B。解析：both+名词+and+名词谓语动词用复数，on sale表示"上市出售"。

15. A。解析：bread and milk表示"面包和牛奶"，所以是整体含义。

16. D。解析：a series of+复数名词谓语动词常用单数，yesterday是过去的时间状语。

17. A。解析：not only...but also谓语动词用就近原则，谓语动词和but also后的谓语动词一致。

18. B。解析：neither...nor谓语动词用就近原则，谓语动词和nor后的谓语动词一致。

19. D。解析：either...or谓语动词用就近原则，谓语动词和or后的谓语动词一致。

20. A。解析：ten minutes是时间做主语，谓语动词用单数。

21. B。解析：as well as谓语动词用不管原则，谓语动词和as well as前的名词一致。

22. B。解析：three sevenths of+名词，其谓语动词和名词有关，名词若是可数名词复数，谓语动词用复数，名词若是不可数名词，谓语动词用单数，melt不用被动语态。

23. A。解析：who引导的定语从句谓语动词和先行词有关，students是复数，从句谓语动词用复数。

24. B。解析：who引导的定语从句谓语动词和先行词有关，students是复数，但是students有only修饰时，从句谓语动词用单数。

25. B。解析：ten percent of+名词谓语动词和名词有关，名词若是可数名词复数，谓语动词用复数，名词若是不可数名词，谓语动词用单数，the apples是可数名词复数，go bad表示"变坏"。

26. B。解析：two thirds of+名词谓语动词和名词有关，名词若是可数名词复数，谓语动词用复数，名词若是不可数名词，谓语动词用单数，the forest是不可数名词，所以谓语动词用单数，而且forest是被destroy的，所以用被动语态。

27. A。解析：本题考查附加疑问句的谓语动词形式，the Smiths表示"Smith一家人"，是集体名词，用复数。

28. A。解析：every+名词+and+every+名词，其谓语动词用单数，every强调每一个。

29. B。解析：politics是复形名词表示单数，谓语动词用单数，本句表示"政治比历史更难"，是一般现在时。

30. C。解析：all是集体名词，all have left表示"所有人都离开了"，谓语动词用复数，all is quiet表示"一切都安静了"，谓语动词用单数。

31. A。解析：to know是不定式做主语，谓语动词用单数。

32. C。解析：the+形容词表示一群人，谓语动词用复数，live是不及物动词，不能省略介词in。

33. A。解析：more than+名词，其谓语动词和名词有关，名词是可数名词复数，谓语动词用复数；名词是可数名词单数，谓语动词用单数。last year是过去的时间状语。

34. B。解析：one or two months是时间，做主语时谓语动词用单数。

35. C。解析：本题考查复合不定代词anyone的替代情况，一般用his替代。

36. D。解析：本题考查附加疑问句的用法，I don't think属于插入语表示观点，附加疑问句与he is honest有关，但是要注意否定转移。

37. A。解析：with的谓语动词属于不管原则，句子谓语动词与with之前的名词形式有关，the teacher是单数形式。

38. C。解析：not all children是复数形式，所以用物主代词their。

39. A。解析：where to go and how to go是两件事，用and连接，谓语动词用复数，本句表示"地点和方式没有被决定"，用被动语态。

40. A。解析：what you said just now是主语从句，谓语动词用单数，have nothing to do with表示"与……无关"，从句用一般过去时，主句用一般现在时。

41. D。解析：more than+名词，其谓语动词与名词有关，名词若是可数名词复数，谓语动词用复数，名词若是可数名词单数，谓语动词用单数，one people是单数。

42. B。解析：more+名词+than+one，其谓语动词用复数，句子表示"多个朋友被邀请去聚会"，用被动语态。

it的用法练习

1. C。解析：it在句中替代that引导的从句，it是形式宾语，that是真正的宾语。

2. B。解析：本题就星期几进行提问，It's的完整形式是It is。

3. C。解析：本题考查强调结构的用法，强调结构是It+be动词+强调部分+who（指人）/that（指物）+其他部分，that后的句子中是一般过去时，主句也应是一般过去时。

4. B。解析：It+be动词+形容词+of+sb.+to+do+sth.，本句表示"你说谎是错误的"。

5. A。解析：It is reported that+从句表示"据报道……"。

6. A。解析：they在本句中替代food and service in this restaurant。

7. D。解析：本题考查it，one和that做替代词时的不同，it指一模一样的物体，one指可数名词的单数，that指前者物体的某一方面或是句子，本题比较的是钢笔的颜色，所以是某物体的某一方面。

8. B。解析：本题考查强调结构的用法，强调结构是It+be动词+强调部分+who（指人）/that（指物）+其他部分，that后面的句子是一般过去时，主句也应是一般过去时。

9. A。解析：It+costs+sb. +钱+to do sth. 表示"花某人多少钱做某事"，yesterday是过去时间状语，所以本句用一般过去时。

10. B。解析：本句就时间进行提问，回答是it is+时间。

11. C。解析：it在句中替代the baby，it可以替代刚出生的婴儿。

12. B。解析：it替代问句中的the bird，一模一样的物体用it替代。

13. B。解析：take it for granted that表示"理所应当认为……"，是固定搭配。

14. B。解析：it是形式主语，用以替代真正的主语，即不定式to do sth.。

15. D。解析：it是形式主语，用以替代真正主语if we will visit Paris，是主语从句的替代词。

16. D。解析：it seems that/to do sth. 表示"看上去好像……"，是固定搭配。

17. A。解析：it替代问句中的my book，一模一样的物体用it替代。

18. C。解析：It+be动词+not until+时间状语+that+句子表示"直到……才……"，是固定搭配。

19. C。解析：It+be动词+before long+that+句子表示"不久之后就……"，是固定搭配。

20. A。解析：本题用how long就距离进行提问，应该用it进行回答。

21. B。解析：it在句中是形式宾语，to tell him不定式做真正的宾语。

22. D。解析：It+be动词+useless+to do sth. 表示"做某事没用"，是固定搭配。

23. B。解析：it在句中替代my watch，change sth. for sth. 表示"用……替代"。

24. B。解析：It+surprised+sb.+that+句子表示"某事让某人很惊讶"，是固定搭配。

25. A。解析：it在句中替代her English book，问句的正常语序为It is what that she is looking for，是强调结构，表示"某物是她正在寻找的东西"。